Introduction to Intersectional Qualitative Research

Dedicated to the ancestors.

Sara Miller McCune founded SAGE Publishing in 1965 to support the dissemination of usable knowledge and educate a global community. SAGE publishes more than 1000 journals and over 800 new books each year, spanning a wide range of subject areas. Our growing selection of library products includes archives, data, case studies and video. SAGE remains majority owned by our founder and after her lifetime will become owned by a charitable trust that secures the company's continued independence.

Los Angeles | London | New Delhi | Singapore | Washington DC | Melbourne

Introduction to Intersectional Qualitative Research

Jennifer Esposito
Georgia State University

Venus Evans-Winters
Illinois State University

Los Angeles | London | New Delhi
Singapore | Washington DC | Melbourne

FOR INFORMATION:

SAGE Publications, Inc.
2455 Teller Road
Thousand Oaks, California 91320
Email: order@sagepub.com

SAGE Publications Ltd.
1 Oliver's Yard
55 City Road
London EC1Y 1SP
United Kingdom

SAGE Publications India Pvt. Ltd.
B 1/I 1 Mohan Cooperative Industrial Area
Mathura Road, New Delhi 110 044
India

SAGE Publications Asia-Pacific Pte. Ltd.
18 Cross Street #10-10/11/12
China Square Central
Singapore 048423

Acquisitions Editor: Leah Fargotstein
Product Associate: Ivey Mellem
Production Editor: Megha Negi
Copy Editor: Erin Livingston
Typesetter: Hurix Digital
Proofreader: Ellen Brink
Indexer: Integra
Cover Designer: Scott Van Atta
Marketing Manager: Victoria Velasquez

Printed in Canada

Library of Congress Cataloging-in-Publication Data

Names: Esposito, Jennifer, author. | Evans-Winters, Venus E., author.

Title: Introduction to intersectional qualitative research / Jennifer Esposito, Georgia State University, Venus E. Evans-Winters, Illinois State University.

Description: First Edition. | Thousand Oaks : SAGE Publications, Inc, 2021. | Includes bibliographical references and index.

Identifiers: LCCN 2020053034 | ISBN 9781544348520 (paperback) | ISBN 9781544348537 (epub) | ISBN 9781544348544 (epub) | ISBN 9781544348551 (ebook)

Subjects: LCSH: Social sciences—Research—Methodology. | Intersectionality (Sociology)—Research. | Qualitative research.

Classification: LCC H62 .E737 2021 | DDC 300.72/1—dc23

LC record available at https://lccn.loc.gov/2020053034

This book is printed on acid-free paper.

21 22 23 24 25 10 9 8 7 6 5 4 3 2 1

Brief Table of Contents

Detailed Table of Contents

Preface

We have conducted and taught qualitative research for over 20 years. As researchers, we have cobbled together the theories and methods that speak to us as women of color. As instructors, we have searched for the "perfect" text-book that centers race and gender. As years went by and we didn't find that one perfect book, we decided to write one ourselves. Both of us have studied or taught qualitative research methods and critical race theory in education, feminism, and intersectionality extensively. These are the theories and approaches we consistently use with our own research. Sometimes, we have found that traditional approaches to qualitative research were not always compatible with the act of centering race and/or gender. In fact, many introductory qualitative textbooks don't even mention race or gender. We wanted to write a book that introduced students and novice researchers to the basic aspects of qualitative research, including research design, data collection, and analysis. But it was important to us that we do so in a way that allowed intersectional concerns to be infused throughout. What we have done is developed an intersectional approach to qualitative research. We use as our epistemological framing that race and gender matter and that racism and sexism are institutionalized in all aspects of life, including research.

As instructors, we know that students often don't want to pay for multiple textbooks in one class. Thus, we have written this book as a one-stop shop for those interested in learning the basics of qualitative research. Given that we have taught and mentored thousands of students, we have tried to focus on the aspects of research that have been the trickiest for our students to comprehend or relate to their personal histories. Because we have spent countless hours assisting in students' organization, coding, and analysis of data, you will see two chapters dedicated to data analysis. Given that one of the most common questions we are asked in an introductory qualitative research course is "How do I find a theoretical framework?" we have an entire chapter on theory. We stood firm in our desire to focus only on methods and methodologies that are compatible with intersectionality. We know that this may cause the most angst for instructors who feel compelled to teach students a wide variety of methodological approaches. Given our book's approach to intersectional research, we thought it best to delve more deeply into a few approaches rather than try to cover the gamut, especially ones that would not be compatible with intersectional research.

You will see that each chapter opens with a vignette about a struggle a novice researcher is having. We created these vignettes based on our numerous interactions with students as well as our reflections on our own time as novice researchers. Because there is not a rule book—so to speak—on how to do qualitative research, we often encourage our students to learn by trial and error. Reflecting on your mistakes as well as your successes can be a powerful way of learning. We wanted these vignettes to be a reminder to students that they are not alone in their struggles and mistakes. We also end each chapter with some discussion questions that instructors can pose to students in groups or individually. We tried to include a mix of retention types of questions as well as critical analysis/evaluation of content. Additionally, it is important to know that we center intersectionality within qualitative inquiry as opposed to centering qualitative inquiry within intersectionality. What this means is that we wrote the book as methodologists who believe that all research should be intersectional. Intersectionality will be the frame and foundation of every aspect of the research project instead of being inserted in as an add-on feature. Of course, using intersectionality methodologically is unchartered territory, so there may be additional ways to center it that are not apparent to us in this moment. We expect that this book will be a seed to help grow projects that enable students to confidently investigate race, class, and gender as well as other identities in all of their complexities while situating the project within a careful analysis of systemic oppression and privilege.

The organization of the book was informed both by how we like to teach research methods as well as by reviewer feedback. Chapter 1 walks readers through the historical landscape of qualitative research and introduces intersectionality as both theory and methodology. We understand that not all instructors like to take a linear approach to qualitative research, and neither do we; however, an overview of the historical trajectory of qualitative research provides students with insight into the messy and complicated tradition of research with human participants and across cultural contexts. We appreciate the ways the field has shifted over time and think it's important to situate a discussion of those shifts within an understanding of the prominent social, cultural, and historical moments. Obviously, all discussion of research should be situated within an understanding of the ways colonization has shaped research. Chapter 2 tackles theory, something that is often a new or advanced concept for students who are now required to think about *how* and *why* we use theory. We discuss ontology, epistemology, theory, and methodology and how the relationship among these influences the research study. We also spend time teaching about embodied theory, as this is central to understandings of intersectional research. As intersectional researchers, we believe ethical concerns should be at the forefront of all research projects. As such, Chapter 3 delves into ethics. We discuss the disturbing history of the abuses of science, especially in regard to historically marginalized people, especially Black, Indigenous, and people of color (BIPOC). Given that our primary audience will be graduate students conducting research inside institutions of higher education, we also discuss ethics in the context of institutional review boards and informed consent and provide examples for students to examine. Chapter 4 examines different methodologies again with a focus on those most compatible with intersectionality. We spend a lot of time on ethnography, as that is the hallmark of qualitative research, and move to critical ethnography and autoethnography. We also discuss arts-based research, narrative inquiry, and case study, which are all inquiries that are appropriate for intersectional research. We use examples to illustrate how you might design a study within that methodology and, because we know how difficult it is for students to construct good research questions, we provide multiple examples of how to do so. Chapter 5 serves as the data collection chapter. We begin with a discussion of the ways the tenets of intersectional research should guide your decision making and your relationship to power dynamics. We teach students how to conduct an interview, engage in participant observations, and complete a document analysis. Our two chapters on data analysis, Chapters 6 and 7, detail how to engage in interpretation and analysis. Chapter 6 discusses data management and storage—skills that must be taught and developed in novice researchers. We do a lengthy discussion of coding, not because we think it is the most important but because we know it is something that has to be done well in order to be meaningful. We provide examples of how to code while using your chosen theoretical framework. Chapter 7 deals with the complexities of theorizing data. We discuss memoing and engaging in reflexive thinking about data. We then do a brief walk-through of different types of analysis, such as thematic, narrative, and discourse analysis. Chapter 8 deals with the task of writing up your research. We discuss writing rituals, revisions, and perfectionism. But we also take readers through the journey of writing a research proposal and dissertation or research manuscript. We spend time in this chapter discussing the literature review, which is often a struggle for graduate students. Our book ends with Chapter 9, which is a manifesto or call to action. We invite our readers to engage with both the possibilities and perils of qualitative research and help us reimagine it. What are the possibilities and limitations in this current moment?

When we first started writing this textbook, it felt as if we were back in graduate school. Each chapter required us to go back and read what we were initially taught and reflect on how we teach those concepts now. We experienced a variety of emotions—from excitement to disappointment to anger to hope. Much has changed over the past twenty years, including more researchers understanding that research has always been and continues to be a colonial project. We are grateful to our mentors and our students who have pushed our thinking over these years. Although we learned about intersectionality in graduate school, we didn't learn about it in our qualitative research courses. This is a deficit we would like to address.

Writing a textbook is a true labor of love and it sometimes involves more labor than love. In crafting something of this magnitude, it is important to recognize that we didn't do this alone. We have had plenty of assistance along the way. We would like to first thank each other. We have been writing together since we met as graduate students. We attended different institutions, but Dr. Garrett Duncan, in his infinite wisdom, put us on an American Educational Research Association (AERA) panel together. We represented the "next generation" of scholars of color. We immediately connected and have grown up as academics together. Sometimes, it is difficult to tell where Venus's voice ends and Jennifer's begins and vice versa. We have collaborated together for so long that working together is easy. It is hard to believe that the AERA panel was almost 20 years ago! We are no longer the next generation. Instead, we are now training the next generation.

We would like to thank Leah Fargotstein, our acquisitions editor. We didn't always meet our deadlines, but Leah was always there when we were ready to submit another chapter or discuss next steps. Thank you, Leah, for your patience and for your excitement about our project. Thank you also to the multiple reviewers who provided feedback at various stages of this book. We especially appreciated those reviewers who told us how they might use the text in their classrooms and what else they would like us to add. We hope you are satisfied and that the final product will meet your students' needs.

Thank you also to our past and present students. Without you, we would not know what to focus on in an introductory textbook. Because of you, we get to see what it's like year after year learning qualitative research with fresh eyes. Thank you for always being willing to ask the important questions and to push us to go deeper in explanations and practical applications.

Finally, thank you to our families. You may not always know or care what we teach or write about, but you've always encouraged us to keep pushing. We are grateful; we are because you are.

A note on terminology: Ways of describing groups of people have changed throughout the course of time. In this current moment, the acronym *BIPOC* is being used to describe those who identify as Black, Indigenous, or people of color. Just a few years ago, we regularly used the terms *Black* and *Brown*, but we find now that BIPOC is more inclusive and politically intentional. We denote *Black* if we are referring to people of the African diaspora and *Latina/o/x* if we are referring to people of the Latin American diaspora. We have tried to use gender-neutral pronouns throughout. However, as women of color, it remains our political standpoint that we should "Say Her Name," given that race continues to supersede gender, which has a disproportionate impact on hurting women of color. We, therefore, are often deliberate in our use of the *she* pronoun with the recognition that *she* can also refer to transgender women. In response to the vignettes, we vary among *she*, *he*, and *they* as recognition that people do have pronouns that we need to respect. Most importantly, throughout the manuscript, we center our students' histories, memories, and questioning of research and the future of freedom struggles.

Acknowledgments

SAGE and the authors would like to thank the following reviewers for their comments:

Lisa Bajor, St. John's University

Yiting Chu, University of Louisiana Monroe

Leigh D'Amico, University of South Carolina

Rene Guillaume, New Mexico State University

Jaimee Hartenstein, University of Central Missouri

Yasmin Jiwani, Concordia University

Phyllis Jones, University of South Florida

Katharine Keenan, Carthage College

Ksenia Keplinger, University of Colorado Boulder

Esther Kim, University of Southern California

Gita Maharaji, Point Park University

Courtney Lynn Malloy, University of Southern California

Peter Mather, Ohio University

Jan-Martijn Meij, Florida Gulf Coast University

Sylvia Mendoza, University of Texas San Antonio

Elizabeth Pope, University of West Georgia

Andrea Rounce, University of Regina

Rebecca Stone, Suffolk University

Shalini Tendulkar, Tufts University

Barbara Tobolowsky, University of Texas Arlington

Jasmine Ulmer, Wayne State University

About the Authors

Jennifer Esposito is a department chair and professor of research in the department of educational policy studies at Georgia State University. Her research examines the ways race, class, gender, and/or sexuality impact a person's experiences within education, including the educative sites of popular culture/media. She is the coauthor of the book, *Intersectional Analysis of Popular Culture Texts: Clarity in the Matrix*. Additionally, she is the author of over 40 articles and book chapters. She has published in journals such as *Qualitative Inquiry, International Journal of Qualitative Research in Education, International Review of Qualitative Research*, and *Urban Education*.

Venus Evans-Winters is a research and policy scholar, former professor of education, and Senior Researcher at the African American Policy Forum. She is a licensed clinical social worker and psychotherapist in private practice. Her research interests are educational policy analysis, racial trauma inside and outside of schools, and Black girls' and women's psychosocial development across the African diaspora. Dr. Evans-Winters is the author of *Black Feminism in Qualitative Inquiry: A Mosaic for Writing Our Daughter's Body* and *Teaching Black Girls: Resilience in Urban Schools*. She is coeditor of the books *Black Feminism in Education: Black Women Speak Up, Back, & Out, Celebrating Twenty Years of Black Girlhood: The Lauryn Hill Reader*, and *(Re)Teaching Trayvon: Education for Racial Justice and Human Freedom*. She is also the author of numerous academic journal articles and book chapters. She is also the Executive Director of Planet Venus Institute.

CHAPTER 1

(R)evolution of Qualitative Inquiry

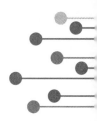

Rosa found herself alienated in research courses because she was hyperaware that traditional research practices did not fully consider her position as a marginalized person in society. The texts she was assigned to read were written mostly by white men (and some white women) and explored how to "capture" reality. The word capture has a differential meaning for many Black, Indigenous, and other people of color (BIPOC) whose ancestors were captured and either annihilated or enslaved. Rosa longed for a research approach that spoke to the ways in which research had been and continues to be weaponized against her and her community. When Rosa read about decolonized research, it made sense to her, and yet, she wondered if it was possible to actually do decolonized research within the walls of an institution that some of her ancestors may have built for free while enslaved. In theory courses, Rosa had been introduced to critical race theory and intersectionality and often wondered how these theories related to research and to the questions she was raising about the nature and purposes of research. She longed to know how to put everything together but, unfortunately, there was no class or book on how to do that.

The questions Rosa has been pondering in this current moment are questions that we, Jennifer and Venus, have asked ourselves throughout our careers as scholars and teachers of qualitative research. We became critical scholars upon being exposed to critical theories because these theories put into words what we had been experiencing in life. Intersectionality was one such theory. Intersectionality originated within Black feminism, and it asserts that there is no singular oppression. Instead, our race, gender, class, sexuality, and other identities are entangled and, thus, it is difficult to parse out why someone has been or continues to be oppressed. This theory is the crux of our book and we will define it more thoroughly soon. For now, we want to explain to you that if you are questioning things, the way Rosa is, you are not alone. We have asked similar questions for the past twenty years and, with each article or book we wrote or with each class we taught, we have generated partial answers.

Our careers (as detailed in Evans-Winters & Esposito, 2019) have been marked by this push and pull between true decolonization and keeping our jobs to sustain our livelihood. On the one hand, we read critical theories that interrogated the nature of race and racism as well as asserted the complexity of oppression. On the other hand, we pushed up against a traditional research system without ever dismantling it completely. We played by the rules, so to speak, by citing the lineage of researchers who we were taught had built the field. We knew there had to be a better way. Though we pushed against the system slowly, we remained confined within it. It is difficult to dismantle a system that you are actively a part of, and we were firmly entrenched in academia as we journeyed toward tenure and promotion. Both of us are full professors now and we have proven ourselves in many ways. We were successful in having been measured against traditional research and scholarship. Yet, we still are clawing our way out of traditional approaches to qualitative research because, as Linda Tuhiwai Smith (2012) states,

> From the vantage point of the colonized, a position from which I write, and choose to privilege, the term "research" is inextricably linked to European imperialism and colonialism. The word itself, "research", is probably one of the dirtiest words in the indigenous world's vocabulary. When mentioned in many indigenous contexts, it stirs up silence, it conjures up bad memories, it raises a smile that is knowing and distrustful. (p. 1)

In this book, you will see us grapple with the traditions of research while centering intersectionality. Like all texts, this text is incomplete and there are things that we left out. Twenty years from now, when conducting intersectional research is as common as conducting an ethnography, people may look back on this text and point out gaps we didn't address or flaws in our thinking. We encourage that. We are writing in a moment when academic libraries are full of articles on the theory of intersectionality. But few scholars have attempted to turn the theory into a methodological approach. This book breaks ground in that we have tried to account for the "how to" of intersectional research. Many of you may be familiar with the theory but may never have learned how to put the theory in practice in the design and conduct of intersectional research. As the field of intersectional research deepens, so too will all of our understandings about best practices or ways to do this. For now, you will see some familiar elements of qualitative research (i.e., research design, data collection, data analysis) but you will see it discussed within the centering of intersectionality. At the root of everything we do in research, we need to be sure we are thinking/acting with intersectionality in mind and enacting intersectionality at all times.

The field of qualitative research is contested terrain and not everyone will agree with who we cite or what we say. You will face this issue as well and, thus, we encourage you to find like minds early on. When you read something that speaks to you, save it, make notes on it, cite it. As a researcher, it will be your job to teach us how to see you and how to interpret what you've done. If you see us citing someone multiple times, you can rest assured that their work spoke to us and continues to speak to us.

In this chapter, we will define intersectionality more fully, trace the lineage of research in general and qualitative research more specifically, and discuss how intersectionality can and should be used in qualitative research. This chapter and the next one are pretty dense theoretically but that is only because we want you to understand that intersectionality means more than being a Black or Brown woman and being oppressed due to the entanglement of your race and gender. We take you through the evolution of both intersectionality and qualitative research. So, be patient with us as we lay out this landscape for you. After we are done laying this out, we will review common aspects of qualitative research that you must consider as you develop a research project. You will see chapters on ethics, methodology, data collection, data analysis, and writing it all up.

Introduction to Intersectionality

Intersectionality evolved from several human struggles of resistance to domination, civil rights movements, social conditions, sets of social experiences, epistemological ruminations, and disciplinary camps, including the abolitionist movement, women's movement, civil rights movement, Afrocentric/womanist movement, Chicano movement, Black feminist theory, critical race theory, and so on. Women of color feminists throughout history have been concerned with how intersectional identities shape their own lives. For example, when Sojourner Truth asked "Ain't I a woman?" at the Seneca Falls Convention on Women's Rights, she was articulating how difficult it was to be both a woman and African. Black women could not be located within deliberations on civil or human rights. The African woman shackled by white supremacy, chattel slavery, and patriarchy was not considered a full human being nor an actual woman, legally or scientifically, which made it nearly impossible for anyone, except for herself, to articulate and justify her civil liberties.

Although it is difficult to pinpoint exactly when or where intersectionality was born, most critical theorists agree that Kimberlé Crenshaw coined the term *intersectionality* in 1991 to describe how Black women experienced workplace racial and gender discrimination due to multiple intersecting identities. Kimberlé Crenshaw (1991) defines *intersectionality* as "the location of women of color both within overlapping systems of subordination and at the margins of feminism and antiracism" (p. 1265). Specifically, Crenshaw argued that Black women were not hired by industries that recruited women applicants because they were not white women; Black women were not hired by industries that recruited Black people because Black women were not men.

In other words, Black women were discriminated against by employees who privileged white women and those who privileged male workers. Crenshaw went on to argue that Black women received no special consideration before the courts, because the discrimination and forms of exclusion that Black women confronted in the labor force did not affect all women (i.e., white females) nor did it affect all

Black people (i.e., their Black male counterparts). Black women workers such as Sojourner Truth, who were discriminated against for their race and gender status in the United States (U.S.), were falling between the cracks of racial and gender protections. Intersectionality as theory entails analysis that includes acknowledging that such a crack exists and how individuals and groups resist falling through the cracks and advocate strategically against power regimes that create such cracks.

Hence, theorists who embody an intersectional perspective consider how people are multiply situated and how coercive power and systematic oppression cannot be fully understood by asynchronous examinations of structural or relational power. Intersectionality recognizes that identities are mutually interlocking as well as relational (Berger & Guidroz, 2009; Collins, 1998). Prior conceptions of societal relationships regarded social identity as additive and ordinal, with one identity being the primary identity and most important identity while other identities were subsequent or secondary to the main identity (Evans-Winters & Esposito, 2019).

A singular analytical focus on one identity ignored and erased the multiple identities and lived realities of women of color and others who were impacted in multifarious ways by systemic inequality and thus were more vulnerable to structural violence. Intersectionality concerns itself with the multiple ways in which one's identity makes one simultaneously invisible and hypervisible. And born out of standpoint theory (Collins, 2000; Smith, 1983), intersectionality as an analytical and methodological tool presupposes that the multiple perspectives of the marginalized and oppressed offer unique and, at times, divergent viewpoints of the social world and thus research experience.

Accordingly, intersectionality as research methodology is about contemplating, interrogating, naming, and simultaneously reclaiming and rejecting that nexus between the *known and unknown, invisible and (hyper)visible*, and *humanizing and dehumanizing*. Further, besides intersectionality as advocacy and political strategy, intersectionality might be considered as a vantage point and embodiment. Intersectional viewpoints contemporaneously concern themselves with racial domination and gender-based oppression along with other forms of discrimination related to social class, sexuality, disability, language, citizenship status, religion, age, and so on.

Intersectionality goes beyond simplistic one-dimensional critiques and analyses of power and domination, such as traditional feminism's singular focus on gender oppression. Instead, intersectional methodologies juxtapose social categories to systems of power and social phenomena to power relations. Consequently, qualitative inquiry from an intersectional perspective unashamedly and ardently concedes that individuals can be multiply situated in the world and, thus, the researcher must be prepared to accept complexity as a part of the research process.

We present intersectionality throughout the book as a methodological matrix of analysis (which includes ethical considerations) and interrogations of relationships embedded in power and influence. Intersectionality has been described as a theoretical framework born out of the lived experiences of Black women and other critical race feminists of color. Intersectionality is both a theory and a methodology that recognizes that oppression cannot be understood as additive or in terms of a single axis. Single-axis methods and modes of analysis privilege one form of oppression over others and presumes that all members of one category of race, for example, will have the same experiences by virtue of being in the same group (Grzanka, 2014). These single-axis methods position racism, sexism, and classism as parallel instead of as intersecting.

As human beings, we have several markers of identities such as race, class, gender, and sexuality along with other individual and group identities that are then enmeshed within systems of oppression. These systems of oppression sustain social inequality at the systemic level. Collins (2000) refers to this as the "matrix of domination" and explains how interlocking and mutually reinforcing systems of domination sustain themselves. As an example, Crenshaw's (1991) analysis of Anita Hill as both Black and a woman (part of two oppressive regimes—racism and sexism) instead of as a woman (presumed white) or a Black person (presumed male) was integral to illustrating how multiple oppressions shape a person's legal outcomes. Oppression must be understood as intersecting, interlocking, and co-constitutive because that is how it is lived (Collins, 2000; Crenshaw, 1991).

We do not mean to give the impression that intersectionality began with Crenshaw's analysis of the Anita Hill case. This moment in history is important because it did allow intersectionality to move from a more specialized form in critical legal studies to a wider use across disciplines. However, intersectionality predates Crenshaw's and Collins's use of it. Intersectionality's origins are difficult to neatly map out, given that historically, the theory has been discussed in various ways in different social movements. The earliest forms of intersectionality date back to women of color activists in the 19th century (Collins & Bilge, 2016; Grzanka, 2014). Sojourner Truth, Maria Stewart, Ida B. Wells, and Anna Julia Cooper are only a few of the Black women activists whose writing and political speeches included attention to embodied ways of knowing as well as the systemic oppression they lived within given their race, class, and gender positions (Cooper, 2017).

origins

The use of intersectionality within women of color's political and activist work continued. Because various U.S. social movements within the 1960s and 1970s were often framed around men's concerns, many women of color continually pressed for recognition of their unique contexts. Gloria Anzaldúa and Cherríe Moraga, who were early Chicana feminist intersectional scholars wrote important work (Moraga & Anzaldúa, 2015/1983) that allowed women of color to speak from their multiple positionalities. There were also other women of color scholars/activists who wrote from the standpoint of being multiply oppressed and argued directly against many of the single-axis social movements such as Black Power, feminism, and Asian American activism, to name a few (Lim & Tsutakawa, 1989; Smith, 1983).

Methodologically, intersectionality is presented throughout this book as a tool to examine the ways in which multiple oppressions manifest in a person's life (Collins, 2000; Crenshaw, 1991). From a critical race feminist perspective, intersectionality concerns itself with how racism, sexism, classism, heterosexism, and xenophobia, and other interlocking systems of oppression impede on the rights and dignity of women of color, Indigenous communities, queer women, youth of color, poor and working-class people, and other similarly situated subjugated people. The rest of this chapter provides a more in-depth discussion of the evolution of intersectionality theory.

Reframing critical qualitative inquiry from an intersectional perspective is a starting point in efforts to de-marginalize the intersection of race and gender (Crenshaw, 1989, 1991) and decolonize our research methodologies (Smith, 2012). Intersectionality as a methodological tool in qualitative inquiry pursuits also serves as a conceptual device for the consideration and interpretation of how social forces construct theory and praxis and how theory and praxis construct political-economic forces and body politics.

As you think about conducting intersectional research, we invite you to reflect upon the following questions: How might qualitative research take up intersectionality in all its complexities? How can intersectionality as a critical methodology help critical scholars radically excogitate matrixes of domination across social contexts, relationships, and academic disciplines? As a praxis, how might intersectionality as a methodological device move qualitative inquirers toward critical action as we strive for humanization, democratization, and emancipatory pedagogies?

Evolution of Qualitative Research

Some of you may be brand-new to the field of qualitative research, so we are going to start from the beginning. Qualitative research has been metaphorically described as a bricolage, a montage, quilt-making, and musical improvisation (Denzin & Lincoln, 2000) and, more recently, as a mosaic (Evans-Winters, 2019). The dynamism and cultural malleability of qualitative research projects, approaches, and interpretative processes makes it nearly impossible to assign one single definition to qualitative research methods. We might agree that qualitative research is an interpretative project that produces text(s) as a set of representations, and it is these sets of interconnected representations that connect parts of the whole of qualitative research. However, an interweaving (Sherman & Torbert, 2013) of all of the threads of qualitative research shares a familiar relatedness in characteristics and features.

Qualitative inquiry typically encompasses an intentional contemplation of meaning making in the examination of human behavior and interactions across and within social contexts. Denzin and Lincoln (2000), in an attempt to synthesize the landscape of qualitative research, suggest that qualitative research moves toward interpretative theory; contends with politics of representation; partakes in textual analysis of literary and cultural forms, including their processes of production, distribution, and consumption; and explores novel pedagogical and interpretative praxes that serve to collectively instigate critical cultural analysis in our teachings inside classroom spaces. Qualitative research takes an interpretive and naturalistic approach to the study of social and cultural phenomenon and consists of a set of interpretive practices that endeavors to make social life more known through a series of analytical representations.

Accordingly, the task of the qualitative researcher is to "study things in their natural settings, attempting to make sense of, or to interpret, phenomena in terms of the meanings that people bring to them" (Denzin & Lincoln, 2000, p. 3). Gubrium and Holstein (1997) succinctly articulated,

> The commanding focus of much qualitative research is on questions such as what is happening, what are people doing, and what does it mean to them? The questions address the content of meaning as articulated through social interaction and as mediated by culture. The resulting research mandate is to describe reality in terms of what it naturally is. (p. 14)

Further, qualitative research concerned with *how* questions emphasize the production of meaning and *how* the production of everyday life is accomplished in each setting (Gubrium & Holstein, 1997).

Qualitative researchers seek to assiduously investigate the everyday interactions and taken-for-granted happenings of individuals and groups while seeking to interpret what those conscious and dysconscious (King, 1991) happenings mean to the social actors themselves. Just as importantly, qualitative researchers attempt to comprehend the role of cultural forces on individuals' and groups' (a) behaviors and interactions, (b) interpretations of those behaviors and interactions, and (c) values, beliefs, and attitudes. Thus, qualitative research concern lies in the depiction of the reality of social life in what some might assume is in its "naturally" occurring state but also what seem to be patterns of social forces occurring in a setting. From an intersectional perspective, qualitative pursuits concern themselves with all the aforementioned but also with the political and/or intellectual intent to understand how people come to garner collective agency, resilience, and forms of resistance against oppressive institutions, policies, and practices.

Although there are a shared set of presuppositions that determine the theoretical and pragmatic work that qualitative researchers set out to accomplish as scientists, qualitative research as a field of inquiry is interdisciplinary, multifarious, and informed by many genres. Since the early 1900s, qualitative research, as we know it today, has endured through many evolutions. These evolutions within the U.S. have been conveniently explained as "moments" that occurred in a somewhat linear fashion and yet, Denzin (2001) notes, all moments "operate in the present" (p. 25). Not all qualitative researchers agree with the way these moments have been outlined and many would argue that they were never as linear as they are made to appear. We find this linear overview useful and we discuss each moment in further detail. The eight moments are outlined as follows (Denzin & Lincoln, 2000, 2004):

evolution of qualitative research

- **The first moment.** Represents the traditional moment (1900–1950) and is associated with the positivist paradigms and notions of objective science. Researchers (i.e., the lone ethnographer) wrote objective colonizing accounts of their observations in the field.

- **The second moment**. Signifies the modern or golden age (1950–1970) phase in which qualitative researchers attempted to position their pursuits and research products as formalized and rigorous, similar to quantitative traditions.

- **The third moment**. Denotes blurred genres (1970–1986) and a time when the humanities became a resource for the critical interpretation and exemplification of qualitative research projects.

- **The fourth moment**. Characterizes the crisis of representation (1986–1990) and marks a point in qualitative history in which researchers called for systematic reflection of their own beliefs and values.

- **The fifth moment**. Characterizes the postmodern period of new ethnographies (1990–2000) in which researchers and audiences began to challenge grand narratives. There was an ideological turn toward multiple realities and socially constructed truths and research was characterized by specific, local, and historical representations.

- **The sixth moment**. Represents postexperimental inquiry (1995–2000) in which qualitative research was linked with democratic policies and no discourse had a privileged place. Qualitative researchers began to use performative strategies to communicate their findings.

- **The seventh moment**. Indicative of the methodologically contested period (2000–2004) and included more intentional conversations about the limitations and possibilities of qualitative research. Questions about race, class, gender, sexuality, and location arose in research pursuits.

- **The eighth moment**. Representative of the fractured future (2005–present) and includes interrogations into the innocence of qualitative research and research in general. Written cogitations about who is the known and who is the knower, the purposes of research, and pushback against authority and authorial voices are prevalent.

The traditional period of qualitative research begins in the early 1900s, with early iterations akin to anthropology and continued until World War II. During this period, researchers (primarily white European anthropologists) traveled to distant lands and set out to write "objective" accounts of their observations and interpretations of their encounters. However, many scholars of today, and some of the past—including Black scholars such as W. E. B. DuBois, Zora Neal Hurston, John St. Clair Drake, and Frantz Fanon—might describe their accounts as simply fragments of the colonizers' imagination. The purpose of the research was to justify and learn how to colonize better and more efficiently. Indeed, all research was a colonial project that relied on a deficit notion of the *Other* or the *Savage* (Bishop, 1998; Smith et al., 2002). Research became the groundwork for reporting and representing this Other and was intimately linked to the colonial project that sought to dominate and control. As Denzin, Lincoln, and Smith (2008) argued, "as agents of colonial power, Western scientists discovered, extracted, appropriated, commodified, and distributed knowledge about the indigenous other" (p. 5). In no uncertain terms, anthropology was an agent of Western domination. Falling under the positivist science paradigm, the white European colonizer anthropologist claimed to offer the scientific world valid, reliable, and objective firsthand accounts of his experiences in the field.

These lone ethnographers' colorful representations asserted laws and generalizations of the cultural Other, which became depicted as scientific truth. Of course, this is the history of anthropological research that many of us were taught. But, similar to much of the knowledge that is privileged in the academy, it is not the whole truth and this tale seeks to continue to privilege a Western way of knowing over an Indigenous way of knowing. Margaret Bruchac, an Indigenous anthropologist, used archival and oral history data to engage in what she termed *reverse ethnography*—the practice of reenvisioning relationships between anthropologists and their informants. Although much early anthropological work is characterized by the lone ethnographer's account, Bruchac's work revealed that "despite class, gender, and ethnic divides, anthropology was often a collaborative endeavor. Indigenous individuals were enlisted as guides, interpreters, artisans, procurers, and translators. These relationships began to blur the roles of anthropologist/informant, kin/outsider, and collector/collected" (2018, p. 9). The early anthropological accounts we read today were filtered through a Western lens and were written for an audience who expected and needed this exotic Other to be presented as savage to justify colonialization, religious domination, and scientific exploration. Bruchac uncovered personal letters that were written to anthropologists by Indigenous informants who criticized the Western interpretations. According to Bruchac, these Indigenous informants "rarely gained credit as intellectual equals. Their efforts were largely obscured by power relations and cataloguing practices that separated people from objects, objects from communities, and communities from their stories" (p. 10). The residual effects of the traditional moment are still very much present in qualitative research. Even today, anthropologists specifically and qualitative researchers in general grapple with the notion of telling a community's story without "othering their research participants, exploiting them, or leaving them voiceless in the telling of their own stories," (Liamputtong, 2007, p. 165).

Much of the traditional moment, which spilled over and influenced the second moment (or modern phase), is representative of present-day ethnographic texts and didactics. Building on the convention of the traditional period, the modernist phase yielded texts that appeared to provide insight not only into other cultural worlds but also introspective literatures of the author's worldview. These insights were posited as objective and rigorous studies of social life. The intent during this moment was to formalize qualitative research so it could be recognized as legitimate.

Described as postpositivism by Denzin and Lincoln (2000), the second moment of qualitative research was marked by standardization, generalization, frequency and patterns (of behavior), and causality. This period was noted for qualitative researchers of positivist and postpositivist leanings. On the one hand, qualitative researchers compared their cultural productions to quantitative research while on the other hand, they believed that their role was to represent the marginalized in society. At this time, sociologists also began to greatly influence the field of qualitative research (mainly the sociologists at the University of Chicago during the first half of the 1900s). These sociologists later became known as part of the "Chicago school."

As described by Cortese (1995),

> Chicago sociology methodological innovations occurred, chronologically, between earlier social surveys, aimed at social reform, and later highly scientific social surveys. Some of the distinctive research methods linked to Chicago sociology are personal documents, intensive field research, documentary sources, social mapping, and ecological analysis. (p. 238)

The Chicago school of sociology particularly influenced the field of qualitative inquiry. Sociologists who blended the social sciences and called for interdisciplinary approaches and reflexivity, drawing upon symbolic interactionism, sought to understand behavioral patterns. What distinguished members of the Chicago school from anthropologists at the time is that sociologists from the Chicago school decided to investigate the Other within their nation-state. Thus, instead of traveling to foreign lands, these sociologists investigated the colonized people living among them, including racialized minorities, ethnic and immigrant groups, sexual minorities, the southern poor, prostitutes, alcoholics, and urbanized cultures (Blumer, 1967; Bulmer, 1984; Humphreys, 1970; Wirth, 1928).

Taking the stance that reality was a social construction (Blumer, 2000), reminiscent of popular research methodologies of later qualitative phases, the Chicago school is known for the case study approach; historical analysis, which embraced the use of autobiographies, diaries, and personal letters; and the statistical method. There was a sequence in the use of methods during the process of a research project. An emphasis was placed on the study of subcultures and necessitated field research and participant observation. The Chicago school's prominence began to fade in the late 1960s and was followed by the *blurred genres* moment of qualitative research.

The blurred genres (1970–1986) moment stands out as a time in which the humanities became a resource for the critical interpretation and exemplification of qualitative research projects. During this period, researchers not only pushed back against "tales from the field," but they also constructed counter-narratives by presenting participation observation as stories, artistic formations, and literary representations of social life. In this phase, researchers such as Geertz (1973) called for "thick description"—thinking and reflecting on symbolic acts—and generalizations within cases as opposed to across cases. The focus on thick description in ethnographic work is still present in much of qualitative research as traces of the fourth moment.

Whereas much of the responsibility of the researcher in the third moment was to provide a detailed account of what the researcher observed or the analysis of the artifacts collected, the fourth moment marked an emphasis on the researcher's values, beliefs, and understandings of what was under observation and their own set of lived experiences. During this period, qualitative researchers began to question their own assumptions and biases and explore how such preconceptions about the social world and social identities influenced their approaches to research and interpretations of what they saw, smelled, or heard. By the sixth moment, influenced by the fourth (1986–1990) and fifth moment (1990–2000), ideas regarding the role the researcher plays in the creation of the research became a part of research discourse. Terms such as *positionality* (the researcher's subject position especially in relation to the researched's position) and researcher *reflexivity* (self-awareness and criticality of the researcher's subjectivity) became commonplace topics of discussion for researchers. Revelations of one's own beliefs and experiences and how they (un)intentionally shaped the research became important expectations of the written record.

For example, in *Writing Up Qualitative Research*, Harry Wolcott (2001) pointed out that participant observation has become virtually synonymous with ethnography and fieldwork. Therefore, he argues that it is essential that the researcher details exactly how participant observation played out in the research process. Research became recognized for the embodied practice that it is, and with that recognition came an understanding of the need to interrogate the researcher's subjectivities because research is "fully embodied in the sense that all of who we are—spiritually, emotionally, physically, and intellectually—is part and parcel of the research process" (Edwards & Esposito, 2019). Many qualitative researchers began to explore their own proximity to privilege and power while others openly claimed the margins and/or (re)claimed the center (Lather, 1992; Tillman, 2002; Villenas, 2000). For example, Tillman (2002) describes culturally sensitive research as those approaches to the study of education "that place the cultural knowledge and experiences of African Americans at the center of the inquiry and emphasize the relationship of the researcher to the individual or the community under study" (p. 6).

With no distinct lines of demarcation, the seventh (2000–2004) and eighth (current) moments in qualitative research distorted the disciplinary/cultural boundaries between research and literature and performance and art (Bochner & Ellis, 2002; Ellis, 2004). At present, more qualitative researchers than ever grapple with the meaning of research in the first place: Who does research benefit? What is the role of research in larger freedom struggles? Who benefits and profits from research? And how might research be used to transform communities and counter hegemonic institutions? The role of research within academia has been necessarily interrogated for its role in propagating what Delgado Bernal and Villalpando (2002) termed an *apartheid of knowledge*. Chela Sandoval (2013) notes that this racialized apartheid between knowledges that are accepted in academia (Eurocentric epistemologies) and culturally informed knowledges continues to marginalize

[handwritten margin note: positionality/ self-reflexivity]

research produced outside of these Eurocentric ideological frames. While research based on Eurocentric theories is viewed as objective, Indigenous and racially sensitive research is viewed as inherently biased and non-rigorous (Buendia, 2003).

Critical qualitative researchers have actively located qualitative research within the colonial project, claiming that this research relies too much on a deficit perspective of the Other (see Bhattacharya, 2009; Bishop, 1998; Dillard, 2000). Denzin, Lincoln, and Smith (2008) place Indigenous and critical researchers in the eighth moment of qualitative research because researchers are "performing culture as they write it" (p. 4). As part of the eighth moment, intersectionality as a research methodology was born out of critical theories, activists' praxis, and multiple ways of knowing. It crosses cultural bridges and epistemological borders and recognizes that all critical research must be grounded within the specific cultural meanings, traditions, and understandings of the culture(s) under study. In the next section, we explore in more detail the evolution of intersectionality as both theory and methodology. By acknowledging that research is a significant site of struggle (Smith, 2012), we propose intersectionality as a tool of intervention.

Centering Intersectionality in Qualitative Inquiry

Black feminist, mother, lesbian, and poet Audre Lorde once stated in a 1979 conference during a panel presentation:

> Those of us who stand outside the circle of this society's definition of acceptable women; those of us who have been forged in the crucibles of difference; those of us who are poor, lesbians, who are black, who are older, know that *survival is not an academic skill.* It is learning how to stand alone, unpopular and sometimes reviled, and how to make common cause with those others identified as outside the structures, in order to define and seek a world in which we can all flourish. It is learning how to take our differences and make them strengths. For the master's tools will never dismantle the master's house. They may allow us temporarily to beat him at this own game, but they will never enable us to bring about genuine change. (p. 95)

We see Lorde's 1979 proclamation above as a call to action for qualitative researchers who seek to become change agents. Lorde emphasized that marginalization and the social status of the Other—and sometimes hatred of the Other—shapes the consciousness and actions of minoritized women. For Lorde, it is from lived experience and this consciousness that forms of resilience and resistance arise.

Lorde's insight raises multiple questions for qualitative research. First, how might one's lived experiences shape our research questions? How might a critical consciousness informed by one's multiple realities influence our relationships with research participants? How might an intersectional perspective inform research reflexivity or how we understand the role of personal taste, biases, struggles, identities, and privilege in the research process? How can we take into consideration differences in our research interpretations and analysis? As qualitative researchers investigating the social world from an intersectional perspective, we enter the research process with the intent to make any real or perceived differences between researchers and research participants a strength.

You may be wondering what Lorde means by "the master's tools" referenced above. The master's tools are state apparatuses of control, manipulation, and surveillance, including all forms of scientific investigation. This means that scientific research, including qualitative research, is a tool of the master. The proverbial "master's house" above refers to white supremacist patriarchal capitalism and its ghostly apparition in academic research and discourse. We discussed previously how research has functioned as a colonial project. It has been allowed to do so invisibly because when researchers of color have called it out, we have been silenced with claims regarding our biases or agendas.

> Because identity and/or body politics is our starting point, positivist researchers charge that our studies only work to explain what we already believe to be true. We push back on this perspective because it does not interrogate how "neutrality" itself is a particular standpoint steeped in relations of domination. (Edwards & Esposito, 2019, p. 49)

We will no longer remain silent. We will continue to call out research as a colonial project and continue to teach about ways to do decolonized research. Intersectional research is one such approach. Intersectionality as methodology attempts to directly take up the fact that the master's tools will never dismantle the master's house. Instead, we need new tools—in this case, new ways of conducting research—in order to call out and disrupt oppressive regimes. In order to think intersectionally and to use intersectional methodology and methods, we must accept the following claims:

claims required for intersectional research

1. Academe or formal education represents only one way of getting to know the social world. Assumptions and theories about social relationships and institutional authority are also born out of having to survive under hostile conditions and (unequal) power relationships.

2. We must accept our own lived experience and how it shapes our critical consciousness and approach to the research process.

3. We must embrace differences within and across communities to better understand the social world and how our research participants, especially those multiply marginalized, operate within and across communities.

4. Research is the opportunity to learn with and from the Other; we challenge the assumption that researchers only have something to give or take from participants.

5. We seek a collaborative research experience in which our differences can help us imagine a better world where we all can do more than coexist; we can thrive together.

Intersectionality as methodology is a complementary tool—to other forms of knowledge—for combating white racism, sexism, classism, homophobia, elitism, ageism, xenophobia, ableism, and ethnocentrism in qualitative research practices and paradigms.

Decolonizing Methodologies

By ignoring power differentiations across race, class, and gender and the effects of social exclusion on individuals' and groups' choices in our research paradigms and relationships, qualitative researchers inadvertently maintain the status quo under the guise of *mutually beneficial* (Coburn et al., 2013) partnerships. However, as Lorde expressed in her panel discussion, the master's (theoretical and methodological) tools

> may allow us temporarily to beat him at his own game, but they will never enable us to bring about genuine change. And this fact is only threatening to those women who still define the master's house as their only source of support. (p. 95)

Not much can change when qualitative researchers only find comfort in age-old academic modus operandi built on segregation, marginalization, and hierarchy. With Lorde's main point in mind, we cannot expect societal transformation out of qualitative research if it only periodically invites researchers of color and other marginalized people to the table, if it is expected that we will continue to borrow the same old theories, if we engage in the same old methodologies, and if we embrace the same old buffet of protocols set before us by the beneficiaries of academic apartheid.

Presented as an oppositional paradigm, intersectionality begins with the standpoint that the marginalized and Othered have our own ways of knowing, doing, and interpreting our social and political circumstances. "It appalls us to know that the West can desire, extract, and claim ownership of our ways of knowing, our imagery, the things we create and produce," points out Smith (2012), "and then simultaneously reject the people who created and developed those ideas and seek to deny them further opportunities to be creators of their own culture and own nations" (p. 1). Linda Tuhiwai Smith argues that academic research has historically erased Indigenous people from human history and scientific knowledge. Indigenous people, colonized people, enslaved people, poor people, immigrants, women, and prisoners across the world have been vetted as objects of science but not as meaningful producers of knowledge, culture, or scientific methodologies.

Academic research has a way of ordaining the qualitative researcher as "the expert" of a social group or cultural community but only if the researcher is not a member of that social group or cultural community. Indeed, academia still privi-leges researchers who study the proverbial Other, who cross race, class, and gen-der lines in order to make known and make palpable the dangerous Other. This qualitative researcher is rewarded (e.g., tenure, publications, keynote presenta-tions, salary increases, etc.) for having extensively studied and *captured* in their research *exhibitions*[1] the practices, norms, rituals, and beliefs of a specific cultural group or cultural context. The assumption is that in their copious accounts of people, places, and things, the qualitative researcher has accurately portrayed the beneficial evidence (i.e., data, artifacts, etc.) needed to understand a group to solve a social problem—whatever that social problem might be—and its impact on the rest of the civilized world.

Such social problems are typically referred to as the *research problem*; other times, the problem is never specifically exposed but is implied as indicated by codified phrases such as *research implications, suggestions for policy or practice,* or *implications for future research.* The assumption is that the researcher is accessing the research context for the greater good of humanity or in the "spirit of scientific exploration" itself. In *Decolonizing Methodologies* (2012), Smith writes,

> Many researchers, academics and project workers may see the benefits of their particular research projects as serving a greater good "for mankind," or serving a specific emancipatory goal for an oppressed community. But belief in the ideal that benefiting mankind is indeed a primary outcome of scientific research is as much a reflection of ideology as it is of academic training. It becomes so taken for granted that many researchers simply assume that they as individuals embody this ideal and are natural repre-sentatives of it when they work with other communities. (p. 2)

In the search for "serving the greater good," there is little or no acknowledge-ment of the labor and cultural insights shared by the community participants of the particular social phenomena studied. For example, how did the Samoan mothers and daughters of Margaret Mead's (1928) ethnography benefit from the study? This classical text was required reading in many undergraduate sociology and women studies courses and graduate research programs. Mead was lauded for doing the groundbreaking work of actually talking to women and girls instead of focusing on chiefs, political systems, and war/conflicts. While Mead's work is important for recognizing that women and girls had something important to say, the question remains as to what they gained for teaching Mead about their lives and culture. In the not-so-distant past, qualitative researchers loved to say (and still sometimes say) they "give voice" to their participants, as if the participants are voiceless. The girls and women in Mead's study were not voiceless but they were

---

[1] We have noted in italics the terms *captured* and *exhibitions* because, as noted at the beginning of this chapter, these are colonial terms that have become commonplace in qualitative research. We encourage you to become cognizant of how easy it is to emulate the colonial relationship in research and to continue to push against that practice.

silent because their ways of knowing were not considered important until a white researcher validated them. Intersectional research understands from the beginning what is at stake in continuing to invalidate cultural knowledge while at the same time privileging Eurocentric knowledge.

In this current moment of qualitative research, many students of research might problematize the taken-for-granted observations and suppositions put forth in classical research texts, but hardly in our research graduate programs do we bring attention to the fact that the majority of our qualitative research theories, research how-to handbooks, and professors represent and are grounded in white Western middle-class culture. The descendants of the colonizers profit from their inheritance of stolen culture and consumption of Indigenous ethos.

Paradoxically, qualitative research is a knowledge economy at once built on distortions of Indigenous people, lands, and culture and draws upon the observable and shared ("discovered" during the research process) traditions of the Other. Rarely, if ever, are the cultural insiders themselves acknowledged, celebrated, or rewarded as the rightful authorities, producers, and bearers of the culture researched and presented before the scientific world. Somehow our ways of life, problems, and strategies of survival are examined under a microscope, presented to a world outside of our own, and archived as absolute and foreign (and important only because a researcher "discovered" them).

Consequently, our own cultures, dissected and parsed, presented as linear and formulaic—palatable to the Western academic gaze—become unfamiliar and distant even to us. Intersectional methodologies resist exorcising cultural insiders from conversations about (a) theoretical underpinnings of research, (b) research protocols, (c) considerations of what constitutes data, (d) data representations, and (e) ethical considerations of research. An additional aspect of intersectionality in qualitative research is to acknowledge the intellectual and emotional labor that Black, Indigenous, and other people of color (BIPOC) have contributed to understanding and documenting the lives of the marginalized and oppressed.

Intersectionality and Identity Politics

As mentioned earlier in this chapter, traditional academic ponderings about systemic racism were also imagined to be additive or ordinal as opposed to interlocking, multifarious, and synchronous. Intersectionality shifts conversations on theory and practice beyond the simplistic confines of singular identities and instead toward conscientious reflections on how institutions, social structures, and policies construct specific identities and groups as disposable. Intersectionality reveals power relationships and individuals' and social groups' proximity to power.

Intersectionality prompts researchers interested in issues of discrimination, marginalization, abuse of power, and authority to contemplate their own interpretations of the self and Other in more nuanced as well as complex ways. There is a strong relationship between intersectionality and reflexivity; interlocking systems of oppression demand one to be self-aware as a survival strategy. In order to survive an openly unjust world, Black people, Indigenous people, women of color, and many other members of subjugated groups (e.g., gender nonbinary, trans people, etc.) are required to continuously think of their behavior and very presence in relation to those with power to control social norms and rules of regulation.

The act of people of African ancestry existing in the U.S. looking at themselves through a Black cultural lens and the white gaze was referred to by W. E. B. Du Bois (2008) in his 1903 autoethnography, *The Souls of Black Folk*, as a *double-consciousness*. Deborah Gray White (1999) later coined the term *triple consciousness* to describe how Black women, specifically, are forced to see themselves through a Black cultural identity, white supremacy, and patriarchy. Recently, *triple consciousness* has also been used to describe the histories and tensions that Afro-Latinxs encounter in the U.S. due to white racism, xenophobia, and linguistic discrimination within and outside the Black community (see Flores & Jiménez Román, 2009).

[handwritten margin note: double / triple consciousness]

Especially from a critical race feminist perspective, such imparted or instinctual self-awareness of the "double jeopardy" (King, 1988, p. 42) of race and gender from the cradle to the grave in a white supremacist patriarchal capitalist society fosters a multiple consciousness that is associated with the development of critical theory (i.e., Black feminism). Below is a diagram that illustrates the interconnectedness of self-awareness, a group's shared collective consciousness, and ongoing strategies of resistance to hegemony and other forms of structural (and interpersonal) violence. Our methodologies can become a tool for resisting various forms of hegemonic power, including economic exploitation, patriarchy, racial domination, and gender oppression. Figure 1.1 illustrates an interconnectivity between our methodological underpinnings and larger social issues as individuals and members of various social groups.

Reflexivity is the practice and process of being aware of one's own values and personal tastes and purposeful examination of one's feelings, behaviors, and motives. Intersectionality calls for *critical reflexivity* in the research process, which is a conscientious effort on the part of the researcher to examine their own personal biases, motives, beliefs, and thought processes in relationship to the research study. Critical reflexivity as an intersectional methodological tool entails revealing how the researcher's own personal tastes, values, and belief system shapes their choice of research question, theoretical assumptions, research site, relationship with research participants, and interpretation and analysis. Critical reflexivity presumably discloses the researcher's proximity to power.

Below is a writing prompt for students considering intersectionality as a methodological approach. An intersectional approach in qualitative inquiry entails conscientious reflection on one's own value system, cultural upbringing, and experiences with unequal power relationships. Moreover, intersectionality calls for thoughtful consideration of how multiple and interlocking oppressions bear equally or differently for the academic researcher and research participants. Now, take a moment to think through and respond to the questions below to better

Figure 1.1   Intersectionality and Critical Reflexivity

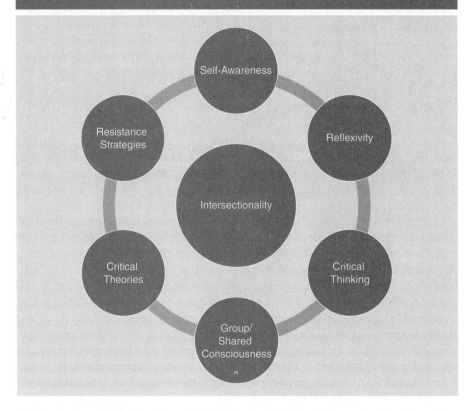

The image represents the interconnectivity of critical reflexivity and intersectionality. Intersectionality is synchronously born out of a personal self-awareness and a shared consciousness with a cultural group(s) and interaction with a group's sociocultural context.

understand how culture and context have shaped your identity, research interests, and interpretations of the social world.

1. Identify three of your strongest personal values. In what ways did your family, community, and/or schooling shape your values and beliefs? In your own words, describe how these values shaped your ideas about the purpose of research and your research interests.

2. When did you develop your first understandings of what science entailed (e.g., television, social media, a textbook, a religious experience, etc.)? What was considered science or scientific? What individuals or groups of people were portrayed as scientists in books or

media? Were members of your own racial, ethnic, gender, or cultural group represented as scientists?

3. What do members of your primary cultural group think about science and/or research? Do they trust scientists and/or researchers? Why or why not? Do they view science as safe? Accurate? Do they consider research findings to be useful to themselves or the community? Why or why not? If you cannot recall any members of your cultural group discussing science or research, why do you think this is the case? Do you personally find research to be valuable to yourself or your respective communities? Why or why not?

4. Think of a life experience that challenged one or more of your deeply held beliefs about research or science. Describe that experience in detail. Who were the people present and what was the context? How did you respond when your beliefs were challenged?

5. How might you share information about your family, cultural upbringing, and other important lived experiences to help research participants and/or research audiences learn how you came to embrace your personal values and how they became a defining part of who you are and how you approach the study and interpretation of the social world?

The above prompts can help you begin to think like an intersectional researcher. Also, the questions demonstrate the role and usefulness of intersectionality in qualitative research by prompting the qualitative researcher to examine her own socialization and personal values. For example, Venus can recall when Pluto was no longer determined to be a planet; after much deliberation privately and publicly, scientists decided to demote Pluto to a dwarf planet. During all of her childhood and most of her college years, Pluto was considered a planet. We learned "**M**y **V**ery **E**ager **M**other **J**ust **S**erved **U**s **N**ice **P**ie" to remember all nine planets (Mercury, Venus, Earth, Mars, Jupiter, Saturn, Uranus, Neptune, and *Pluto*) in the solar system. Alas, it was in 2006 that it was announced that Pluto had been demoted!

Venus was not taken aback that Pluto was not a planet; instead, she simply became more cynical of scientific proclamations overall. The demotion of Pluto from planet to dwarf planet, along with the ongoing frantic debates from laypersons and career scientists alike, signified to her that science is a process of discovery, deliberations, negotiations, and compromises. Reflecting on question four above, Venus's views of science were changed when a group of scientists gathered around and decided together, and not without debate, that a long-standing fact ("Pluto is a planet") was no longer a scientific fact!

Jennifer's example of learning that scientific proclamations do not always hold up came when she studied for a master's degree in education. There, she learned that the blank slate theory (the theory that children were born as empty vessels waiting to be filled with knowledge) popularized by John Locke was simply not true. As we learn more about genetics, scientists are discovering that our ancestors' cultural and survival knowledge lives in our DNA. Since our DNA resides with us at birth, this means that we are not merely empty vessels or blank slates and that, instead, we have generations of knowledge waiting to be utilized.

Of course, Venus and Jennifer have had many other intellectual and nonacademic encounters before and after Pluto and the blank slate theory that have required them to question science, their relationship to science, and how they participated in scientific inquiry. We hope you use the questions above to evoke your own critical consciousness as a qualitative researcher. You may want to use a research journal to reflect on the questions with depth, scope, and clarity. Further, consider how your personal values influence why you think research is important and how (or if) qualitative research aligns with your value system. How might your values shape your ideas of scientific research, power and authority, truth, or intersectionality? We hope you will respond to the above in the written/oral/signed language that comes naturally to you!

Intersectionality in Qualitative Research

The previous section raised important questions for examining one's own personal belief system. Now, we turn to a broader examination of institutionalized power and social justice struggles. We have raised the following questions elsewhere (Evans-Winters & Esposito, 2019): How does intersectionality in qualitative research further decolonial, anti-racist, and feminist social justice pursuits? Simultaneously, how does intersectionality in qualitative research expose sexism in anti-racist inquiry and make racial hierarchy in feminist qualitative inquiry visible? These questions serve as a catalyst for entering into discussions about racial and gender discrimination in academic hiring practices, epistemic apartheid in academic discourse, and debates about whose knowledge is of value.

> Whether we turn to anthropology, psychology, sociology, medicine, philosophy, literature, theology, history, or elsewhere in cultures of knowledge production, we find mounting dilemmas and controversies over whether there is only one way of knowing . . . the whole messy issue of what we know and, more importantly, how we know in an age in which hegemonic cultural authority is under unprecedented attack become even more confusing. (Stanfield, 1994, p. 167)

As pointed out by Stanfield (1994) above and emphasized throughout this chapter, science has found itself in "confusing" times as more scholars call for cultural, epistemological, and methodological representation(s). Certainly, calls for intersectionality from Black, Indigenous, and women of color has instigated such confusion and concurrently embraces such confusion in the social sciences.

Qualitative researchers generally confess that the scientific method is intrinsically subjective and value laden. Yet, qualitative research deliberations neglect to consider how researchers and the research process can simultaneously *interrupt* and *perpetuate* cultural hegemony.

Intersectional methodologies are an intentional interruption to Western Eurocentric male-centered knowledge claims and productions because intersectional methodologies attempt to center the cultural experiences, values, and beliefs of the research participants, including the researcher herself. Inherent in intersectional methodologies is the desire to convalesce cultural pluralism within and across sociocultural contexts as well as in academic institutions and disciplines. Intersectionality is also born out of the recognition that some people's knowledge claims are taken more seriously and viewed as more objective than others' assertions and declarations. Therefore, intersectional methodologies challenge authoritarian (and majoritarian) conceptualizations of credibility and validity. Intersectional critical race feminist methodologies pursue research relationships and experiences that "educe" (Akbar, 1999) authentic representations of people, places, emotions, stories, texts, and the sacred. As once explained by Na'im Akbar, the true purpose of education (and in this case, research for consciousness raising) is to educe or bring forth one's true power.

Intersectional scholars unapologetically rely upon cultural knowledge and intuition (Ahmed, 2017; Delgado Bernal, 1998) to counter hegemony, cultural domination, and master narratives. Specifically, critical race methodologists actively endeavor to challenge misrepresentations of cultural outsiders; for instance, using research to challenge medical exploitation in the name of science (see Roberts, 1999; Washington, 2006), investigate violence against multiply marginalized youth in school environments (Evans-Winters & Girls for Gender Equity, 2017; Simson, 2013; Watts & Everelles, 2004), theorize necropolitics in U.S. urban schools and neighborhoods (Evans-Winters, 2019), openly confront the whitewashing of academic labor (Darder, 2012), and demarginalize the legal rights of women around the world by blurring the boundaries between research, legal practice, and social activism (Wing, 2000).

As both researchers and the researched, women of color, Indigenous people, racial and ethnic minoritized people, queer and gender nonconforming people, and the economically disenfranchised especially draw upon cultural intuition and collective knowledge as methodological tools to disrupt knowledge apartheid. With an intentional concern for social groups' relationship to power, scholars who embrace intersectional methodologies directly respond to the nearly three-decade-long apothegm, "what knowledge is and what knowledge should be" (Stanfield, 1994).

Intersectionality is an epistemological stance and modus operandi for the examination (and interpretation) of (a) complex relationships, (b) cultural artifacts, (c) social contexts, and (d) researcher reflexivity. Consequently, intersectionality acknowledges and affirms the knowledge productions of BIPOC. In our intersectional methodological performances/productions, we incessantly demonstrate that there are multiple ways of existing in the social world; therefore, there are multiple ways of knowing it—understanding, navigating, and interpreting the social world. Accordingly, intersectionality facilitates methodological procedures that account for complexities and obscurity in our research pursuits and cultural interactions.

An intersectional perspective in qualitative inquiry raises the question, "What is the researcher's sociopolitical proximity to the research topic or issue, the cultural context in which the study takes place, and to the research participants themselves?" This question prompts the researcher to examine their own relationship to power. Accordingly, we posit that intersectionality methodologies approach the research process by seeking to more effectively comprehend the following (see Evans-Winters & Esposito, 2018):

1. How power and authority are concurrently fixed and static within and across social contexts

2. How individuals and groups resist, confront, and/or placate oppressive authority and structural power

3. How space (social and spatiotemporal) affects how social actors perceive and enact power

4. How one's place in history and contemporary society influences their approaches to qualitative inquiry and forms of knowledge production

Intersectional Research

In *Intersectionality: Key Concepts*, Collins and Blige (2016) assert that the core ideas of intersectionality are social inequality, power, relationality, social context, complexity, and social justice. To this point, intersectional methodological invocations grapple with the ways in which social inequality persists through the academic research process and in how research is disseminated. Intersectionality as a methodological (and ethical framework) mandates that we pause and reflect on how research protocols might evolve from "doing no harm" to furthering human and civil rights. To further human and civil rights, one will have to accept that resistance against inequality is an ongoing struggle, and researchers at any given moment are complicit in protecting the status quo or intentional in eradicating racism, sexism, classism, and xenophobia.

As methodology, intersectionality consistently engages in self-reflection as it relates one's power and proximity to power. Most—if not all—social actors, regardless of their race, class, and gender status, have the ability to possess power and the equal capability to abuse power. Of course, some people have ascribed (e.g., white, middle class, or intellectual privilege) or achieved (e.g., professor, president, social worker, etc.) power that gives them more control over the lives of others. In our roles as intersectional qualitative researchers, we engage in consistent cogitations with ourselves and others on our own (earned or unearned) power, empowerment, and shared powered in the research process.

We also acknowledge the agency of our research participants and/or collaborators; we also—to the best of our ability—make space for shared recognition, including financial gain, promotions, publications, and so on. This might require creativity on the academic researcher's part. For example, the authors of this textbook have coauthored publications with research participants, presented at conferences with research collaborators, created programs with research participants, and participated in fundraising activities at the close of research projects. Authentic collaborative relationships foster opportunities to become lifelong friends or organization partners. That is why it is important to understand the significance of mutuality, collective responsibility, and reciprocity in the research process. Intersectional qualitative researchers accept that power influences relationships in our research endeavors.

Power differentiations in research relationships determine types of human subject reviews (i.e., expedited, exempt, or full review), how we obtain consent and from whom (Bhattacharya, 2007; Limes-Taylor Henderson & Esposito, 2019), how and where we collect our data (Evans-Winters, 2005), what research questions are asked and how they are responded to (Green-Powell, 1997), and what research theories and methodologies we use to study social problems (Edwards & Esposito, 2019). Indubitably, intersectional methodologists' intentional stances for taking on research as a site of struggle means centering in the research process any ethical considerations that serve to (a) foster coalition-building and/or (b) threaten possibilities of meaningful symmetrical relationships with individuals, communities, or organizations while (c) recognizing the limitations and the possibilities of qualitative research for combating structural violence and hegemony.

[handwritten margin note: how power differences affect the research process]

In sum, intersectional methodologies are one more step forward in decolonizing methodologies and recentering the priorities, values, ontologies, and epistemologies of the historically oppressed and multiply marginalized.

How to Read This Book

Because qualitative research is such an iterative and emerging process, it often can't be done in a neat and linear fashion. We wrote the chapters in the order we, as experienced researchers, would think about things as we design a study. However, we understand that people have different needs and desires as they conduct research. While the chapters build somewhat on each other, they can also be read as stand-alone chapters. Additionally, we open each chapter with a vignette. These vignettes are loosely based on the experiences of our former and current students. Each vignette is a story that poses a problem or challenge someone faced related to the chapter's topic. Chapter 2 provides a closer look at what theory in general is and how it functions in intersectional research. Chapter 3 explores ethics in qualitative research. Chapter 4 explores various methodologies and research design. You won't see all qualitative methodologies presented in this chapter. We chose to focus only on those that can be done in an intersectional manner. Chapter 5 explores methods of data collection. We dedicated two chapters (Chapter 6 and Chapter 7) to data analysis. Since we have taught research methods for almost 20 years, we have seen students struggle the most with analyzing their data. We try to walk you through coding and other forms of analysis. Chapter 8 is about writing. Once you have collected and analyzed data, you will need to know how to write up your results. We end the book with a short epilogue titled "The Reimagining and Possibilities of Qualitative Inquiry." Intersectional research is a relatively new field and our book attempts to incorporate this theory into all aspects of the research process. As a conclusion of sorts to an emerging field, we look back on our knowledge of qualitative research with an eye for the incredible possibilities the future holds.

DISCUSSION QUESTIONS

1. The authors state that they are still clawing their way out of traditional approaches to qualitative research. What does that mean exactly? Can any qualitative researcher ever be truly free from the constraints imposed by colonization? Why or why not?

2. Which of the eight moments in qualitative research spoke to you the most?

3. What is intersectionality? Trace its historical evolution and note which social movements may have impacted the theory. Who are the important theorists to cite and why?

4. In what other spaces have you heard of intersectionality (i.e., classrooms, popular discourse, books, etc.)? How have your understandings of the theory shifted?

5. What is the difference between intersectionality as a theory and intersectionality as a method/methodology of research?

Theoretical Underpinnings of Qualitative Research

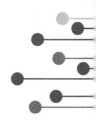

Tasha is a graduate student interested in Black girls' literacies. Her coursework included work in her content area (literacy) as well as within social foundations in which she examined the ways that race, class, and gender shape educational experiences. A course on the politics of education introduced her to critical race feminism (CRF; which is an outgrowth of critical race theory), a theoretical framework that places gender and race privilege and oppression at the center of our lives. Tasha was excited because this theory provided an academic language to describe some of her life experiences. In previous courses, she had discussed what it was like to be a Black woman in the United States, speaking from personal experience. She always wondered if her professors thought she was uneducated, not well read, or speaking too much about her opinion. Yet, CRF was premised on the experiential experiences of people like Tasha. CRF spoke to Tasha. It was a theory that made sense and it was a theory she found comfort in. She realized that she had read many CRF theorists before, but she had not realized that she was actually reading CRF. This theoretical framework would allow her to center her participants' lives as Black girls. Tasha knew right away that CRF was the right theory to frame her study.

In this chapter, we discuss the philosophical and theoretical underpinnings of qualitative research. Theory has a complicated place within qualitative research, as there is no consensus regarding its role (Anfara & Mertz, 2015). Many positivists who believe that research is objective think theory should be an overlay on your study. This understanding neglects the very fact that no research can ever be objective and that all research has something at stake. Some naturalistic researchers, ethnographers, and grounded theorists would say that using previous theories will bias your data or that the theory should "emerge" from the data, as if it will magically appear (Lincoln & Guba, 1985; Merriam, 1998). This more-open stance on conducting research without being first informed by previous literature might have sufficed before institutional review board (IRB) regulations became so stringent and before graduate students had to defend research proposals before they could actually go into the field to collect data. Now, given current constraints of the university, including IRB regulations, students must read theory before they propose their research. Yet, even if students are not reading theory per se, they are theorizing about their research topics. *Theory* has been referred to as a map that explains why the world is the way it is (Strauss, 1995) and as a set of "orienting ideas" (Miles & Huberman, 2013, p. 17). We agree with Merriam (1998), who cannot imagine a qualitative study without a theoretical framework. Because of this, we encourage students, such as Tasha in the opening vignette, to embrace theory in all its complexities. We believe that theory is a way of exploring someone else's mind and perceiving the world in the way they perceive it (Anfara & Mertz, 2015). When Tasha expressed that CRF spoke to her, it was her recognition that she had felt this theory all along. She had lived this theory. But she did not have the language to articulate it. This is the problem we see with a traditional understanding of theory. We are intimately connected to theory. It is part of our bodies and minds. Yet, our claim to embodied understandings of theory are often labeled as "subjective" or "anecdotal." These are not innocent claims. They come from a history of colonialism and imperialism—a history that has Othered us and distorted our versions of truth. These claims originate from a history that created "different and competing theories of knowledge" and "structures of power" (Smith, 2012, p. 45). This history worked hard to teach us to believe that our ways of knowing, being, and understanding were deficient, that they were colloquial and not scientific enough. We reject these understandings of theory outright and claim that it is time for researchers to recognize the important work being done outside of Western colonial–settler frames. This is a concern for all intersectional research and, thus, is important to consider when conducting qualitative research.

As such, we take the stance that theory is always intimately connected to research, even before you begin to collect or analyze data. Stanley and Wise (1993) have argued that we cannot separate what we experience as people versus what we experience as researchers. The two are intimately connected. And, just as we theorize about research, we also theorize about our everyday life experiences. We attempt to understand and explain what is going on in our personal lives as we do in our research. In other words, the theorizing that we do to understand our life experiences is the same theorizing we will do in our research. For us, similar to other feminist, Indigenous, and critical scholars, there is no way to separate theory from your research; this is partly because theory and experience are intermingled, and you need an understanding of both to conduct a research study. It is impossible to separate oneself from one's research. We are embodied researchers who are conducting research in particular historical, political, economic, and social moments. This matters.

Similar to Gloria Anzaldúa (1990), we argue for a "theory in the flesh." We need transformational theories because for too long we, as social justice academics and as women of color, were denied access to theories to use, to critique, and to create.

> Theory, then, is a set of knowledges. Some of these knowledges have been kept from us—entry into some professions and academia denied us. Because we are not allowed to enter discourse, because we are often disqualified and excluded from it, because what passes for theory these days is forbidden territory for us, it is vital that we occupy theorizing space, that we not allow white men and women solely to occupy it. By bringing

in our own approaches and methodologies, we transform that theorizing space. (p. 25)

We want you to know that theory can be useful. It can come directly from your embodied experience, which we will address more of later in this chapter. Theory is not something to fear. But theory does not have to be defined in narrow ways that make sense to only particular segments of the population. Theory can be and should be for everybody.

In the following sections, we will outline the differences between ontology, epistemology, theory, and methodology. We will discuss the ways in which these inform each other to help ground a study in a way that makes sense. We also introduce the concept of critical research with a call for all research to have critical aims. We end the chapter with a list of recommended readings.

chapter outline

Ontology

Qualitative research must be fundamentally concerned with the nature of reality and knowledge production. In Chapter 1, we addressed positivism and how that paradigm has been given so much power within social science research. We also illustrated that the ways we think about reality shape the type of research we are drawn to. These are ontological concerns. While we identify as methodologists over philosophers, we believe that one should not do research without considering some fundamental philosophical issues, such as the nature of reality, what it means to know, and how we come to know. *Ontology* is the study of the nature of reality or of being. In qualitative research, we have some commonly accepted assumptions about reality that align with the constructivist paradigm.

In Chapter 1, we discussed the positivist paradigm that has been contested by qualitative researchers and feminist theorists. In an attempt to shift how scientists thought of objectivity, Donna Haraway (1988) referred to the *God-trick*, which was positivism's belief in objective knowing and a knower/researcher who can attach himself (gender use intentional) from the objects under study. There is no "outside" from which we can conduct research as outside knowers and observers. She argued instead for *situated knowledge,* which was a version of feminist objectivity that insists upon embodied knowing and truth that is always situated within particular cultural, historical, and political moments. Any knowledge production—and this includes research inquiry—should be situated within the powerful social forces and institutions that shape our lives (Anzaldúa, 1987; Collins, 2000).

situated knowledge

Intersectionality takes as a core claim that lived experiences are important sources of data. While examining lived experiences through the lens of race and gender are important, we also must attend to the many ways these lived experiences are mediated by power and privilege. It is not enough to say you are studying Black girls. Instead, you must study the ways all forms of oppression mediate the lives of Black girls. Interviewing Black girls who have been adjudicated to discuss their experiences is not enough. The next step in intersectional research would be to contextualize their lives within the school-to-prison pipeline, to truly interrogate the various ways Black girls are disciplined in schools, in their communities, and even within popular culture. Black girls' bodies are not their own. Any qualitative researcher who wants to study Black girls, for example, must understand the complicated history of slavery, colonialism, patriarchy, and white supremacy. Black girls—and no one for that matter—do not live lives disconnected from power. They are implicated within power relations. This must be teased out as part of intersectional scholarship.

One of the main ontological assumptions within qualitative research is that there is not a single truth or a single reality. Postmodernists refer to Truth with a capital *T* and claim that this is an impossibility. There is no such thing as a single truth or a single reality, but we have been led to believe that there are Truths through what are called *master narratives*. These narratives rely on ideologies that masquerade as common sense. Often, the people or institutions who have the most power are the ones who get to write or determine the master narrative (Foucault, 1972). Those who have the least amount of power are the ones who are forced to accept these narratives and pay the price for that acceptance. Black, Indigenous, and people of color (BIPOC) have often been complicit in the telling of these master narratives (Smith, 2012) because we have been Othered in such drastic ways. We have been colonized and yet we submit to this continual colonization project every day. Before we can disrupt these master narratives, we must first identify them and call them what they are: a settler–colonial project. While we embrace the idea of multiple truths, we cannot simply relinquish the understanding that a master narrative has shaped our lives and the lives of those who came before us. We agree with Smith (2012), who states, "Our colonial experience traps us in the project of modernity. There can be no 'postmodern' for us until we have settled some business of the modern" (p. 35). What this means is that while we understand that there are multiple truths, we also know the insidious ways in which one truth gets valued over another. We cannot simply embrace the idea of multiple truths without continually recognizing that truths have different levels of acceptance by the powerful majority. We cannot pretend that this does not matter.

In order to better understand this concept, let's think about a car accident for a moment. Imagine that you have witnessed two cars crashing into each other. The reality is that an accident has occurred. Your evidence for this reality is the physical evidence you see (dents in the cars, windshield glass in the road). But the particulars of this accident will lend themselves to interpretation. For example, we know that two cars crashed into each other, but Driver A may interpret the situation as Driver B crashed into their car. In other words, the blame will be placed on Driver B and Driver A may not recognize their role in the crash.

There may be witnesses who saw what occurred. However, each will have their own vantage point. Perhaps one was sitting in a coffee shop looking out on to the street. Maybe their vision was partially blocked by a telephone pole or by

master narratives

pedestrians walking by. Another witness may have been sitting at a red light and could see the two cars parallel to their position. A third witness may have been following behind one of the cars and was able to see the accident from that standpoint.

A police officer might be called to take a report. It is the officer's job to collect witness accounts as evidence of what occurred and then write an objective account of the accident. Each witness (including the drivers) will explain their vantage point and their experience of the accident. Each person contributes to truth with a small *t*—that is, their truth cannot stand in for everyone's truth. The way the coffee shop patron experienced the accident will be very different from the way the person following behind a driver involved in the accident has experienced it.

You may be wondering whether the police report then becomes a Truth with a capital T? You might think that because the officer has interviewed all the witnesses that the officer can then approximate what happened by including a mix of witness accounts. Yet, the officer's report is still not the whole truth. The officer interpreted the witness accounts based on their interactions with an assessment of the witnesses. Maybe the coffee shop patron was a businessperson in a suit while the driver sitting at a red light was a construction worker in jeans and steel toe boots. Perhaps because of socioeconomic bias, the officer might give the businessperson's account more weight. Or perhaps one of the drivers involved in the accident was an older woman (senior citizen) while the other driver was a middle-aged man. It is likely that, due to sexist assumptions about each driver, the officer placed the blame on the older woman. Are there other factors that could shape the officer's ultimate account of the situation? Yes. What if the businessperson was a Black woman and the construction worker was a white man? Could racial perceptions and stereotypes change the police officer's account? The point of this example is that there is no such thing as a single reality. Our perceptions of the world shape our realities. Not everyone believes this, however. For example, in a court of law, it is most likely that the police officer's account will be considered the most valid account of the accident because, by virtue of their badge, the officer is assumed to know how to take an objective view of a situation. The police report then becomes a master narrative and becomes difficult to question because it is assumed to be more valid than the personal experience of one of the accident victims. But, if the court of law really wanted to do its due diligence, it would investigate how each witness and participant came to their understandings of what occurred. This concern with how knowledge is produced and acquired leads us to an examination of epistemology.

Epistemology

Epistemology is simply how we know what we know. Our knowledges have been informed by a variety of factors, though as intersectional scholars, we give primacy to experience. Philosophically, epistemology is concerned with the nature of knowledge. It asks, "How is knowledge constructed? How is knowledge acquired?"

You may have heard the saying that knowledge is power. From a philosophical standpoint, this means that knowledge is intimately connected to power relations (Foucault, 1972) and is produced by relations of ruling and relations of knowing (Smith, 1987). How we know is tied to our identities as well as to what knowledges have been passed on to us and what knowledges we've had access to.

Jennifer remembers learning in grade school about Rosa Parks, who had been portrayed in books and lessons as a tired seamstress. Jennifer had been taught that Parks worked all day and couldn't stand on the ride home; thus, she sat on a bus seat reserved for whites during Jim Crow segregation. Jennifer was astounded to learn in college that Parks was actually a well-trained civil rights activist and that her actions had been planned, rehearsed, and prepared for. Parks was not a lone, tired seamstress. She was networked and connected to a well-organized civil rights group who was tired of racism and injustice but also unified in that tiredness. Jennifer's knowledge about Parks and her overall understanding of the civil rights movement had been limited and constrained. Her epistemological framework had been informed by a white supremacist patriarchy that could not and did not credit Parks for being the activist that she was. Thus, this example is an illustration of how power relations inform our epistemologies. It is also an example of how master narratives become replicated. Institutions—in this case, the institution of education—plays a part in the crafting and communication of master narratives.

We are left to ask ourselves, why was Rosa Parks taught this way? Perhaps you may be thinking, "I am sure this author was in grade school many years ago and things have changed since then." Well, yes, but that is only partially true. The author attended grade school in the late 1970s and early 1980s in New York City. The surprising thing is that the author's daughter attended grade school forty years later in a different state and was *still* taught that Rosa Parks was a tired seamstress. That is not much by way of progress. We share this story with you to show how powerful master narratives are. The stories that get told again and again become knowledge. Those who want to disrupt these master narratives face a huge challenge, as the opposition is strong and so many people fear change. In an interview with Linda Tuhiwai Smith (2002), she wonders how to include people in a movement for social change when they fear the very change you are fighting for. When you grow up being fed a particular narrative, it becomes difficult to accept that there might be other versions of the truth, other ways of knowing and being, and other ontological positions. If your ontology shapes how you live your life, then it stands to reason that it shapes your research project, too.

We want to draw your attention to Figure 2.1, which illustrates how your ontological standpoint shapes all aspects of the research study.

You can see from Figure 2.1 that ontology informs epistemology, which informs theory, which informs methodology, which informs methods. We will discuss each of these in further detail, but it is important to understand that, for example, the theory that you use in your study will be informed by your epistemological standpoint, which has been informed by your ontological standpoint. Some researchers will combine ontology and epistemology into one category

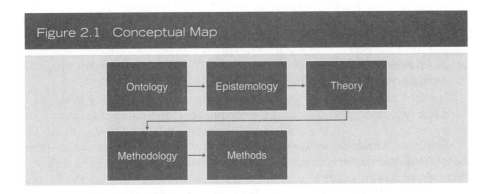

Figure 2.1   Conceptual Map

Ontology → Epistemology → Theory

Methodology → Methods

(onto-epistemological standpoint). We are okay with either, as there are many similarities between ontology and epistemology. We believe that theory, which is sandwiched between epistemology and methodology, provides the strongest framework for your study. Crotty (2013) has argued that epistemologies (or theories of knowledge) are embedded in theoretical frameworks. Let us now explore the role of theory and theoretical frameworks in qualitative research.

Theory

We began this chapter by discussing what theory is and how it has been conceptualized and transformed. We want to remind you that embodied knowing is real knowledge. We also want to remind you that there is not one way to write theory or even to "do" theory. Here is where we may differ from other qualitative researchers: We want theory to be inclusive *and* to address the needs and concerns of the most marginalized. As women of color scholars and as intersectional feminists, it is the embodied experiences of power (Ahmed, 2017) that speak to us the loudest. We are moved and we are shaken by theories that recognize our humanity, theories that privilege our experiences. We borrow a lengthy excerpt from Anzaldúa (1990), whose conceptualizations of theory make the most sense to us. She argues that what is considered theory in the academic community is not what counts as theory for many women of color academics and that there is not one way to do theory. Anzaldúa argues for a reconceptualization of *teorías*:

> Thus we need teorías that will enable us to interpret what happens in the world, that will explain how and why we relate to certain people in specific ways, that will reflect what goes on between inner, outer and peripheral "I"s within a person and between the personal "I"s and the collective "we" of our ethnic communities. Necesitamos teorías that will rewrite history using race, class, gender and ethnicity as categories of analysis, theories that cross

borders, that blur boundaries—new kinds of theories with new theorizing methods. We need theories that will point out ways to maneuver between our particular experiences and the necessity of forming our own categories and theoretical models for the patterns we uncover. We need theories that examine the implications of situations and look at what's behind them. And we need to find practical application for those theories. We need to de-academize theory and to connect the community to the academy. (p. xxv)

Similar to Anzaldúa, we do not believe that there is a correct way to write theory. Your dissertation committee or refereed reviewers might disagree with us. However, what is important to us is that you complete research that matters to you and that matters to your communities. To do so, you might have to use theories in a new way. You might have to write your own theory because the previously cited theories in your field do not apply. Many of the commonly accepted theories in many fields became theories because friends and associates of the theorists cited their work. Yes, citational practices matter. As Ahmed (2017) said, "A citational chain is created around the theory: You become a theorist by citing other theorists that cite other theorists" (p. 8). If all the theory previously available was written by white men, guess who got to be called a theorist? It certainly wasn't women of color. We are not the first scholars to say this and we will not be the last. Just know that if you are frustrated by current theories because they seem insufficient (or, in many cases, actually harmful), there are alternatives.

Up until this point, we have not differentiated between theory in general and a theoretical framework. That is because they have the same function. A theory informs your theoretical framework, which informs your methodology. We have cited researchers who spoke of the various utilities of theory, but one thing is common: Theory provides a way to orient you forward. It is similar to using a guide on a hike that already has a set path. The guide has been there before and can help steer you away from pitfalls and dangers but you, as the hiker, will have to move yourself forward. According to Crotty (2013), the *theoretical perspective* is a philosophical stance or set of assumptions that informs the methodology and provides a context for its process. Some researchers discuss a conceptual framework sometimes in lieu of and sometimes in conjunction with a theoretical framework (Ravitch & Riggan, 2012). More in line with Crotty (2013), we prefer the term *theoretical framework*. We do appreciate Ravitch and Carl's (2016) definition that a theoretical framework includes "the ways that a researcher integrates and situates the *formal theories* that contextualize and guide a study" (p. 86). We see the theoretical framework (along with the methodology) as guiding the study from its beginning to end. Schram (2003) states most succinctly what the theoretical framework guides throughout: "how you engage with a preliminary sense of problem and purpose, how you portray your involvement with study participants, the way you define key concepts, how you address assumptions within your research questions" (p. 39).

We tell our students that the theoretical framework doesn't only guide one part of the study. You should and will return to it again and again because it shapes the entire study. The theoretical framework should be put into conversation with different aspects of your research design. For example, when you discuss methodology, you should illustrate the ways in which the theoretical framework informs the methodological framework. When you analyze data, your theoretical framework should guide both your analytic choices as well as your techniques. We want to return to the example of Tasha (who opened our chapter). Tasha's theoretical framework is CRF. As a theory, CRF is premised on five tenets (Evans-Winters & Esposito, 2010). One of the main tenets is that CRF centers the experiences of women of color and articulates, understands, and explains their experiences with multiple forms of discrimination.

If Tasha were to use CRF as a theoretical framework, she would need to explain the tenets in depth, summarize its historical evolution and development, and detail how she would use the theory. She would also need to be clear about the ways in which the theoretical framework would shape how she designs the study and collects and analyzes the data.

It is not a secret that theories that center the experiential lives of people are best used in qualitative research projects. Since Tasha is interested in investigating Black girls' literacy practices, she would center the lives of the Black girls in her study and illustrate the ways in which race, class, and gender oppression have shaped their experiences with literacy. Since Tasha is not yet sure how she will analyze her data, the theory of CRF might assist her. If she is interested in centering the lives of her participants, she might also choose to keep their stories intact and analyze them through narrative analysis. This would be an example of the ways in which your theoretical framework shapes the methods and methodology you might choose for a study. If Tasha is interested in exploring the ways race and gender inform literacy, she would use a sociocultural analysis approach. There would be different possibilities but, as Tasha proceeds in decision making about the study, she would return to her theoretical framework for guidance.

Although we discuss how to write a literature review in more detail in Chapter 8, we will briefly introduce a literature review, since many assume it is part of the theoretical framework. A literature review analyzes and synthesizes previous research. Hart (2001) lists the following reasons for conducting a literature review: tracing the history and development of particular concepts and theories related to your research topic, illustrating the current knowledge of your topic, learning the definitions and vocabulary related to your topic, examining the range of methodologies and methods used to study your topic, conceptualizing key theories related to your topic, and identifying any gaps in the research on your topic. All of these reasons will help you craft a stronger research proposal because you will have an idea of what has come before you as well as how your topic has been conceptualized, discussed, and studied.

While a deeper understanding of your theoretical framework stems from the literature review, the terms are not synonymous. A *literature review* is a comprehensive synthesis of previous research on your topic (some of which you may not want to mimic because of its weaknesses). A *theoretical framework*, on the other hand, is

[handwritten margin note: reasons for conducting a lit review]

more of a guide as you design and carry out your study. It will shape all aspects of the research and is, therefore, a narrowed-down version of the theory on your topic that you think is most important and helpful. While a literature review includes many sources from the past and present, your theoretical framework will be much further refined and will include sources that you have deemed most relevant.

Now let's return to our metaphor of a theoretical framework as a guide helping you to move forward on your hike. To move forward after selecting a theory means that you must choose your methodology. In this section, we discuss what a methodology is and how it is informed by your theoretical framework. We will introduce you to specific methodologies in Chapter 4.

Methodology

Many students ask, "What comes first: your research questions or your methodology?" Before we can answer this question, we must first determine what a methodology is. There is often some confusion between *methodology* and *methods*. Crotty (2013) defines *methodology* as "the strategy, plan of action, process or design lying behind the choice and use of particular methods and linking the choice and use of methods to the desired outcomes" (p. 3). Methodology is why you do what you do in the research project. An example of methodology might be an ethnography: It has a tradition of investigating a cultural group over a long period of time. *Methods*, on the other hand, are quite simply the procedures you use to collect and analyze data. In an ethnography, you might use observations as your primary method of data collection and you might use sociocultural analysis as the method to analyze data.

It is time to return to the initial question: What comes first: your research question or your methodology? While some qualitative researchers might have a hard-and-fast rule about this, we do not. We actually believe that the way you think about knowledge and how you come to know comes first. From there, you will be drawn to specific areas of inquiry. We see your research topic (and your research questions) as emerging alongside your methodology because the two are interconnected. Let's imagine that you have identified a problem in an assessment that is regularly used by a federally funded program. Those who take the assessment do not truly understand certain questions because the questions are culturally biased. If you are interested in investigating this topic, you would not immediately decide to pursue positivist research that might include additional assessments or surveys. Given that your purpose is to investigate a flaw in a survey (in this case, cultural bias), you would look for a way to do so. Instead of providing participants with another survey that they may not understand, you would need to talk to them about their understandings of the questions. Thus, your methodology would be naturally provided to you based on this type of inquiry. Clearly, you would have to select a methodology that allows you to talk to people. Perhaps a case study (methodology) that could involve interviews (method) regarding the assessment as well as your own document analysis (method) of it.

Critical Qualitative Research

In Chapter 1, we defined what qualitative research is and examined the history of this type of inquiry. Given that there are different kinds of qualitative research, we would like to specifically discuss critical qualitative research. Simply put, critical qualitative research critiques systemic inequalities in an ethically responsible and just manner (Denzin, 2017). When we first proposed this textbook, we wanted our book to be marketed as qualitative research in general. We did not see the need to add the qualifier *critical*. This is because we believe that there is an urgent need for *all* research to take up the issues that critical qualitative researchers are interested in. Unfortunately, our society is not yet there; many people *still* believe that research, even qualitative research, should be objective and that there are other pressing issues to research without always investigating race, class, and gender. We respectfully disagree. As Sara Ahmed (2017) stated, "So much feminist and antiracist work is the work of trying to convince others that sexism and racism have not ended; that sexism and racism are fundamental to the injustices of late capitalism; that they matter" (p. 6). We can cite statistics here to support our arguments that racism, sexism, and classism still shape a person's life. There are statistics regarding the school-to-prison pipeline, the medical industrial complex, the dismal state of education for Brown and Black children, housing discrimination, employment discrimination—the list goes on. Yet, even in the face of statistics, even in the face of hearing people's stories, those who do not want to believe that injustice is everywhere will still pretend not to see. They have the luxury and the privilege of not seeing the injustice because it is not their children who are suffering. Not noticing or recognizing racism is a privilege. And when you do not have the privilege to not notice, you must become engaged in the labor of helping others notice. We face the dismay and dehumanization of our communities every day and we cannot be silent about it. Similar to Ahmed (2017), we recognize that "if a world can be what we learn not to notice, noticing becomes a form of political labor" (p. 32). Writing this book was political labor for us. Yet, any author who writes and who makes choices about what to claim as important is engaged in political labor. We say this to share with you that all research is a political act. It is tremendously tiring to have to continuously defend the fact that our stories matter. While Ahmed speaks specifically about a feminist movement in her book, *Living a Feminist Life*, the ideas are applicable to critical qualitative researchers as well and, more importantly, to intersectional qualitative researchers. Throughout our careers, we have had to continually validate our work and our claims in front of a research community who was quick to label us as "having an agenda" or "being too involved in the research." Our stories, our histories, our traumas, and our joys matter. We should not have to continually insist that racism or sexism exists. And yet, here we are, still insisting.

As mentioned in Chapter 1, the history of qualitative research, though it has been shaped by colonialism, causes many qualitative inquirers to try to be cognizant about power relations, subjectivities, and voice in ways that many positivist researchers do not have to be. Yet, it is a reality that most of our research epistemologies and frameworks "arise out of the social history and culture of the dominant race" (Scheurich, 1997, p. 1414). This means that researchers must be purposeful about interrupting the status quo. And they must be comfortable using theories and methodologies that may not always be well accepted within the academy. This is especially true of scholars who use intersectionality, as they may be in the "margins of their disciplines" (Cho et al., 2013, p. 793) and be wary about including mainstream theories and methodologies, given that these may not be culturally situated. To truly investigate social life in all of its complexities, the critical qualitative researcher must be open to being a pioneer in our adaptations of traditional frameworks or in our creation of new, culturally situated and race- and gender-centric frameworks.

Critical qualitative research has been, unfortunately, relegated to an outside position. If the center is what some might call "traditional" qualitative research, then critical qualitative research is pushed to the margins. This marginal status means that critical qualitative research is not viewed as the norm. It is, instead, viewed as somehow deficient because of its liberatory potential.

> Together, they seek morally informed disciplines and interventions that will help people transcend and overcome the psychological despair fostered by wars, economic disaster, and divisive sexual and cultural politics. As global citizens, we are no longer called to just interpret the world, which was the mandate of traditional qualitative inquiry. Today, we are called to change the world and to change it in ways that resist injustice while celebrating freedom and full, inclusive, participatory democracy. (Denzin, 2017, p. 9)

Yet, similar to other critical qualitative researchers, we view our work as central to the project of what should be social research's main goal. No longer can we merely interpret the world (as if interpretation were not a political act). As Denzin says, as qualitative researchers, we are called upon to change the world. We heed this call, and our hope is that you do as well. Now you may be wondering what the difference is between intersectional qualitative research and critical qualitative research. While critical qualitative research may interrogate and investigate issues of power, it does not always center race and gender. Intersectional research is critical in that it always interrogates power while at the same time centering race and gender in its attempt at an analysis of and accounting for systems of oppression.

Conclusion

The theoretical and methodological framework that guides this textbook is intersectionality. The text will be infused with attention to race, class, and gender epistemologies—something that is missing from traditional qualitative textbooks. It will be grounded within intersectionality. Intersectionality is both a theory and a methodology that recognizes that oppression cannot be understood as additive or in terms of a single axis. Single-axis methods and modes of analysis privilege one form of oppression over others and presumes that all members of one category of race, for example, will have the same experiences by virtue of being in the same group (Grzanka, 2014). These single-axis methods position racism, sexism, and classism as parallel instead of as intersecting.

Part of recognizing why research should be intersectional means, as Collins (2000) points out, that we must redefine what counts as intellectual. In doing this, by recognizing embodied theory and research as important intellectual endeavors, we can help reclaim much of the work that has been silenced in the past by being discounted as biased. As Grzanka (2014) argued, "Intersectionality imagines alternative ways of knowing and doing in the interest of forging efficacious tools for social justice" (p. xix). Given how the field has been emerging and how it has become more institutionalized, many things are being called intersectional without actually engaging in systemic critique (Cho et al., 2013). Dill and Kohlman (2011) have argued that there are actually what they term "weak" and "strong" intersectional analyses. Weak approaches include attention to difference but the methods normalize whiteness. In this way, hegemonic knowledges are reproduced. Strong approaches critique systems of oppression. We encourage qualitative researchers to be attuned to race, class, and gender epistemologies precisely because multiple oppressions shape the individual's lives under study. However, merely including BIPOC or the working poor in your study is not enough. You must go one step further in your analysis and discussion to critique how the identities that you label in your study shape the material lives of your participants. This is something we will return to in different chapters to explain how to do so in all aspects of your research project.

DISCUSSION QUESTIONS

1. What is embodied theory? How does it differ from traditional conceptions of theory? Which version of theory (embodied versus traditional) are you most comfortable with and why?

2. What are the differences among ontology, epistemology, and theory?

3. The authors include a quote from Ahmed (2017): "A citational chain is created around the theory: You become a theorist by citing other theorists that cite other theorists" (p. 8).

How has this pattern of citational practices impacted qualitative research? How has it impacted your field?

4. What is the purpose of a theoretical framework? What theoretical framework(s) might you use in your study? In what ways will it shape the study?

5. What are the differences between methodology and method? How will your theoretical framework impact both method and methodology?

RECOMMENDED READINGS

Anfara, J., & Mertz, N. T. (2006). *Theoretical frameworks in qualitative research*. SAGE.

Anzaldúa, G. (1990). *Making face, making soul/ Haciendo Caras*. Aunt Lute Books.

Anzaldúa, G. (2012). *Borderlands/La frontera: The new mestiza* (4th ed.). Aunt Lute Books.

Charmaz, K. (2006). *Constructing grounded theory: A practical guide through qualitative analysis*. SAGE.

Collins, P. H. (2000). *Black feminist thought: Knowledge, consciousness, and the politics of empowerment*. Routledge.

Crenshaw, K. W. (1989). Demarginalizing the intersection of race and sex: A Black feminist critique of antidiscrimination doctrine, feminist theory, and anti-racist politics. *The University of Chicago Legal Forum, 140,* 139–167.

Delgado Bernal, D. (1998). Using a Chicana feminist epistemology in educational research. *Harvard Educational Review, 68*(4), 555–583.

Edwards, E., & Esposito, J. (2019). *Intersectional analysis as a method to analyze popular culture: Clarity in the matrix*. Routledge.

Evans-Winters, V. E. (2019). *Black feminism in qualitative inquiry: A mosaic for writing our daughter's body*. Routledge.

Sandoval, C. (2000). *Methodology of the oppressed*. University of Minnesota Press.

The Ethics of Intersectionality

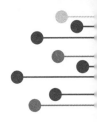

Toni is a seasoned qualitative researcher who has spent years, in her words, "giving voice" to marginalized people. She views her research as part of a social justice plan of action that tries to purposefully disrupt deficit narratives about those with less power in the world, such as Black and Brown people, the working class, and/or members of the lesbian, gay, bisexual, transgender, and queer/questioning (LGBTQ) community. Toni likens herself to someone who knows the dominant language and is able to use her position as a researcher to provide an avenue for those she considers voiceless to tell their stories. The problem with this standpoint is that Toni has never been asked by any of these marginalized groups to study and/or represent them. She takes it upon herself to include them in studies and has convinced herself that only good can come from their stories in research.

Ethics are concerned with the principles that govern a person's conduct, behavior, or activity. Research ethics, more specifically, have been defined as the "justification of human action" (Schwandt, 2015, p. 91). Accordingly, ethics in qualitative research is concerned with the shared principles that qualitative researchers purport to uphold that guide our behavior in the field and our varied interactions with research participants. We may go even further and suggest that such principles shape our approaches to qualitative inquiry, including the type of research questions we raise, how we raise said questions, our choice of observational sites, and the kinds of stories we choose to share and those we choose not to tell. Ethics also concerns itself with the protection of human participants in research. As such, ethics in qualitative inquiry contends with issues of confidentiality, privacy, anonymity, advocacy, and even human dignity. When we ponder Toni's role as a researcher, we must do so under the guise of ethics. Is Toni acting in the best interest of her research participants? We will address possible answers to this question later in the chapter. For now, we will take a broad look at research ethics and the role intersectionality plays.

How might intersectionality inform research ethics or the ethics of the researcher? Specifically, what are the ethics of the intersectional researcher? Who gets to decide what qualifies as ethical research? When should conversations about the ethics of qualitative research or the ethical quality of the research take place? What role does ethics play in qualitative research that claims to approach inquiry from an intersectional perspective? Depending upon whom you ask, you might get very different answers to these questions. Broadly speaking, ethical research is research that does no harm to research participants. Yet, the term *harm* might be defined in different ways. Some researchers believe that research ethics should concern itself with the protection of citizens and, specifically, the protection of human participants in qualitative research pursuits. This is because, historically, research and science have harmed and continue to harm. We cannot think about research ethics and the notion of harm without acknowledging that scientists/researchers are capable of causing harm and have, unwittingly or sometimes knowingly, contributed to harm.

Historically, scientists, including qualitative researchers in the social sciences, claimed a stance of "value neutrality" and insisted that moral issues, political agendas, and social envisages were of little or no concern in the pursuit of scientific truth. Science conceptualized as value neutral or amoral may present an intellectual provocation for many of us who embrace an intersectional standpoint. Therefore, intersectional feminists should consistently engage in reflection that examines their own values, institutional values, disciplinary values, and the values and guiding principles of communities and other organizations that they partner with in their research. Where can you compromise? Where are you inflexible? This type of reflection may not be monitored by your institutional review board (IRB) but nevertheless is an important endeavor as you conduct research.

As intersectional researchers and women of color, we take a strong stance in this chapter regarding ethical decision making in research. That is because, for too long, our people have been used, abused, and denigrated with research. It is not merely the outright unethical research that we are referring to. Of course, we will discuss the infamous Tuskegee experiment, where medical treatment was deliberately withheld from Black men and their partners. But we also want to educate you on the fact that research, however well-meaning it may have attempted to be, has contributed to an ongoing deficit narrative about communities of color. One of the most famous examples would be what has come to be known as the Moynihan Report. Daniel Moynihan was a sociologist who served as the assistant secretary of labor for President Lyndon B. Johnson. In 1965, he wrote *The Negro Family: The Case for National Action* as an internal document to explain rampant poverty among African American families. The document was leaked to reporters shortly after the Watts riot in Los Angeles. Although Moynihan wrote it in order to call for government intervention for solutions to poverty, many felt that the report blamed the victim. Moynihan focused on absent fathers and mothers on welfare without a historical and sociological analysis of this country's attack on the Black family. Moynihan was hurt by critics who believed he blamed Black people without examining structural factors. The intent of his report was, of course, to help Black families and write policy to address racialized poverty. However, similar to Toni in our opening vignette, Moynihan could not speak for Black families, especially not without their input. And similar to Toni, Moynihan never anticipated how the data he collected and analyzed would be used against Black families for decades afterward. The term *welfare queen*, which has been used to discuss Black women who collect public assistance, originates from Moynihan's portrayal of Black women in the report. Whether well intentioned or not, the Moynihan report has had lasting implications for the ways Black mothers were represented in public discourse.

The important thing to know as we think about ethics is that these conversations should extend beyond debates about whose values and morals are honored or privileged in the research process. In fact, research ethics debates stem from historical patterns of harm and abuse of research subjects; in particular, harm of the most vulnerable groups and individuals in society at the hands of scientists. Women, children, ethnic minorities, prisoners and captives of war, poor people, and those with disabilities have been subjected to some of the most evil and inhumane experiments in the name of science.

Human Experimentation

For instance, during what is now known as the "Nazi experiments," Nazi doctors clandestinely (yet openly at times) conducted experiments on Jewish women, men, and children. While held captive at Dachau, Auschwitz, Buchenwald, and Sachsenhausen concentration camps, Jewish people were intentionally poisoned with chemicals, viruses, and diseases; exposed to high altitudes and extreme temperatures to the point of induced hypothermia; underwent surgery (e.g., limb amputations and transplants, artificial insemination, etc.) at the hands of Nazi doctors without anesthesia; and women and men were sterilized unknowingly or against their will in concentration camps. So horrific were these Nazi experiments that many of the subjects were presumed to have not survived (Weindling et al., 2016).

Despite present-day consensus on the immorality and evilness of these experimentations on human test subjects, procedures and methods by which the so-called data were collected continue to be cited and debated amongst medical research circles and the scientific community as reputable researchers and lauded as "good" science. According to record, Nazi experiments fell into three categories: (1) medical military research, (2) miscellaneous or ad hoc experiments, and (3) racially motivated experiments. In brief, Nazi medical military experiments were to be undertaken in efforts to investigate ways to improve the life circumstances of those in the Nazi military or to simply explore ways humans could possibly survive extreme environmental conditions. Jewish and other prisoners became the sacrificial lambs of such military pursuits.

Similarly, ad hoc experiments used prisoners in the concentration camps as living and breathing human test subjects without justifiable cause but only because the prisoners were doomed to die anyway. Not much justification was required for miscellaneous experiments beyond the rationalization that the prisoners were readily available and deemed disposable. Lastly, that which is of more common knowledge is the known fact that the Nazi research community routinely starved, sterilized, tortured, and murdered concentration camp prisoners with the intent of "purifying the Aryan race." In some cases, the human subjects were alive; and at other times, scientific exploration took place on the corpse of the victims (Spitz, 2005). In life and in death, Jewish people and other prisoners became available as "data" for scientists, without the ability to consent or assent. Some researchers have called these disgusting experiments cutting-edge science. As intersectional researchers and ethical humans, we would respond that these horrific experiments were not cutting edge simply because the participants were not even recognized as human. Nothing inhumane should ever be called cutting edge. Therefore, we will not cite these studies nor entertain the idea that they were "good" science.

Although most researchers prior to conducting a study concern themselves with ethical procedures for obtaining consent or the opportunity to rescind agreement to participate in a study, there were times in history when moral law superseded ethical judgement. Enslaved African women were determined to be less than human and were considered property with no protection of human or civil rights in the United States (U.S.). If a society's moral law determined them to be without soul, then how could scientists decide the most ethical conduct in which to approach their interactions with enslaved people? Steeped in moral turpitude (and propagated by a slavocracy) and clouded by ideas of racial and moral superiority, European scientists easily decided that they had a right to experiment on African women's bodies.

During the era of slavery, doctors who were owners of enslaved Africans would merely experiment on their African captives while other doctors would seek the consent of enslavers of African women to pursue their medical experiments. One notable medical scientist who experimented regularly on African women was James Marion Simms, a southern gynecologist who actually never received formal gynecological training. Simms and other medical researchers operated under the racist notion that Black people felt no pain and thus proceeded ethically under the pretense that human property needed to be sustained and in a healthy enough state to produce and reproduce for the purpose of gaining profit for their enslavers (Washington, 2006).

Simms conducted countless gynecological experiments on African women in his custody for which he is remembered today. He is not only remembered for his undoubted cruelty to his victims but also for his invention of the vaginal speculum and a surgical technique used to repair vesicovaginal fistula (Washington, 2006). All of his scientific trials on African women's bodies (and African children's skulls) took place without anesthesia and with little or no regard for Black women's cries and screams, interminable pain, and death caused by shock, blood loss, fever or infection. Simms himself and other physicians documented the enslaved women's torture, merely as a matter of medical record. Their unceasing suffering became data.

Native American boarding schools ("schools" in which Indigenous children were stripped of their culture and forced to assimilate to a colonizer's mindset and culture) were considered an experiment led by Richard Pratt. In 1879, Pratt decided to recreate a prison experiment with Indigenous children. Pratt had given Indigenous prisoners the choice of a longer prison sentence or to assimilate by learning to speak English and accept Christianity into their lives, along with learning a trade. Pratt deemed his experiment successful because so many prisoners chose a shorter prison sentence. He decided to continue this experiment with Indigenous children and convinced 80 families to let him "educate" their children in Carlisle, Pennsylvania. He ran the school as a military regime and punished children for speaking their Native language. His motto was to "kill the Indian, save the man." By 1893, mandatory education for Indigenous children became federal policy and many were forced into boarding schools modeled after Pratt's experiment. Of course, there are some misguided supporters of these schools because they allowed Indigenous children the chance to learn a trade, and many of the children refused to go back to their Native roots and, instead, preferred a Westernized life. We use the example of the Carlisle school to show you how research or experiments, perhaps well intentioned, may have disastrous effects on participants. In this case "the Indian" was killed literally (many children died while at these schools) and figuratively (children were stripped of their Native heritage and culture).

Even though research ethics inevitably grapple with questions of right and wrong, such as what is morally wrong and what is righteous behavior expected of research scientists, there is probably less attention given to what to do with data that were gathered unethically (Moe, 1984). Some in the scientific community might shame the Nazi doctors and other racist physicians such as Simms; others are grateful for the results that their scientific explorations yielded. As morality shifts in this society, so do understandings of what is considered moral and ethical. It is important to note, however, that even though the scientific community would not allow the outright torture of research subjects in the same way they did 200 years ago, the experiments that occurred under a different set of moral standards are considered major contributions to science (Weindling, 2004). We have made our stance clear on this, however. We would never use terms such as *cutting edge* or *thorough* to describe experiments that tortured, maimed, and killed people. If scientists have learned from these unethical studies, then perhaps they should pay homage to the cultures whose bodies were destroyed in the name of science.

The Right to Consent

Post-chattel slavery U.S. researchers continued to deceive and exploit Black people. In 1934, at the height of the syphilis epidemic, the Tuskegee Institute and the Public Health Service collaborated to study the progression of syphilis in African American male subjects in Macon County, Alabama (Jones, 1993). Researchers told the men they were being treated for "bad blood," a local term used to describe several ailments, including syphilis, anemia, and fatigue. Of the subject pool, 399 of the men had syphilis and 201 men did not have the disease. Syphilis is a sexually transmitted infection that can cause serious health problems when untreated.

Without medical treatment, syphilis can spread to the brain and nervous system or to the eyes, including changes to vision and even blindness. Other symptoms include severe headache, difficulty coordinating muscle movements, paralysis, numbness, and dementia. The participants in the "bad blood" study did not receive the proper treatment needed to cure their illness; instead, researchers were interested in studying the long-term effects of this disease on people. Researchers were waiting on and documenting the disease spread to participants' brains. The problem with the infamous study is that the men involved in the study had agreed to participate in the study and believed they were being treated. Instead, the male participants (as well as their partners who were continually unwittingly exposed to the disease) were left to deteriorate. Additionally, there was no evidence that researchers actually informed participants of the real purpose of the study.

In fact, when a more effective treatment (i.e., penicillin) was discovered for syphilis in the mid-1940s, the African American men in the study (as well as their partners) were not given the treatment nor were they provided the option to quit the study, since a real cure had been discovered. The Tuskegee syphilis study lasted 40 years, from 1932 to 1972! Generations of men, women, and children have been impacted. The Tuskegee research experiment is common knowledge amongst Black people living in the U.S and is often touted as a major ethical breach.

A lesser-known unethical syphilis study is the Guatemalan study (Rodriguez & Garcia, 2013). Beginning in 1946 and ending in 1948, the U.S. government knowingly and unethically injected syphilis and other sexually transmitted diseases (STDs) into over 5,000 Guatemalan citizens. Of particular note is that the director of this research study, Dr. John C. Cutler from the U.S. Public Health Service, was also a lead scientist in the Tuskegee study. The National Institutes of Health (a U.S. government organization) had been unsuccessful in their STD testing on U.S. prisoners. They therefore turned to Guatemala and injected its citizens (without their knowledge or consent) with various STD bacteria. Many of those infected people have still not been treated today and were never compensated for this torture. This study was only discovered after Dr. Susan M. Reverby, an expert historian on the Tuskegee experiments, found papers related to the Guatemalan study in Cutler's publicly archived documents. In those papers, the abuse and torture of vulnerable people such as children, indigent people, and mentally disabled Guatemalan citizens is documented in horrific detail. In 2010, President Barack Obama apologized to the Guatemalan president and the Guatemalan people, pledging that the U.S. would uphold more stringent ethical (and legal) research standards.

Most of our parents or grandparents were alive during those times and can recall numerous uncited medical "experiments," "treatments," "diagnoses," and "cures" that seemed to impact the quality of life and/or death of unnamed Black, Indigenous, and people of color (BIPOC). We previously discussed Indigenous children, who were taken from their homes and forced to live in assimilating boarding schools. While at the boarding schools, they were also subject to experiments regarding nutrition. This was especially common in Canada as thousands of malnourished children in the 1940s and 1950s were experimented on with nutritional supplements. Mexican American and Indigenous women were forcibly sterilized without their knowledge through the 1970s. It is difficult for those of us in Black and Brown communities to decipher scientific social truths from urban legend. Consequently, many BIPOC have a legitimate fear of doctors, researchers, and medical facilities (Shavers et al., 2000; Washington, 2006). Abuse of research participants has historically occurred on already-marginalized and powerless people who became easy fodder for scientists (Mitchell, 1994). This category included disabled people and orphans of all races in addition to BIPOC. Other similar studies have exposed the less-than-innocent history of medical science research. One such notable study is the Willowbrook hepatitis study that took place at the Willowbrook Institute, which housed children with mental disabilities.

Beginning in 1955 and lasting for nearly 15 years, Saul Krugman of New York University exposed children housed at the Willowbrook Institute with the hepatitis virus. Early on in the study, Krugman took positive antibodies taken from the blood of hepatitis patients and injected the antibodies into children at the school. Krugman theorized that children exposed to the gamma globulin antibodies would develop only a mild case of hepatitis, which would cause their body to naturally develop the antibodies needed to protect them against future, potentially more serious infections. Later experiments included giving positive antibodies to a group of children newly admitted to the school while other students were intentionally infected with hepatitis. Parents who consented to participate in the study were promised housing in a newer part of the facility. The Willowbrook hepatitis study begs the question: Is it possible to induce consent under desperate circumstances?

For example, parents who wanted their children to receive care at the facility or to be shielded from overcrowded conditions at the site might have consented to the experiment out of desperation and not out of trust in science; desperation might supersede the shame, guilt, or fear of participating in a scientific experiment. In fact, some parents reported that care at the institute was not possible if the child did not participate in the study. In this case, consent was obtained from parents of the children housed in the facility. It was not possible, however, for the mentally disabled children themselves to give consent to participate in the study.

Further, if the virus affected both children and adults at the facility, then why were adults not invited or given the opportunity to participate in the study? Not extending the opportunity for adults to participate in the hepatitis experiments make it appear that something nefarious was taking place ethically; if the positive antibodies or hepatitis exposure caused no known harm or undue suffering, why not provide an intervention to all who may be affected at the institution as opposed to only the most vulnerable and those intellectually unable to make an informed decision?

The studies we have shared with you are some of the most notably heinous experiments we know of. We described this section as "The Right to Consent" because these research studies effectively took participants' rights away. They were not able to give consent to have their bodies experimented on in this way. When we begin to discuss modern-day negotiations of ethics, you will see that one part of your role as researcher is to obtain consent from the people you study. They have to know the purpose of your research, their role in the research, and whether there is a personal or societal benefit to their participation. You can no longer deceive people in research, though this was a common study tactic before more stringent IRB regulations.

Deception in the Name of Science

Yale psychologist Stanley Milgram studied research participants' response and obedience to authority figures who asked them to perform tasks which, under ordinary circumstances, would be in conflict with one's beliefs and values. In 1963, Milgram set out to investigate whether Germans were particularly obedient to authority figures, as this was a common explanation for the Nazi killings in World War II. During the recruitment phase of the study and throughout the implementation of the study, Milgram, instead of informing potential recruits about the actual purpose of the study, informed prospective participants that the study would investigate learning and memory. Specifically, participants were told that researchers were interested in understanding the effects of punishment on learning, such as "Do people learn best after they have been punished for making a mistake?" The experiment included randomly having one participant play the role of the teacher and another participant play the role of the learner. The only problem is that the selection of teacher and learner was not actually random; the experimenter (an actor in cahoots with the researcher) always played the role of student while the actual participant was assigned the role of teacher. As a matter of procedure, the teacher was instructed to teach the learner a set of word pairs, and upon failing to correctly recall a word pair, the learner would endure a series of electrical shocks by the teacher.

In some versions of the study, the learner would inform the experimenter— aware that the teacher was listening—that his heart condition caused him some worry about being shocked. The experimenter would then, following a script, explain aloud to the teacher and learner that there was no need to worry because even though the shock would cause pain, the shocks overall were not dangerous. Eventually, the teacher would be sitting in another room, separate from the learner. At this point in the study, the teacher was provided a faux shock box machine that was labeled to incrementally administer fifteen-volt shocks (e.g., 15 volts up to 450 volts). Along with the pretend voltage readings, labels on the switches also read *slight shock*, *moderate shock*, *intense shock*, *extreme shock*, *danger XXX*, and so on.

As a part of the study, the teacher delivered the word pairs to the student. The teacher was then instructed that each time the respondent gave an incorrect response, the teacher should shock the student at intervals of 15 volts. Initially, the respondent (or actor) would give correct answers, but soon enough, the actor would provide wrong answers. As the shocks were administered, the actor would gasp lightly; eventually, as the voltage increased, the respondent would shriek as if he was being tortured to death. In due course, the respondent would scream out and remind the teacher of his pending heart condition. The respondent would eventually call out that he wants to quit; soon after, there would be dead silence and no communication from the other room. When research participants (i.e., teachers) looked to the experimenter for guidance, the experimenter would inform them that they must continue or that they had no other choice. Again, this was to test their obedience to authority. Would participants continue administering electrical shocks at the risk of harming another human merely because a scientist told them to do so?

The study would only come to an end after four verbal protests from the teacher or after 450 volts was administered to the learner (who was now expected to be silent, perhaps dead) three times. This study is notable in social psychology, because 65% of research participants shocked all the way up to 450 volts, despite general consensus that most people would not cause undue harm or knowingly cause severe distress to another human being within earshot! Further, the study is notable because many of the participant teachers themselves conveyed discomfort with the task at hand during the experiment, yet the majority of participants chose to continue to follow the experimental scientist's commands. Needless to say, the Milgram study is often cited in the social sciences because (1) deception was intentionally and systematically utilized throughout the study's research protocol, (2) the study informed the research community and laypersons alike of the significant influence that those in authority have over everyday people, and (3) people will comply with authority even when it might go against their personal morals and beliefs (and will even blame the victim to justify their own behavior).

For some researchers, deception should never be considered in scientific pursuits; for other researchers, there is the belief that deception is sometimes necessary to achieve scientific truth. According to Milgram, deception caused no harm to the participants' psyche at the close of the study and the benefits of the study outweighed the risk involved. Ethically, researchers should protect participants from harm. The historical record, however, suggests that the benefits of the Milgram study also apparently outweighed the physical and psychological distress some participants encountered. Follow-up research reports that Milgram did debrief his participants to account for the state of their mental health after their participation. Most reportedly were doing fine after the study and thought their participation had been beneficial.

In the end, the undebatable conclusion reached about Milgram's study is that he failed to extend to the participants the opportunity to withdraw from the study at any time without penalty. In fact, Milgram did the opposite. When his participants expressed discomfort and attempted to verbally rescind from the experiment, they were told by the researcher "please continue," "the experiment requires that you continue," "it is absolutely essential that you continue," and "you have no other choice, you must go on." Because the experiment was about giving commands and obedience to authority, Milgram felt his approach to handling participants' dissension was justifiable and in alignment with the objectives of the study. Regardless of Milgram's justification for his research procedures, enough of his peers in the academic community questioned the ethical boundaries of his research. Even though his research findings are considered to have made a significant contribution to social science, he was ultimately denied tenure.

In the early 1970s, another researcher knowingly engaged in deception and trickery to collect data on his participants. Laud Humphrey's tearoom sex study included disguised identities, role playing, collecting study participants' personal information without their permission, and pretending to be a professional gathering health data. More specifically, as a part of his dissertation research, Humphrey decided to go undercover as a "watchqueen" in a public restroom where men had consensual sex with other men. The role of the watchqueen was to watch out for police while the men exchanged money for fellatio.

In some cases, Humphrey revealed his identity to those who visited the tearoom; in other cases, he was required to sneak the license plates of visitors and then look up their home addresses. It was at their homes that he disguised himself as a health worker and asked questions about their sexual identities, marital relationships, sexual behaviors, and motives for having sex with men. In Humprey's mind, the harassment and shame these men experienced at the hands of law enforcement warranted such a clandestine study. He believed that by proving that these were merely ordinary men pursuing intimate desires outside of their marriage and not a criminal threat to society, the study would alleviate injury to the men involved in these sexual exchanges and the undue burden to law enforcement in that these men were engaged in sex that harmed no one and that they were, overall, good citizens.

From his participant observations and interviews, Humphrey proclaimed that tearoom sex was a benefit to the men who chose to engage in tearoom sex, their families and marriages, and society at large, because tearoom sex saved the former and latter; thus, the benefits of the study overshadowed the ethical violation of one's right to privacy as well as the risk of publicly outing the men observed in the study (or jeopardizing their social standing). At the time of his study, IRBs did not exist but, disgusted with Humphrey's breach of ethics in the now infamous tearoom sex study, Washington University's sociology faculty petitioned the president of the university to rescind Humphrey's doctorate degree.

Nuremberg Code and Belmont Report

Despite historical and contemporary documentation of unethical research (or outright human rights violations), there is a history of U.S. bodies attempting to govern (or, at the least, guide) researchers' conduct and approaches to scientific investigations. During World War II, Germany actively engaged in human experimentation and Nazi scientists were summoned to stand trial before the court in Nuremberg, Germany. The Nazi scientists were tried for war crimes in Nuremberg; out of this reprehensible moment in human history came the creation of the Nuremberg Code 10-point statement issued by the Nuremberg Military Tribunal in 1947. The Nuremberg Code was established with the intent to prevent future abuse of human subjects. With that aim in mind, although specific to that time period and the trial at hand, the 10-point code influenced future research guidelines. The following ethical principles were put forth:

- Participation in research must be voluntary.
- Results of the research must be determined to be useful and unobtainable by any other practical means.
- The purpose of the study must be reasonably based on knowledge of the disease or condition to be studied.
- The research must avoid unnecessary suffering of participants.
- The study cannot include death or disabling injury as a foreseeable consequence.
- The benefits of the study must outweigh its risks.
- The study must use proper facilities to protect participants.
- The study must be conducted by qualified individuals.
- Research participants have the right to withdraw from the study at any time during the study without penalty if they so desire.
- Investigators are responsible for stopping the study should participants die or become disabled as a result of participation.

Later, in 1974, the National Research Act was signed into law, creating the National Commission for the Protection of Human Subjects of Biomedical and Behavioral Research (Canella & Lincoln, 2011). The Commission produced a report—the Belmont Report—that outlined basic ethical principles and guidelines that should underlie the conduct of biomedical and behavioral research with human subjects. The Belmont Report (National Commission, 1978) seeks to resolve the ethical problems that surround the conduct of research with human subjects. The commission concluded that the primary principles that should undergird ethical research with human beings are (1) respect for persons, (2) beneficence, and (3) justice. As outlined in the Belmont Report, the means used to recognize these principles are (a) informed consent, (b) risk/benefit analysis, and (c) appropriate selection of patients.

More recently, guidelines on key protections for research participants were revised in 2018. Known as the Common Rule, these guidelines intend to make the risks and benefits of participating in a study clearer. Additionally, and importantly for you as a qualitative researcher, studies deemed "lower risk" will have less paperwork as you seek institutional approval to conduct the study. If your study is classified as "exempt" by the new guidelines, you will not have to submit a full proposal application. Additionally, you may not have to renew your study on an annual basis.

Informed Consent

Informed consent requires that the researcher(s) share details of the study, including the research procedures, purposes, risks and anticipated benefits, alternative procedures (where therapy is involved), and a statement offering the subject the opportunity to ask questions and to withdraw from the study at any time without penalty. The Belmont Report makes it clear that some potential participants may not be able to comprehend the provided information and give informed consent or voluntarily agree to participate in the research.

Consent and Assent

Children, those with a mental disability, the terminally ill, and the comatose may not be capable of comprehension, but these members of vulnerable population groups must also be given the opportunity to assent to the research if they are able. In any case, a parent, guardian, or other representative who has the person's best interest in mind could consent to participation. Power dynamics and the influence of authority on decision making was also taken into consideration in the Belmont Report. For instance, threats of harm or offering excessive, unwarranted, inappropriate, or improper reward for participation and/or pressure coming from a position of power to obtain consent is considered unethical. This is, of course, a slippery slope. If a researcher offers remuneration in exchange for participation in a research study, how do we adequately determine that a poor person is not unwittingly pressured into participating because they are in desperate need of the money? The scientific community has left it up to us to decide what counts as harm and what does not (Stark, 2012).

The notion of vulnerable populations has been contested in the research literature. There are federal mandates designating certain groups as "vulnerable." In the U.S., for example, "special care" should be given to children, prisoners, pregnant women, mentally disabled persons, or economically or educationally disadvantaged persons. Given that there may be increased scrutiny around these vulnerable populations, needed research may be affected or decreased (Juritzen et al., 2011; White, 2007). There have been some researchers who have argued for the dissolution of the label *vulnerable* because it strips people of any agency they might have (White, 2007). We disagree. Given the heinous history of research abuses, we encourage you to err on the side of caution. Groups have been designated as vulnerable for a reason and there might be some groups without a federal designation that are still a very vulnerable population (undocumented people, for instance). Although your institution will do their part in protecting human subjects (see section on IRBs below), we also encourage you to examine the ethical codes your scientific community may have devised for its professional members. Obviously, we can all heed the Belmont Report. But there are also ethical codes from a variety of disciplines. For instance, both authors adhere to the American Educational Research Association's (AERA) ethical codes, which assert professional competence and integrity at all times. The American Psychological Association (APA) has a set of ethical codes that include justice, among other stances. The American Sociological Association (ASA) also has their own set of codes. These are only a few discipline-specific examples. The responsibility lies with you to investigate and then adhere to your specific discipline's ethical codes.

Institutional Review Boards

Today, research that is affiliated with a university is monitored by an IRB. The IRB's role is to evaluate and approve or disapprove research proposals (to ensure that no harm will be done to potential participants) as well as to monitor approved projects and demand that research cease if harm has occurred. While the Belmont Report is certainly used as a guideline, the National Institutes of Health (NIH) also established the Human Research Protection Program, which many IRBs use as a framework for monitoring the protection of human subjects. Many researchers bemoan the IRB and argue that it is based on a biomedical model that automatically favors a particular methodology or creates unnecessary scrutiny due to methodological ignorance (Israel, 2015). IRBs have often been accused of being overly bureaucratic and seem to exist to protect the university (which often receives much federal and national funding for research) instead of protecting research participants (White, 2007). Shea (2000), in his article on the bureaucracy of IRBs, shares a story of a University of California, Berkeley professor, John Wilmoth, who engaged in a series of interviews with a 112-year-old man, Christian Mortensen, he met in a retirement home. Wilmoth began the interviews after consulting with Mortensen's legal guardian and physician. Both agreed that some mental stimulation would only help Mortensen. Wilmoth, who had no training in qualitative research, reached out to his university's IRB after the interviews had been conducted when he decided he wanted to administer psychological instruments on Mortensen to determine his mental capacity. Wilmoth, familiar with psychological testing, knew he had to get IRB approval to administer these tests. Yet, in 1996, the IRB unleashed an investigation into Wilmoth's study, citing that he had engaged in scientific misconduct by not revealing his research relationship with a human subject. The university took six months to investigate and, eventually, Wilmoth was cleared of the charge of scientific misconduct and granted tenure at the university. Yet, many academics believe that this case illustrates "the unwarranted and intrusive policing of social science research by human-subject committees" (Shea, 2000, para. 6). Shea's ultimate point is that the IRB is not always a good fit for social science research. Part of qualitative research involves hanging out with and getting to know people. If, in that initial meeting, "a researcher whips out a consent form on a street corner, with warnings like those on a thalidomide bottle, people might run—or laugh" (para. 33). This can be a real concern for researchers who merely want to talk and build rapport.

Whatever your stance on the bureaucracy of the IRB, before you conduct any research, you must get IRB approval. These applications may look different, depending upon the institution, but will include information regarding how you will collect and store data, what exactly participants will be asked to do, and how you will obtain consent. In addition to the proposal, you will also need to create a consent form (for any participant 18 years old and older), an assent form (for any participant under 18 years old), and a parental consent form (for the parent of any child under 18) for your study. We have included an example consent form to use as a guide (Figure 3.1). Your institution may, however, have a template or specific language that you must incorporate into the forms. At one of the author's institutions, the IRB checks readability statistics of consent forms. They must be written on an eighth-grade level or below to ensure that all participants will understand what they are reading (presuming they read in the language the form is written in). This is because consent forms are often written at a reading level higher than that of the general population (Ogloff & Otto, 1991). If the participant cannot read the language in which the consent form is written, many IRBs will require that a certified translator translate the form into the potential participant's native language. In addition, assent forms for children must be written at their grade level so they can better understand what they are agreeing to.

Protecting Confidentiality

Anonymity and confidentiality are similar terms and are often used interchangeably in the research literature. We rarely can have anonymity in social science research; such a concept is used in biomedical studies that are double-blind (meaning even the researcher does not know who is part of the experimental group and who is in the control group). As a social science researcher, you could collect anonymous data through a survey. If you utilized a survey web tool, such as Qualtrics, you could collect data that is de-identified (i.e., you will never know who answered the survey questions). There is no way that a person could remain completely anonymous in studies that utilize interviews or observations. We can, however, help to ensure confidentiality of a participant's identity. This means that while you as the researcher will know the real identity of the participant, it is your job to protect your participant's identity from being revealed. There are a variety of ways you can do this. The first is to use pseudonyms (fake names) for all people and places involved. The pseudonym should not be easily discoverable (i.e., avoid using a pseudonym such as *Bob* for *Robert* and avoid the practice of using the same first letter, such as *Eliza* for *Elizabeth*). Sometimes it is helpful to ask participants to select their own pseudonyms so that they can identify themselves when the study is in print. Of course, there is not always consensus on the use of pseudonyms in research.

Figure 3.1   Example Consent Form

(Name of your university)
Informed Consent

Title: Perceptions of Teachers during a Global Pandemic
Principal Investigator: (Researcher name)
Student Principal Investigator: (Student name)

I. Purpose:
You are invited to participate in a research study. The purpose of the study is to analyze teachers' perceptions regarding teaching during a global pandemic. You are invited to participate because you are a teacher who taught either online or face-to-face during the COVID-19 global pandemic. A total of 30 participants will be recruited for this study. Participation will require one hour of your time.

II. Procedures:
If you decide to participate, you will be interviewed by the researcher for one hour in a virtual format.

III. Risks:
In this study, you will not have any more risks than you would in a normal day of life.

IV. Benefits:
Participation in this study may not benefit you personally. Overall, we hope to gain information about how teachers perceived their roles during the COVID-19 global pandemic.

VI. Voluntary Participation and Withdrawal:
Participation in research is voluntary. You do not have to be in this study. If you decide to be in the study and change your mind, you have the right to drop out at any time. Whatever you decide, you will not lose any benefits to which you are otherwise entitled.

VII. Confidentiality:
We will keep your records private to the extent allowed by law. (Name of researcher) and the research team will have access to the information you provide. Information may also be shared with those who make sure the study is done correctly (institutional review board). We will use a pseudonym rather than your name on study records. The information you provide will be stored on (name of researcher)'s firewall- and password-protected computer. Your name and other facts that might point to you will not appear when we present this study or publish its results. The findings will be summarized and reported in group form. You will not be identified personally.

VIII. Contact Persons:
Contact (name of researcher) at (phone number and email address) if you have questions, concerns, or complaints about this study. You can also call if you think you have been harmed by the study. Call (IRB officer's name and contact information) if you want to talk to someone who is not part of the study team. You can talk

(Continued)

(Continued)

about questions or concerns, offer input, obtain information, or suggest improvements about the study. You can also call (IRB officer's name) if you have questions or concerns about your rights in this study.

IX.   Copy of Consent Form to Participant:
We will give you a copy of this consent form to keep.

If you are willing to volunteer for this research, please sign below.

_____   _____
Participant   Date

_____   _____
Principal Investigator   Date

While you may be required by your IRB to hide the identity of participants, some participants may want to be publicly named. This may be especially true in situations where historically disenfranchised people's stories have not been part of the research canon. They may want to be noted for their time and effort and for sharing their stories. In this case, you may have to work to get special permission from the IRB to do so. There are cases where it is allowed. One example would be oral histories in which the researcher lets the participant know upfront that their identity will be revealed as part of the research. The participant consents to this type of disclosure. Revealing someone's name in the context of research is something you and the participant must think carefully about and it is something you should investigate with the IRB before any research commences.

You also want to be careful regarding the protection of places. This can be difficult, especially if you are a doctoral student. You generally will conduct research in places that are convenient to where you are located geographically. Therefore, if you are doing research at Delaware State, you cannot merely provide a pseudonym for the university and tell your readers that you conducted research at a historically Black college and university (HBCU) in Delaware. At the time of this writing, there is only one HBCU in Delaware (Delaware State), so it would be easy for readers to figure out your research location. In this instance, it might be best to be general and say, "I conducted the research at an HBCU in the Northeast." As another example, if you are doing research at an HBCU in Georgia or Alabama, you might be able to identify the state in which you conducted the study because there are more than one in each state, but you would still need to be careful with the pseudonym you chose for your study. For example, you would not call *Alabama A&M* something like *Alabama B&N*. We know this must sound asinine to you or more like common sense, but you would be very surprised by how careless researchers can be with pseudonyms. They may think they are being clever, but if readers can identify the location and/or people involved in your study, then you have not worked hard enough to protect their anonymity.

To be truly ethical and aware of issues that could arise, you may also have to think about the ways already marginalized participants might be further marginalized. For example, one of the authors was, at one time, the only Latinx faculty member in her college. She participated in a campus climate focus group but feared the entire time that if her words were connected to her identity as Latina, she would be outed or exposed. The facilitator of the focus group assured her that her words would be de-identified and that no reference to her specific identity as Latinx would be included. Issues similar to this might be prominent in your study, depending upon your topic and participants. We suggest that you develop a culturally responsive framework to ethics. Lahman (2018) has written a text on culturally responsive ethical practice and we certainly cannot do the book justice here. We encourage you to read it and develop your own ethical stance. Your ethical stance should include aspirational ethics, which are the highest ethical stance a researcher tries to attain (Southern et al., 2005) and which compel you to go above and beyond the minimal ethical requirements. Lahman (2018) developed what she terms a Culturally Responsive Relational Reflexive Ethics (CRRRE) stance. CRRRE researchers must be culturally responsive, which entail us first understanding our own culture before we can begin to study someone else's. Lahman's framework includes eight different strands, including continually employing reflexivity throughout the research and developing the skills needed to be agents of change through research practices (p. 36).

Ethical Dilemmas

IRBs are interested in your compliance with their rules and regulations. However, IRBs cannot anticipate everything that may happen nor is an IRB member in the field with you, looking over your shoulder as you collect data. Thus, it becomes your job as a researcher to aspire to ethics that are "beyond regulatory compliance" (Israel, 2015, p. 191). It is your role as the researcher to anticipate ethical dilemmas and be as thorough as you can in their resolution. We will pose a few ethical dilemmas for you to think about now. While there are no easy answers and certainly not one "right" answer, it is important that you consider multiple approaches to these common ethical issues before conducting research.

- After an explicitly racist incident on campus, a researcher is interested in interviewing college students of color about their perceptions of the campus climate. What are some ethical issues the researcher should anticipate?

- The IRB wants the researcher to put the phone number to the campus psychological services on the consent form. What are the pros and cons of doing this?

- If a participant gets upset (cries) during the interview, what should the researcher do?

- A researcher is interested in interviewing high school students (ages 14–17) about sexual activity and STD prevention. What ethical issues might the researcher anticipate?

- If a participant reveals sexual abuse, what are the researcher's legal and ethical responsibilities? Are these responsibilities the same?

- A researcher is conducting observations in an elementary school. She is witness to a teacher belittling and insulting her students to the point that some cry and/or become visibly upset. How should the researcher handle this?

- An evaluator of a program knows that his report will help determine whether or not the program will be funded next year. The program's (afterschool tutoring for underprivileged students) overall goals are noble and there is evidence that the tutoring is making a positive impact. However, the researcher observes overt sexism and sexual harassment throughout the program. The male counselors favor the boys, and the boys are allowed to explicitly sexually harass the girls (for example, the researcher witnessed a male student physically hold down a female student on a desk and threaten to rape her while the counselor did nothing). What should the researcher do both in the field and in the report?

Conclusion

We have spent a lot of time discussing unethical research for two reasons: The first is that we want you to be aware of what has been done in the past and how people's notions of ethics and what is right and wrong have changed over time. The second reason is that because ethics can be complicated and situation specific, it is sometimes easier to tell you what not to do than to provide you with rules about what to do. We suggest you use the Belmont Report, your own discipline's ethical codes, your university IRB's regulations, and a trusted mentor as you think about the best ways to conduct ethical research. As an intersectional researcher, you will have the additional task of making sure that your research does not participate in deficit narratives about already marginalized people. This is no easy task, as you may not always be able to anticipate how your research findings will be used in the future. But we believe that if you proceed cautiously and ethically in all decisions, you will stand a better chance of conducting research that benefits instead of harms.

DISCUSSION QUESTIONS

1. What are research ethics? Who or what governs them?

2. How have researchers' understandings of ethics shifted throughout history?

3. In what ways were unethical experiments shaped by colonialism and racism?

4. What unethical experiments had you heard about previously? Which ones were new to you? Why do you think there were some that you had never heard about before?

5. What is the purpose of the IRB? What is your university's process for submitting research to an IRB?

Methodology

Mateo was enrolled in an introductory qualitative research course. He found himself intrigued by various methodologies but did not know how to select one for his study. His professor asked him to reflect on what questions he wanted to ask. Mateo was interested in understanding how undocumented immigrants and refugees negotiated schooling for their children. His professor pointed out that because he was mostly interested in their experiences, which would be recollected best by interviews, he should choose a methodology that centered interview data. In other words, Mateo would not conduct an ethnography because there really wasn't much to observe unless he sat in on school meetings between the parents and school administrators. Basically, his data collection methods would consist of interviews and, thus, he needed a methodology such as phenomenology, case study, or life history—all methodologies that can primarily utilize interview data.

There are a variety of methodologies to choose from in qualitative research. We will provide you with a general look at some of the more popular methodologies but encourage you to delve further into these. Before we begin examining different methodologies, it will be important to review the difference between *methodology* and *method*. Remember that a methodology undergirds your study. It provides a framing for the methods (data collection and analysis tools) that you select. Before you can choose a methodology, as Mateo did in the example above, you first should think about what research questions you need responded to and what methods will allow you to have those questions answered through the research process. We also suggest thinking about your ontological and epistemological frames—specifically how they inform your methodological choices. In other words, if your onto-epistemological frame is intersectional and/or critical, then your methodological choices would align with that perspective. In the next section, we introduce a few methodologies that student researchers typically draw upon to address qualitative research questions. Each methodology will be discussed from an intersectional perspective.

Ethnography

Ethnography is often defined in terms of its hallmark method, which is participant observation. Ethnographic research entails a sustained exploration of a cultural group or setting through participant observation. Sustained exploration generally means that the researcher is required to fully immerse themselves into the research context or within a group for at least one year. Obviously, if a researcher is physically present every day or a few times a week over the course of at least one year in the research site, it would be strange not to speak to or engage with participants. When we say participant observation is the hallmark method, we also recognize that in order to fully understand people and their culture, the researcher must frequently engage and cannot merely sit back and observe. Thus, in the course of these observations, formal and informal interviews may occur and the researcher may also collect other forms of data while in the field.

Ethnography has been influenced primarily by two traditions, British anthropology and the Chicago school. British anthropologists from the 19th century include E. B. Taylor, who is often called the father of anthropology. The field during this time was primarily survey and questionnaire based and most of the questions asked were predetermined and served the interests of the colonial empire (Davis, 1999). Over time, it became clearer that this method of observing and documenting people's way of life lacked sincere in-depth analysis at best and accounts were more than likely a distortion of the cultural group. We would be remiss if we did not point out that the original aim of ethnography, which emerged in anthropology, was to scientifically explore the Other—in particular, the exotic Other living in faraway lands and places. These early ethnographers had their own religious, scientific, and political motives for exploring and documenting foreign cultures. Sometimes the intent of anthropologic fieldwork was to spread the lie or to prove that natives of a land were uncivilized savages, while at other times, European men set out to document the lack of intellect or moral aptitude a cultural group had in comparison to European cultures with the intent to rationalize their colonization, enslavement, or even genocide. In the end, as is more than obvious today when we look at the historical role of science in colonization and imperialism, traditional ethnography proliferated European power and domination. Early European anthropologists, such as Rosalie Wax, described ethnographic fieldwork in ways that continually dehumanized the cultures they studied. For example, Wax (1971) stated, "A good many literate and reasonably well-educated men—government officials, administrators, missionaries, and political exiles—were obliged to spend many years and sometimes most of their lives living and working with an alien or 'backward' people" (p. 23). These were not classically trained anthropologists, but in an effort to appear sincere or rigorous, they did live among the Other long enough to provide accounts of their lives, albeit from the perspective of the European-biased outsider. Early anthropologists, including Franz Boaz, were considered to be "armchair anthropologists" because they rarely immersed themselves with a culture group or setting for a long period of time. In many cases, if the armchair anthropologists did take time to interact with the cultural group they studied, the visitor did not stay long enough to learn the language or meaning of customs or rituals.

Anthropology as a field of study began to change as more detailed accounts were expected of anthropologists. Bronislaw Malinowski was the first documented

British anthropologist to actually live amongst the cultural group he purported to study. The British anthropologist's stay occurred by chance—once Malinowski arrived in New Guinea in 1914, World War I began. He could not travel and thus ended up staying in islands near Australia until 1918 (Wax, 1971). By the late 1800s and early 20th century, anthropologists sought to engage in more extended periods of study of a cultural or ethnic group. The Chicago school of urban sociology (mentioned in Chapter 1) began to gain prominence in the 1920s and 1930s. During this period, sociological researchers began studying urban life in the United States (U.S.) and focused on "outsiders" living on the fringes of society in metropolitan areas. This was a departure from more traditional anthropologists, who believed the exotic Other was to be found in other countries and on other continents. Using anthropological and sociological research methods, the Chicago school turned away from the tradition of Othering while studying marginalized outsiders in faraway lands but continued this tradition by Othering local marginalized outsiders such as the Black urban poor, immigrants, gay men, prostitutes, and criminals.

During the time of British anthropology and the Chicago school, Indigenous, Latina, and Black women anthropologists were pushing the field to consider concerns around race and gender in ways that did not Other people or feed the narrative of the Savage (McClaurin, 2001). However, given the ways in which whiteness and maleness are glorified and privileged in academia, their work was given little credibility.

Zora Neal Hurston, a Black writer, began her career as an anthropologist (she was a student of Franz Boas) and published a 1930 study called *Dance Songs and Tales from the Bahamas*. Manet Fowler was the first African American woman to earn a PhD in anthropology from a U.S. higher educational institution (Cornell) in 1952. Vera Green was a founding member and the first president of the Association of Black Anthropologists in 1977. Johnetta B. Cole, who eventually served as the president of Spelman College, published *Women in Cuba: The Revolution within the Revolution* in 1980. For more names, please review Irma McClaurin's (2001, pp. 6–8) timeline of selected Black women/feminist anthropologists in her anthology, *Black Feminist Anthropology: Theory, Politics, Praxis, and Poetics*.

In addition to Black women, Indigenous anthropologists such as Gladys Tantaquidgeon entered the field. Dr. Tantaquidgeon was a Mohegan medicine woman who studied anthropology at the University of Pennsylvania (as a student of Frank Speck) and wrote *A Study of Delaware Indian Medicine Practices and Folk Beliefs* (1942). Ella Cara Deloria (Anpetu Wastewin), born on the Yankton Sioux Reservation, received a bachelor's degree from Columbia Teacher's College in 1915. Though she was not formally trained as an anthropologist, she worked with Franz Boas as a translator of Dakota Sioux texts. Deloria grew close to Ruth Benedict (a white female anthropologist), who encouraged Deloria to focus on kinship and the role of women in the culture of Lakota and Dakota Sioux. Deloria then engaged tribal elders in interviews and this cultural knowledge was preserved. A notable Latina cultural anthropologist/ethnographer includes Elena

Padilla, who was the research assistant to sociologist C. Wright Mills. Her ground-breaking work, titled *Up from Puerto Rico* (1958), challenged deficit narratives about race and poverty.

Some might argue that traditional ethnography has morphed and shifted from its early days (Madison, 2005; Noblit et al., 2004) but this was not without much feminist and race-conscious uprising. Lamphere (2006) argues that

> African American and Chicana/Latina feminists were crucial in bringing the issue of difference to the forefront of feminist anthropology in the late 1970s and early 1980s and in deconstructing the emphasis on the commonalities among women assumed by early US feminism. Because race and ethnicity were so salient in shaping their own lives, these anthropologists were drawn toward research on African American and Chicana/Latina women to articulate the intersection of race and gender in individual lives. (pp. 49–50)

The civil rights movement and feminism exacted a toll on the traditions of ethnography, and researchers of all races and genders were forced to come to terms with power. Coming to terms with power is not the same thing as accounting for it. By *coming to terms*, we mean that researchers began recognizing the subjective nature of all research. They also became more aware of the process of Othering. They asserted, "Ethnographic truths are thus inherently *partial*—committed and incomplete" (Clifford & Marcus, 1986, p. 7). The text this quote is from, *Writing Culture: The Poetics and Politics of Ethnography*, was heralded by some in the field as groundbreaking and as a testament to postmodernism's influence on how observation is done and stories are told. Yet, women anthropologists of all races were left out of the book because Clifford claimed in his introduction that they had not produced innovated writing. It was clear that even in 1986, women's scholarship continued to be devalued. Cultural critic bell hooks (1990; who, by the way, prefers her name not to be capitalized), critiqued the book and its cover:

> I look at it and I see visual metaphors of colonialism, of domination, of racism. Surely it is important as we attempt to rethink cultural practice, to re-examine and remake ethnography, to create ways to look at and talk about or study diverse cultures and peoples in ways that do not perpetuate exploitation and domination. (p. 128)

Clearly, we still have a long way to go in terms of how power gets accounted for in the research process. In 2020, for example, as we began writing this textbook, our review of current qualitative textbooks showed few to almost none that mentioned the words *race*, *class*, *gender*, or *power*. Thus, researchers are still, 150 years later, not being held accountable for all the dimensions of power in their studies. Consequently, there is little analysis of how race, gender, and other social identities overlap to influence how we justify the use of ethnography, which cultures are studied and by whom, and how ethnographic accounts are influenced by power and privilege. Intersectionality in qualitative inquiry offers a new approach to understanding how race and gender influences how one perceives culture, interacts with culture, and shapes culture. Critical ethnography is more complementary to the main goals and objectives of intersectionality in qualitative research. Next, we discuss critical ethnography as a qualitative research methodology.

Critical Ethnography

As a derivative but critical critique of traditional ethnography, critical ethnography attempts to account for interpersonal and structural power in research and society. Some have argued that critical ethnography is the research method more aligned with critical theory (Kincheloe & McLaren, 2000; Madison, 2005). Critical theorists who engage with research enter into the research process with the understanding that (1) society privileges members of the dominant group, (2) social identities such as race and gender are social constructions, and (3) social structures impede on people's daily lives, thus influencing individuals' and groups' behaviors and opportunities. Critical theorists seek to examine the relationship between power and science and how science becomes a tool of hegemonic power to justify and reinstate power. Accepting the limitations and possibilities of science, critical theorists such as critical race theorists, feminists, and Marxists seek to return the research process to the people; stated differently, they strive to involve everyday people in the research process with the intent to use research as a tool to change communities and societies based on the needs of members of the community. Critical ethnography is a methodological tool for critical theorists. Although we argue that all researchers must pay careful attention to the ways their studies may impact research participants, critical ethnographers consider critical reflection or *reflexivity* to be an essential part of the research process. You are not a critical ethnographer if you do not address the ways in which your interpretations and representations of peoples' lives might impact them. Critical ethnography from an intersectional standpoint especially takes into consideration how race, class, and gender influence the researcher's perceptions and interpretations and how race, class, gender and other social identities converge to shape our participants' lives in a particular sociocultural context. We believe that you should not engage in ethnographic research unless you are cognizant of the ways in which power and privilege shape your interactions with participants and your interpretations of those interactions.

Autoethnography

As a derivative of ethnography, autoethnography is a methodology that turns the researcher's focus on themselves. It is a "process, product, and possibility for learning" (Hughes & Pennington, 2017, p. 1) about a single subject of study in which the researcher becomes the subject of research. Ellis (2009) notes,

> As an autoethnographer, I am both author and focus of the story, the one who tells and the one who experiences, the observer and the observed,

the creator and the created. I am the person at the intersection of the personal and the cultural, thinking and observing as an ethnographer and writing and describing as a storyteller. (p. 13)

Autoethnography is an *embodied* process (Ellis & Bochner, 2006), which means that the researcher is intimately involved in the data collection process and the telling of the story that unfolds. Autoethnography as a qualitative research approach has grown and expanded quickly to the point that Hughes and Pennington (2017) were able to provide an outline and description of at least twenty-one different types of autoethnographies! We will not cover every type of autoethnography here, but we will briefly provide an overview that will focus on what we consider to be important to the intersectional project. Autoethnographies must pay close attention to what is called "relational ethics" (Ellis, 2007), which involves a critical examination of the ways relationships are impacted by the telling of one's story. The autoethnographer should be cognizant of the ways others are portrayed in their stories and how the researcher's representation of someone else may impact them socially or personally. While it is not always possible to mask the personal identities of the people connected most intimately to you as the researcher, you have an ethical obligation to try to alter (as much as reasonably possible) characteristics and details about people or places that you include in your telling in order to try to safeguard people's privacy. When engaging in autoethnography from an intersectional analytic framework, the researcher intentionally examines their own multiple social identities and seeks to understand how race, gender, and other forms of oppression transverse in their lives, including those around them, to create barriers and opportunities. Intersectionality would require the critical (recall that intersectionality is a critical theory) autoethnographer to center conversations of power and privilege in their personal narrations and to examine how their lived experiences have contributed to their cultural insights, perspectives of the social world, and social phenomenon under study.

A Note About Methodological Choices

Above, we covered ethnography and its variants because it is the hallmark of qualitative research. Undertaking the study of one's own or other people's culture is fraught with complexities but also possibilities. If qualitative researchers truly set out to privilege lived experiences, then there is no better way to understand someone's experience than through a systematic and engaged study of their life. Of course, there are other ways, outside of ethnography, to study culture and how people make meaning of their lives. Remember that in critical research, the goal is to articulate and critique ideologies that assert themselves as realities. Ideologies function to keep structures and mechanisms of oppression in place, and because they structure all human interactions, they masquerade as common sense and are taken for granted. It becomes the critical qualitative researcher's role to unveil the familiar and taken for granted. Intersectionality positions race, class, gender, and the researcher's mediating identities at the center of the research process. In *Fictions of Feminist Ethnography*, Kamala Visweswaran (1994) attempts to explain the relationship between identity, ethnography, and representation. The feminist ethnographer writes,

> Rather, I have wanted to detail how those of us engaged in identifying ethnography may be moved by different sets of questions concerning power, domination, and representation; how we may ourselves be positioned (and not always by choice) in opposition to dominant discourses and structures of power. The oppositional sense of such ethnography shows that these questions are not only important, but indeed vital for reshaping the practice of anthropology, and point again to the double sense of "identifying ethnography." (p. 140)

As indicated by the Visweswaran, personal history and systems of power influence the types of research questions we ask and the kinds of stories we tell. Furthermore, the anthropologists reveal that those multiply situated at the margins will, at times, develop an oppositional stance that intentionally or unintentionally repurposes the meaning and functions of ethnography. Researchers from marginalized communities, for instance, who investigate social reality from an intersectional perspective strive to conduct research in relationship with and for our respective communities. Because traditional qualitative research has been concerned with the opinions and perspectives of everyday people, there is an assumption that qualitative research is inherently critical. However, not all qualitative researchers purport to be critical nor is all qualitative research critical. Therefore, in this book, we will not discuss all methodologies available to qualitative researchers, but we will privilege those qualitative methodologies that allow researchers to engage in more critical studies. If we take seriously the notion that research should be "a conscious political, economic, and personal conduit for empowerment" (Tyson, 2003, p. 24), then we must carefully consider the best means to achieve that objective. In other words, it is not fruitful to research simply for the sake of research or for personal or institutional gain. Instead, intersectionality as a critical standpoint theory in qualitative research calls for us to learn more about what social actors in our own or other communities need and how we can use research to meet those needs. Furthermore, intersectional analysis sets out to examine how we learn to access our collective knowledge to resist domination and enact transformation as needed. In this same vein, intersectionality frames ethnography as limited and partial knowledge. Specifically, "ethnography, like fiction, no matter its pretense to present a self-contained narrative or cultural whole, remains incomplete and detached from the realms to which it points" (Visweswaran, 1994, p. 1).

Arts-Based Research

Arts-based research (ABR) is another relatively new methodology compared to other qualitative research methodologies like ethnography. ABR actively avoids the dichotomy between art and science by blurring the boundaries of the two genres (Barone & Eisner, 2012). Artistic and scientific methods are used to explore, investigate, and creatively (re)present social life. According to Barone and Eisner (1997), there are seven main features of ABR (pp. 73–83):

1. The creation of a virtual reality

2. The presence of ambiguity

3. The use of expressive language

4. The use of contextualized and vernacular language

5. The promotion of empathy

6. Personal signature of the researcher/writer

7. The presence of aesthetic form

ABR is most notable for how it is represented. For example, a researcher could design and implement what most would consider to be a traditional ethnography, but then the researcher could present the data in the form of a novel or as a screen play. Research such as ABR makes positivists a bit nervous because they wonder about its scientific impact and validity, since the boundaries between art and science become nearly indistinguishable. Our response to those who critique or reject ABR due to questions of validity or legitimacy is that there are other methodological approaches that blur the line between fact and fiction. For instance, although positivists do not talk about it much, statistics or quantified data tend to generalize or even conceal social phenomenon in order to capture the bigger picture or trends. They also blur the lines between art and science but are not transparent about it, hence the use of tables, histograms, bar graphs, pie charts, line charts, and so on. Similar to presentations of statistical information, there are a variety of different forms of ABR, each with their own styles and methods. In poetic inquiry, for example, you can use data to write poetry with the goal of synthesizing "experience in a direct and affective way" (Prendergast, 2009, p. xxii). This enables a more creative way to present findings. From an intersectional standpoint, we are drawn to poetic inquiry because it allows research to be an embodied process informed by the lived experience and knowledge base of the researcher. Given that poetry engages both the cognitive and sensory arenas (Sparkes et al., 2003), it allows the reader to experience the research findings in a more visceral way. Besides poetry, researchers have used the collected data to write screenplays, short stories, or novels (sometimes referred to as *social fictions*; Leavy, 2013). Depending on the researcher's previous training, skill set, or talents, the options for presenting data or social facts are limitless in ABR. You merely have to be willing to be creative and not remain boxed into traditional ways of presenting research.

Example 1: Methodology
Poetic Inquiry (Interview Based)

Research Question(s)

1. How do managers who are a part of racial minoritized groups, living and working in a predominately racially and ethnically working-class neighborhood, experience being recently laid off from employment during a health pandemic?

2. How do these layoffs affect local managers differently from their colleagues who live outside of the local neighborhood and are not a part of a racial minority group?

3. How do women of color managers experience the layoffs similarly or differently from their male counterparts? What strategies do racial/ethnic minorities and/or women of color use to cope during this time?

Methods

The researcher, a Muslim American male business major, will interview 30 managers who have been laid off since the onset of the health pandemic that caused the layoffs. Interviews will last 1–2 hours with follow-up interviews as necessary. As part of the poetic inquiry, the researcher will read and reread the transcripts to develop poetry that captures the feel of the experience. In alignment with intersectionality, the researcher may decide to focus on the experiences and insights of people from racial/ethnic backgrounds and those living and working in racial/ethnic minority communities. Thinking from an intersectional perspective, the researcher understands that race, gender, class, and location converge to make certain groups of people more vulnerable to social forces such as a health pandemic and economic crisis. Further, working from within an intersectional framework allows the researcher to have a better understanding of power and agency; thus, the researcher would also be interested in analyzing pain/frustration alongside of coping or agency in the face of a health pandemic that led to economic shifts. Because personal and collective knowledge are important tenets of intersectionality born out of critical race feminism (CRF), the researcher may choose to employ poetic inquiry as an embodied form of expression and representation.

Narrative Inquiry

Narrative inquiry is often discussed as both a methodology and a method of collecting and analyzing data. In this chapter, we will briefly focus on its use as a methodology and later consider narrative inquiry from an intersectional framework. First, narrative inquiry methodologically centers narration and sets out to capture stories. With shared stories as its focal point, the overall objective of narrative inquiry is to capture a glimpsed understanding of lived experience. As Clandinin and Connelly (2000) state, experience is studied narratively because "narrative thinking is a key form of experience and is a key way of writing and thinking about it" (p. 18). Narrative inquirers recognize that both research participants and researchers lead storied lives. Our stories as researchers cannot be separated from the meaning we make of participant stories.

Robin Boylorn (2017), in her ethnography of rural southern Black women's lives, explains that

> telling is not without controversy. There are multiple versions and multiple truths. A common characteristic of these women's stories, including my own is resilience. . . . I examine our lives, over generations, to determine how black women use narratives to cope and communicate about their experiences and as acts of social resistance. (p. xxi)

Using intersectionality as her analytical framework and narrative inquiry as her methodological tool, the Black feminist researcher teaches that (a) embedded in the process of inscribing other people's lives, which is what we ultimately are doing in ethnography and narrative inquiry, is the risk of not always precisely portraying the characters or their lives in the same way that the participants see themselves and (b) there is an understanding in narrative inquiry that researchers are interested in patterns of shared stories and the meanings that individuals give to the stories. In the case of narrative inquiry taken up from an intersectional perspective, as indicated by Boylorn, is an intentional focus on research participants' strategies of coping and forms of resistance. Recognition of our own subjectivities and how they shape understanding is a crucial aspect of critical work.

Indeed, narrative inquirers view social identities themselves as narratives and believe that people construct identities through storytelling, for it is through stories that people come to understand who they are and how they are positioned in the world (Riessman, 2008). Critical theorists also believe that narratives can be utilized for political mobilization. All too often, social science research such as sociology and education have told majoritarian stories. For researchers exploring the social world from an intersectional framework, then, narrative research can be used as a way to "defy historical and contemporary racial oppression" (Tyson, 2003, p. 24), because reality is told from the perspective of the marginalized. By telling the stories of those who have been historically marginalized, researchers are able to center "discussions of race, gender, class, and sexuality as part of a larger political and epistemological struggle for a better and just future" (p. 25). A narrative inquiry can be interview based or it can be part of a study of previously collected stories (which include documents written on a topic). Because of this, we will provide two different example designs of narrative research.

Case Study

Simply put, a case study is an exploration of a bounded system made up of single but related foci of study. The actual case can be a program, event, activity, or group of individuals (Stake, 1995). The boundary of the case is often determined by the researcher. For example, a researcher might be interested in studying math

Example 2: Methodology
Narrative Inquiry (Interview Based)

Research Question(s)

1. How do adult refugees and/or asylum seekers who were forcibly separated from their children navigate the application process?

2. What sources of support did they draw upon through the process?

3. How are their stories impacted by trauma, despair, hope, and resilience?

Methods

The researcher will interview 25 adult refugees/asylum seekers who came to the U.S. within the last four years but were separated from their children during the time of an anti-immigrant administration known for the inhumane immigration policy of family separation. Interviews will last 1–2 hours at a location designated by the participants and follow-up interviews will be scheduled as necessary.

Example 3: Methodology
Narrative Inquiry (Using Documents)

Research Question(s)

1. How is the story of breast cancer told from pamphlets and other propaganda (e.g., posters, brochures, handouts, etc.) provided in oncologists' offices?

2. What characters are present in the stories and what are their roles?

Methods

Researchers will collect a variety of pamphlets from oncologists' offices nationwide (U.S. offices) that deal with the topic of breast cancer or breast cancer awareness. A narrative analysis will be performed using the pamphlets with particular emphasis on how characters in the story are represented and what discourses are relied upon in the story of breast cancer. Special attention will be given to an intersectional approach, particularly in looking at how people from various racial, ethnic, linguistic, and age groups are represented in the propaganda and what stories are being told with them in mind.

teachers' perceptions of social justice while working in a diverse urban school district. The researcher might choose to study all math teachers in the district but then bound the cases by school. If the researcher wanted to study math teachers nationwide, the boundary of the case would be a group of U.S. math teachers or even cases bounded by city or state. In a case study, the context of the case is crucial for a researcher to understand the context in which participants experience life. In the case of math teachers' perceptions of social justice, the location and the cultural context in which one teaches is significantly important to beliefs about social justice and equity. A case study serves the purpose of understanding how one's perception or behaviors are influenced by those around them, programs and policies, and physical environment. The researcher is interested in how the case relates to other cases to form a whole.

In fact, a hallmark of a case study is that it investigates a contemporary phenomenon in its real-world context (Yin, 2018). The focus on a nationwide context, for instance, will be different than a focus on a single school, school district, or person. In this example, if the researcher focused on teachers' perceptions nationwide, then the researcher would have to consider how their perceptions influence and/or are impacted by the public education system nationwide, not simply at the local level. For a single school, the researcher might be most interested in standards, type of school (rural, urban, suburban), size of school, accountability practices, and school demographics but might be less concerned with how the single school is contextualized within a larger federal and state system. Unlike an ethnographic study, which takes place over time within a specific cultural context, a case study does not have strict time boundaries. Yet, you may want to maintain prolonged engagement in the field site and with your research participants, even though there is not a minimum time requirement to meet.

Below, Table 4.1 lists the methodologies we have discussed thus far in this chapter and methods of data collection typically associated with the methodology. Keep in mind that this is not an exhaustive list and we suggest that you check out other methodologies within your respective fields. For example, case studies are very popular in the medical field, but more and more medical researchers are experimenting with phenomenological research. The most important thing to

Table 4.1 Methodology/Method

Methodology	Method(s) of Data Collection
Ethnography	Primarily participant observations, some formal or informal interviews, documented or undocumented conversations, collection of documents and/or artifacts
Critical Ethnography	Primarily observations, open-ended interviews and dialogue with community members, collection of documents and/or artifacts
Autoethnography	Primarily self-reflection through memoing, journaling, or interviewing of oneself (or those familiar with one's life)
Narrative Inquiry	Primarily interviews and storytelling, might utilize analysis of relevant documents
Case Study	A mix of observation, interviews, and document collection
Arts-Based Research	Can include a variety of methods: traditional observation, interviews, reflection journals, and document analysis. What defines arts-based research is less about methods of data collection and more about how the data are represented.

Example 4: Methodology
Case Study

Research Question(s)

1. How do K–12 teachers diagnosed with attention deficit hyperactivity disorder (ADHD) perceive and interact with their students with ADHD?

2. What strategies do K–12 teachers diagnosed with ADHD utilize to manage their job?

3. What strategies do K–12 teachers diagnosed with ADHD utilize to reach their students with ADHD and in what ways are these strategies an outgrowth of their own experiences?

4. Considering the teachers' gender identity, what recommendations might the teachers have for working with and advocating for boys versus girls with this diagnosis?

Methods

The researcher (a middle school art teacher and graduate student diagnosed with ADHD as an adult) will sample 50 teachers nationwide who have been diagnosed with ADHD for at least five years and teach students with the same diagnosis for at least one year. The researcher will conduct initial one-hour interviews with all teachers. From those interviews, the researcher will select 15 teachers to observe in person three times during the school year. The remaining teachers will be provided with recording equipment so they can record their classrooms twice a month over the course of the school year. The researcher will collect lesson plans for the observed lessons. After the observations and recordings have been collected, the researcher will select 20 teachers for a follow-up interview. By adopting an intersectional framework, the researcher shows that they are interested in the differences and similarities between working with boys, girls, and nonbinary students with ADHD and the unique approaches that teachers believe each may need.

remember is that you want to choose a research methodology that best suits your research questions, is aligned with the cultural context under study, and is representative of your chosen theoretical framework. Because intersectionality privileges the stories and ways of knowing of those multiply situated at the margins, we also privilege methodologies that are able to present people, places, and systems in multiple and complex ways.

Research Design

Depth versus Breadth

Once you have selected a methodology for your study, you will need to think carefully about how to design a solid research study. In the following discussion, as we have showcased above in the methodology discussion, we will now turn our attention to how to design a research study with intersectionality in mind.

First, you need to have collected enough data to make valid claims. What we mean by having enough data to make substantiated claims is that even though there may not be stringent guidelines about how long to immerse yourself in the study or to collect data, you need to be sure that you have enough knowledge of the subject under study. We believe it is always better to strive to achieve depth of a topic as opposed to breadth, especially as a student researcher. In other words, it is better to spend more time interviewing a small number of participants over a period of time than it is to interview a larger number of participants for a shorter period of time. People are typically attracted to qualitative research because it is not typically associated with numbers but actual human relationships. People from disciplines such as social work, nursing, criminal justice, or education are usually drawn to qualitative research due to its emphasis on human relationships and communication. Also, people who are a part of cultural communities that value the spoken word or storytelling are typically drawn to qualitative research's focus on rituals, tradition, meaning making, and historical patterns of resilience and agency. Again, in the sciences, many things that have been valued and passed down by Black, Indigenous, and people of color (BIPOC) have been devalued or deemed as less than rigorous. Therefore, qualitative research at one point gained a reputation of being less than serious or easier than quantitative research protocols. However, we want to say here loud and clear, *qualitative research is time and labor intensive* but provides any researcher with a worthwhile research experience that offers depth and insight into human behavior and thought. If you want something less time-consuming or that potentially requires less self-exploration on your part, then you may want to consider quantitative methodology.

To become a good qualitative researcher, you must be willing to invest the time and energy needed to truly understand your participants' perspectives or those shared perspectives adequately contextually. That cannot be achieved with a single 30-minute interview. The same can be said for observations. If you include observations in a study, please know that people will initially be on their best behavior and performing. Your first few observations may be limited because participants are still getting to know you and trust you to tell their story. The longer you remain in the field with your participants and establish rapport, the more open about their lives and responsive to you they will become. This is why prolonged, sustained, and engaged participation in the cultural site under observation is so important. If you have a choice of observing a site three times per week for one hour versus observing once per week for three hours, choose frequency over duration. The more observations you are able to conduct at the same site, the more observant you will be and the more likely you are to identify patterns of behaviors. Also, the more time you spend observing, the better your chances of being able to build rapport with site participants and identify the nuances of social exchanges. On the other hand, if you are given the choice of conducting 50 one-hour interviews versus 20 two-hour interviews, you might want to consider the latter option. Considering that qualitative research sets out to achieve depth as opposed to superficial generalized claims, it would be better to have fewer participants to interview for your study with the capability of spending more time with them than to have more participants but a shorter amount of time to ask and receive more in-depth responses. Sometimes student researchers ask, "How many participants should I have for my study?" Your research professor wants to respond, "There is no magic number!" The number of research participants may be of little relevance, but how many observations or interviews is an important question that requires research expertise and more information on the research topic at hand. So, instead, student researchers should be asking their advisors, "How many observations and/or interviews should I plan to conduct?" To answer this question, you would need to rely on a trusted research mentor to help you determine, based on the research questions, precisely how many observations and interviews are necessary.

Emergent Design

As you think about your research design, you must remember that qualitative research follows an emergent design. You must be willing, as the researcher, to change or adapt your design depending upon what happens at the research site. Let's say you are studying political decision making amongst middle-class Black and Latinx senior citizens living in a suburb in the southwest part of the U.S. You want to interview them to understand what political issues are important to them. Your original research design concentrated on national political issues, such as the presidential election and immigration reform. However, after a few interviews, you discovered that seniors are more interested in local politics, and senior citizens of color are more likely than their white peers to be actively engaged in local politics as evidenced by their participation in election fundraising, voter registration drives, and attending candidate forums in their local churches. Now, as the researcher, you have an important research decision to make. Should you continue studying the seniors' interests in national politics or should you adapt the study to more closely investigate research participants' decision making regarding local politics? We would recommend that you shift your study toward your (emerging) data theme of local political participation. If they do not think much about national elections, then it is better to seek to understand what they do know and reflect upon. You want your participants to be informed on the subject matter under study, which is the researcher's ethical responsibility, and you want your participants to be excited about participating in the study. Be sure that you are asking the right research questions with the right people!

Research Questions

A good research study usually has three to five research questions that frame the purpose of the study. We recommend that a research study begin with one main overarching question and follow with two to four sub-questions. These questions must be open ended and usually are concerned with *who, what, when, where* and *how*. There are some qualitative studies that investigate *why* as well, and other studies that include the term *to what extent* in their research questions. Your research questions should be sufficiently broad enough to understand a social phenomenon of interest but narrow enough that you are sure you are observing the most relevant people and places. Using the above senior citizens' political decision-making study as an example, we came up with the following research questions:

Overarching question:

1. How do middle-class Black and Latinx senior citizens who live in a suburban community in the southwest part of the U.S. participate in local election decisions?

Sub-questions:

1. What sources of information do they most likely rely on to make political decisions?
2. What actions have they taken that might be considered a form of political decision making?
3. To what extent is their active participation in local politics shaping decision making?

Using an intersectional analytical framework, the researcher selects research questions that serve to center the political viewpoints and activities of people who will potentially offer a historical and/or longitudinal perspective on political engagement. Furthermore, the intentional focus on processes of political engagement from the perspective of (a) middle-class (b) older (c) racial minorities (d) living in the suburbs is aligned with intersectionality. An intersectional methodological approach would be interested in highlighting situated knowledge of the seniors and examining their juxtaposition to power and privilege in this suburban context in the southwest region of the nation.

Do note that qualitative research is not interested in proving causality, thus, you should not be raising causality research questions. That means you cannot "prove" that one thing led to another using qualitative research. For example, you would not be able to determine without a doubt that being a middle-class senior citizen from the South led to a particular political decision. This is because your sample size or participant pool would not be large enough to make generalizations about the political habits of all Black or Latinx senior citizens. You could, however, investigate how race and gender might be mediating factors in the political decision making of senior citizens who are racial minorities or how or why race and gender impacts decision making for the group in your study. The key to remember with qualitative research is that you cannot determine outcomes. Working within the field of qualitative research, your intent is to investigate and eventually describe social processes from your participants' perspective.

Finally, we want to stress that your research questions are different than interview questions. While we discuss this further in subsequent chapters, please note that you never ask your research questions in an interview. Your research questions are broad theoretical questions informed by bodies of research, whereas interview questions are more specific and enable participants to discuss their lived experiences. Thus, for this example of senior citizens' political decision making, your interview questions might consist of narrower questions to pinpoint seniors' political participation:

1. What does being active in local politics look like for you?

2. When did you become active in local politics?

3. What event motivated you to become active?

4. Where do you learn about local candidates and policies?

5. Give an example of your last activity concerning local politics. What did you do and why?

You can see that the interview questions function to get the participant talking about their specific experiences with your research topic.

Sampling

Once you have determined your methodology and methods based on your research purpose, you must think about who you will invite to participate in the study. In research, we call the process of selecting participants for your study *sampling.* You may be somewhat familiar with the process of random sampling, since much positivist research requires it and qualitative research adapted the technique in its early years. However, the difference between sampling in qualitative research versus quantitative traditions is that sampling in qualitative research requires more than a random process. Given that qualitative research typically calls for in-depth analysis and systematic observation, sample sizes tend to be smaller in size than those in quantitative studies. Qualitative researchers try to be deliberate in selecting and inviting participants to join in their study. Qualitative researchers, in most cases, rely on what is termed *purposeful sampling.* We are explicitly deliberate in the selection of participants, and while working within an intersectional framework, qualitative researchers will, of course, consider (1) inviting participants from marginalized groups and (2) collaborating with BIPOC as they plan the study. In purposeful sampling, the researcher would make a list of criteria participants must meet in order to be invited to join the study; issues of identity, culture, age, location, and other diversity factors should be considered. Not too long ago, social science research exploited (or experimented on) BIPOC, and other times, they simply left BIPOC out of research pools. Critical qualitative researchers are reflective of who is invited to the study, why they are invited, and what the benefits are to those invited. Additionally, intersectional researchers must be cognizant of the outcomes of the study. If they are inviting BIPOC to participate or collaborate, intersectional researchers must be aware of how the research study results could impact the lives of these participants/collaborators.

Let's return to the earlier example of Tasha. If you recall, she is interested in studying Black girls' literacies. Thus, it would be obvious that one of her inclusion criteria would be that her participant identifies as a Black girl. Now, it would be up to Tasha as the researcher with a main research question in mind to determine the specifics of what it means to be a Black girl. Some questions that Tasha may need to consider include the following: Can a student who is genetically a male but who identifies as a female participate in the study? What does *Black* mean and who can identify as Black? Will she only invite students who have two Black biological parents? If so, how is this going to be determined and what is this criteria's relevance to the study? Will Afro-Latinas be accepted as Black for the purposes of Tasha's study? These may be simple questions for one researcher but more complicated questions for another researcher. Also, Tasha is studying in a U.S. context. Should she limit her research participants to U.S.–born citizens or should she include Black immigrants as well? These are important questions that must be considered by Tasha in deliberation with her research advisor and in consultation with the literature in the beginning of her study.

Besides purposeful sampling, qualitative researchers have a variety of other sampling methods that they could use as well. Snowball sampling is one such method. In Tasha's study, for example, she might find a Black girl student who meets her criteria, invite her to participate in the study, and then ask her to recommend other Black girls who might be willing to participate in the study. The researcher would then follow up on those recommendations and ask those potential participants for additional recommendations—hence the term *snowball*, which means to gather in size quickly! However, there is one limitation of snowball sampling, which is that the researcher will often end up with what is referred to as a *skewed sample,* since it is likely that the recruited participants may be similar to the participant who recommended them. One way to address this would be to recruit a few participants to your study on your own and then ask a variety of them for recommendations. Another way to diversify your *sample pool* might be to circulate information about your study on your social network sites and ask friends/followers to share the study recruitment letter on their sites or email lists as well (pending institutional review board approval). You may reach a wider network this way and, potentially, a larger volunteer pool.

Many grounded theorists use what is called *theoretical sampling.* In theoretical sampling, you make sampling decisions throughout the study and decisions are often grounded within your initial analysis. Thus, in Tasha's case, she might begin her study by interviewing three Black girls who have already been invited to participate in the study. Perhaps one of the student participants is enrolled in a private high school while the other two students attend public high schools. While analyzing the data, Tasha may notice that the private school student appears to have a different understanding of literacy than the two students who attend public schools. Based on this initial analysis of the data, Tasha's interest might pique now that there might be some differences across sociocultural contexts; thus, she might want to split her sample with 50% private school students and 50% public school students to see if she can find patterns similar to the initial differences she noted. Finally, we must add that there are other sampling methods available to qualitative researchers, though the above three are the most widely used. See Table 4.2 below for a brief description of sampling methods and other types of sampling procedures.

Table 4.2 Sampling Methods in Qualitative Research	
Purposeful sampling	Selects participants based on specific criteria instead of random selection
Snowball sampling	Asks participants to identify additional people who might fit the criteria of the study
Theoretical sampling	Makes decisions about who else to include in the study based on preliminary analysis of the data
Critical case sampling	Selects and invites a participant to the study because they are particularly important to understanding the phenomenon under study
Convenience sampling	Selects participants that the researcher has easy access to and who meet the criteria of the study
Confirming and disconfirming	Similar to theoretical sampling; after an initial analysis of the data, the researcher would look for participants who could help confirm or disconfirm emerging patterns

Putting It All Together

In this chapter, we discussed various qualitative research methodologies as well as how to design a research study from an intersectional standpoint. Now, by way of a summary, let's put it all together and design a study around the topic (introduced in the example of interview-based narrative inquiry earlier in this chapter) of the traumatic impact of family separation at the U.S. border. In looking at the different methodologies we could choose from those outlined earlier in the chapter, there are some that stand out as useful and relevant to the research topic. Before we discuss those methodologies that are most fitting, we must first eliminate the ones that would more than likely not work for the research topic at hand (family separation at the border). Ethnography and critical ethnography might be a stretch for this particular subject matter, mainly because the likelihood of a researcher being allowed access to an Immigration and Customs Enforcement (ICE) detention center is highly unlikely; observation of what is actually occurring in the moment would be virtually impossible. This also means that unless you were a person directly experiencing family separation, you would not be able to complete an autoethnography. Therefore, we can easily eliminate ethnography and autoethnography from our choices of methodologies. Narrative inquiry alternatively might be a useful methodological tool, as you can inquire directly about the experiences of parents and their children. The problem with relying solely on interview data is that some families may have already been separated; thus, potential participants may be difficult to locate and/or interview. For this reason, case study might be a more feasible methodology to carry out, since the researcher can utilize a combination of data collection methods in order to better understand the topic being investigated. You might also be thinking, "Could ABR be used for this research?" Well, yes, it could, and it might be quite impactful since ABR would offer the opportunity to showcase the emotionality (e.g., grief, anger, fear, frustration, etc.) of the topic at hand. Nevertheless, for the purposes of this summary, we will decide on case study as the methodology.

Next, we need to devise our research questions. Remember to use *how* or *what* to thoroughly develop research questions. If we are generally interested in the traumatic impact of family separation, we might ask the following overarching question: How have refugee/asylum-seeking/immigrant families been impacted by the current presidential administration's family separation policy at the U.S.–Mexican border?

When formulating research questions, we want to be specific about which families' experiences we are interested in studying. Are we interested in families who were living in the U.S. prior to detainment? Or families who were detained immediately after arrival in the U.S.? Are we interested in mixed-status families or families with no prior citizenship ties to the U.S.? Further, we also want to be clear about which border we are referring to in our research. Because there has been less media coverage of what has been occurring at the U.S.–Canadian border, we will delineate our case boundaries to a specific border. We may even want to go further and specify a specific geographical region.

To gain even more clarity in our research protocol, our next questions can help us narrow the case further to pinpoint exactly what we are interested in. For this case study, we want to investigate psychological and emotional trauma.

1. How do parents describe distressing (or traumatic) events related to the separation?

2. How do children describe distressing (or traumatic) events related to the separation?

Notice that our interests in the parents' and children's experiences are captured in different research questions because it is important for the researcher to understand that separation experiences or distressing events might be described or perceived differently.

And if families have been reunited, one last question might include the following:

3. In what ways have family dynamics changed since the separation and reunification of the family?

And if families have not been reunited, we might ask the following:

4. What are some of the ongoing effects of family separation on parents, children, and/or other family members?

Now that a decision has been made on research questions, the next step would be to decide *how* to sample. There are many types of sampling that are appropriate for this study. However, due to potential issues of access to families, the researcher might lean toward purposeful sampling. Purposeful sampling, in this case, takes into account issues of privacy and safety, migration and mobility, potential language or cultural differences, and legal status—all issues that are beyond the control of the researcher but are certainly worth considering for those invited to participate in the study. Other things to consider are physical access (proximity) to participant volunteers. Will the researcher have to travel to meet with participants? If not, can interviews be conducted via telephone or the internet? Will other volunteers be needed for the study, such as translators, transporters, social workers, and so on?

Finally, the next step is to decide on your methods of data collection. You will not be able to decide on the best methods of data collection for the study until after you read the next chapter. For now, based on the larger overarching question and the related sub-questions, open-ended interviews would be most beneficial in efforts to capture family members' experiences with ICE, but it would also be helpful in a case study to provide a detailed description of the sociopolitical context. Would it be possible to visit a detention center? Could the researcher go to the border where migrants await entry? How can the topic be studied in a way that preserves the dignity of families and presents a well-rounded and thorough account? As you can see, qualitative research decisions are made throughout the course of the study, and each decision plays a role in the type of account that you will provide to your research audience.

Many have argued that traditional research practices are embedded in and reflective of racial and patriarchal hierarchical relationships. When you place qualitative methodologies and methods at the center of analysis of intersectionality, it is easier to understand the importance of adopting methodologies that study race, class, gender, and other intersecting identities synchronously. An intersectional framework allows for methodologies that are person-centered and seek to explore the subjectivity of people multiply situated at the intersection of power and domination. As we invite you to contemplate how your methodological choices align with intersectionality as a framework and analytical tool, also ponder how your research methodology is reflective of agency and resistance.

Summary

As you can see, there is a lot of decision making that goes into an intersectional qualitative research design. Once you have an idea of your research topic, you can choose a methodology. From there, you would develop your design. Decisions about your methods (how you will collect and analyze data) can be thought about somewhat as you select a methodology, write up research questions, and decide on a sampling strategy. In the next chapter, we will focus on data collection.

DISCUSSION QUESTIONS

1. What is the connection between anthropology and ethnography? How do they differ? In what ways have their fields been shaped by colonialism, racism, and sexism?

2. In what ways did social movements push the understandings and practices of anthropologists and ethnographers?

3. The authors state that they chose to cover methodologies that could be used for critical research and that not all qualitative methodologies are inherently critical. Do you agree with their choices? Why or why not? Which methodologies are missing? Could any of them be used as critical methodologies?

4. What methodology do you think best fits your study? Why?

5. Write one overarching research question for your study along with two to four sub-questions. Share these with a peer who can provide feedback. Are the questions broad enough? Are the questions too causal or too theoretical?

Data Collection Methods

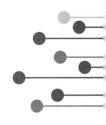

One of the authors of this text recalls an experience that occurred early on in her career as a tenure-track professor and researcher. She once had a graduate research assistant (RA) who was responsible for transcribing interviews conducted between the researcher and research participants. The professor trusted the RA with the de-identified audio files. Not unusually, the professor gave the RA ten interview tapes to transcribe on her own time and in a place that was convenient for her. Many months went by and the RA had not turned in the transcriptions or returned the tapes to the professor. Eventually, the RA admitted that her car had been broken into and the tapes and discs on which she saved the transcriptions were stolen from the car. The professor never questioned or corroborated the RA's claims. However, the new professor learned a hard lesson about backing up interview files. These data were irretrievably lost. She decided that it was best not to conduct the interviews again with the original participants, because she did not want to trouble busy people who had already taken time out of their lives to sit down for an interview in the first place. The author decided it was a lesson learned and since then has tried to be more careful about data access and storage in the future.

Framing the Dialogue on Data Collection

We have discussed methodology in previous chapters and now turn our attention to methods. In this chapter, we will examine methods of data collection from an intersectional perspective. Deciding on which methods of data collection are appropriate depends on your theoretical framework, research questions, methodology, and access to participants. In qualitative research, the four most common forms of data collection are interviews, focus groups, observations, and document analysis. We will examine each of these methods using intersectionality as our methodological framework, then provide tips for efficacious data collection. But first, we will revisit and outline the tenets of intersectionality as a theoretical framework and analytical tool.

Again, you will find dozens, if not hundreds of textbooks and articles on qualitative research methodologies and methods. However, there are few research texts that contextualize qualitative research from an intersectional approach. So, let's revisit the tenets of intersectionality in association with qualitative research.

Intersectional qualitative research focuses on the complex relationship between social identities, power, and knowledge. Intersectionality frames critical qualitative research pursuits in the following ways and with the following assumptions:

1. **Personal and cultural beliefs.** How we come to believe in the legitimacy and value of science and the scientific method is informed by our personal and cultural beliefs and education and schooling.

2. **Emotionality in research pursuits.** We can find pleasure and pain in our research pursuits, especially as researchers from oppressed groups become more conscientious about the relationship between research and power, education and hegemony, and culture and domination.

3. **Collective agency and resistance.** Individuals' and social groups' lived experiences and how they come to make meaning of those experiences represents their agency and resistance strategies.

4. **Research represents power and authority.** The historical knowledge and collective wisdom of those multiply situated along the matrix of domination serve as counternarratives to systemic power and/or oppositional knowledge.

5. **Epistemological understandings.** An understanding of how multiple social identities such as race and gender overlap to shape what people know and how they come to know what they know.

Intersectionality as a theoretical framework and analytical tool informs how we come to our research interests and formulate our research questions, choice of methodology, and methods of data collection. Of course, intersectional research privileges data collection methods that center the worldviews and experiences of those multiply impacted by marginalized identities. Further, intersectional research straightforwardly unveils and deconstructs the formidable relationship among research, power, and authority.

Thus, intersectional qualitative researchers intentionally utilize research processes to expose how research perpetuates deficit perspectives of racialized minorities and women of color and to explore how research can interrupt stereotypes. In fact, there is more than an interest in oppression and marginalization; there is an even more important interest in documenting individual agency, collective knowledge, and the ways of knowing from the standpoint of the Other.

Centering the lived experiences and knowledge of our research participants requires intersectional researchers to be self-aware and to have keen insight into establishing rapport with participants. While the notion of research is quite familiar to us as academics, those outside of academia may not be as familiar with it or the processes involved. Potential participants might be familiar with research that has been represented in popular media (general medical research on animals or clinical trials involving human subjects). Popular media also has its share of representations of anthropological studies, such as documentaries that describe plant, animal, and human life—usually in remote parts of the world where the traveler interacts with Indigenous people or "strange" foods and animals (i.e., as compared to Eurocentric norms).

These documentaries are educational but tend to exoticize habitats and people in an effort to entertain the audience. Unfortunately, the popularization and exoticization of some anthropological fieldwork may lead some participants to enter research studies with preconceived ideas about what counts as research, who research participants are, and how research participants are supposed to act. You have probably noticed that throughout this text, we have been intentional with the use of the word *participant*. The people who participate in our research studies should not be referred to as our *subjects*. In many ways, this dehumanizes them and strips them of agency and self-determination; they become simple props or test dummies in the name of science. People should not be *subjected* to our research; instead, they should be *invited* to be full participants of the study. The term *participant* is a reminder for us to create a mutually beneficial researcher–participant relationship, which is one of the intended goals of intersectional research. A simple change in wording will not erase a history of using and abusing human beings for research; therefore, it is vitally important to be cognizant of how you engage in the research process.

Reflect on the tenets of intersectional research outlined earlier. Here are some questions to ponder as you think about your relationship with participants in the study:

1. What is the purpose of this research and whose interests does it serve?

2. What tangible or intangible benefits will participants receive from their participation in the research compared to the short- and long-term benefits the researcher might receive?

3. What is the role of the participant in the study? What exactly are they being asked to do, to not do, or to give up? How will your request affect them emotionally, physically, or intellectually?

4. In what ways have participants entrusted the researcher with their histories and stories, and how can the researcher protect the stories of their participants and convey those stories justly?

As researchers, we cannot pretend that the benefits we, or our institutional affiliations, receive from research do not outweigh the benefits participants receive. Despite our good intentions, qualitative researchers do use people in our studies. Some researchers will attempt to explain away claims of using people for research purposes by saying that our research benefits society. In many cases, it may be true (or not) that research benefits society, but the real question we must grapple with is whether our research justifies the use of people. We encourage you to read Limes-Taylor Henderson and Esposito (2019) for a fuller exploration of this dilemma. In this article, the researchers confess moral and ethical dilemmas about what it means to research people and then have the power to represent their lives. They refer to research as a colonial project and reflect on the ways they and other researchers are, despite good intentions, complicit in maintaining oppressive structures.

We certainly don't have the answers to the issues and interrogations raised in their discussion, but we encourage you to reflect on them before you begin any research. Intersectional researchers enter the research process with the intent to collaborate with research participants in their social justice pursuits and to avoid the exploitation of participants' shared time, creativity, stories, and knowledge. How can you decenter yourself as a researcher and center the stories and needs of your invited research participants? How can you collaborate with participants in such a way that you and participants mutually engage in the data collection and analysis process and benefits of the study?

Developing Trust

As researchers, we insert ourselves into other people's lives. They usually have not reached out to us first and invited us to study them. We have, instead, sought them out and asked for permission to become a part of their worlds. How do we develop and nurture the researcher–participant relationship when we are outsiders? Many texts mention the importance of building rapport and creating a friendly and open research context. Obviously, you want a friendly and constructive relationship with your participants. Rapport is especially important when you must complete multiple interviews or observations of a cultural context over a prolonged period. Intersectional researchers should strive to move beyond a friendly research context and work to build trust with their participants.

When attempting to immerse oneself in the cultural context, rapport is not enough. You will have to earn the participants' trust as well. You will eventually become somewhat of an insider to the culture or to the site you are observing. And although people will generally open up to you the more time you spend with them, you must still earn their trust through the research process (Glesne, 2011). One of the ways you can become more trustworthy and establish meaningful relationships with participants is through an authentic reflection of (a) what you hope to gain from the research and (b) what you hope to contribute to society at large, to the participants involved in the study, or to a community under study.

You may have noticed that we continually mention the important process of being familiar with who you are as a person/researcher and reflecting on thyself throughout the research process—intersectionality concerns itself with the study of the self in relationship to the Other. This continual reflection process is known as *reflexivity*. Pillow (2013) refers to reflexivity as the critical reflection of the ways in which the researcher, participant, and setting influence and shape each other. Schwandt (1997) has defined reflexivity as the process of "examining one's personal and theoretical commitments to see how they serve as resources for generating particular data, for behaving in particular ways . . . and for developing particular interpretations" (p. 136). In intersectional research, critical reflexivity involves thinking of the self and the multiple social identities one embodies in relationship to other social actors and structures of power.

By embracing an intersectional framework, the researcher takes responsibility for the (ongoing) process of reflection and seeks to understand how she/he/they impacts various aspects of the study—including relationships with participants and their perceptions of the benefits of the study. Indigenous, Latina, Black, and/ or feminist researchers have long recognized that we are subjugated knowers and situated actors who must understand the varying ways we participate in a research project (Collins, 2000; DeVault, 1990; Evans-Winters, 2019; Spivak, 1988). Researchers must include ourselves, implicate ourselves, and situate ourselves so the readers of our texts understand how we may have shaped the study. Yet, dominant paradigms proliferated in academic texts continue to center illusions of objectivity and argue that experiential knowledge is not legitimate science. We completely disagree and believe that experiential knowledge is as important— if not more important—than knowledge collected from a supposedly detached researcher. A detached, neutral, objective position does not exist in research. Therefore, in intersectional research, we conscientiously and consistently reflect upon our own values, behaviors, and emotionality to better understand our role in the research process and how we influence our participants and the study.

Reflexivity

The big question we must ponder is this: Can we ever know how we, as researchers, truly shape a study? We cannot know how we or others shape the research process unless we essentialize identities. Essentialism, as it relates to race or ethnicity, means that researchers sometimes (consciously or subconsciously) attribute characteristics to specific racial or ethnic groups that we presume holds true (sometimes erroneously) for all members of that group. Researchers tend to essentialize all racial and ethnic groups (e.g., Black, white, Indigenous, people of color, Asian, Latinx, etc.).

Of course, as scholars who are critically aware and who operate from an intersectional framework, we know that any generalizations are risky and dangerous. For instance, African, Latinx, Asian, and/or Indigenous diasporas are varied and complicated due to geographical location, tradition, migration and immigration, socioeconomic status, and so on. And we would not even know where to begin with the race that has been termed *white*. Who are white people and what are their common characteristics? Who would get to determine this?

The most we could do is examine the ways in which different racial groups are privileged and oppressed. We know that white privilege exists and shapes all interactions in a person's life; we also know that oppression exists more prominently in the lives of racialized minorities in the United States (U.S.) and across the diaspora due to systemic racism and neocolonialism. We also know that some Latinx people have a closer proximity to whiteness and, therefore, benefit from white supremacy and skin privilege more than someone who identifies as Black/African and/or someone who also identifies as Latinx and has a darker skin complexion (thus seen in opposition to whiteness).

These intersectional ponderings mean that we must truly examine, at the beginning of the study and throughout our studies, (1) the processes of stratification, difference, and power; (2) our own and participants' perceptions of race; and (3) how we make meaning out of our own and others' social identities. Even more important from an intersectional standpoint is how those possessing multiply marginalized identities experience the interlocking systems of oppression. How do our race, class, gender, sexual, and other identities shape the research process? How do our own identities as researchers shape participants' perceptions of us, our relationships with participants, and the research context concurrently? Obviously, as researchers, we will never be able to say with certainty that our visible/invisible or real/perceived identities shaped a project in specific ways.

All researchers possess situated and embodied knowledge; thus, you bring your own subjective perspectives into the research process. However, only some research and some researchers are considered to be objective. An intersectional approach to data collection necessitates that we be critical of who has been "perceived to be an authoritative knower, whose claims have been heard, which forms of knowledge have received recognition (and been recorded, archived, and passed down)" (May, 2015, p. 35). This is a larger philosophical issue about what counts as knowledge and who gets to know and who is the known. Our claims to subjectivity and recognition that objectivity is a fallacy should not dilute the strength of research or invalidate the perspectives of research participants.

It is also okay that we may not be able to pinpoint exactly how we have shaped the research study. We can, however, share what we do know about it. We will know how we developed rapport, how long it took to gain access and entry, and what we needed to do to engender trust and foster mutually beneficial relationships. These are the important fundamental aspects of qualitative research that we can share with research audiences. We also should pay close attention to stories from other researchers about their process when fostering meaningful relationships with participants or other collaborators. We need to begin data collection by understanding that we may never be entirely an *insider* in a cultural context or in a person's life—though we could, if we are not careful, remain an *outsider*.

Sharing a similar gender, racial identity, or sexual orientation with a research participant does not automatically guarantee that we will be given full access to their life nor does it guarantee that they will automatically trust us because of a shared identity (or identities). Interestingly enough, the authors of this book have found that sometimes sharing similar cultural identities with your participant(s) might actually threaten researcher–participant relationships in the research process! Both of us, as novice and veteran researchers, have been in situations where we know for sure that information was kept away from us because research participants were afraid of violating some kind of (perceived or real) cultural taboo (e.g., a teen interested in a same-sex relationship), did not want to offend us (e.g., "professors of color are sellouts"), felt ashamed or embarrassed (e.g., a drug-addicted mother), or were concerned with information getting back to other community insiders (i.e., in racially segregated university towns, degrees of separation are narrow). Intersectional research acknowledges that in some cultures, issues of age, religion, status, and so on can potentially impose boundaries between insiders of that culture, whereas it would be easier (if not safer) to speak to a cultural outsider.

As a self-reflective researcher, you will need to decide, as a cultural insider or outsider, which questions or conversations are culturally appropriate or *aligned* based on the topic at hand. As academia becomes more racially and ethnically inclusive, more and more researchers will begin to reflect the cultural identities and shared experiences of their research participants and sites of study, which is one of the objectives of this book—to encourage researchers from marginalized groups to bring cultural awareness to the research process and, hopefully, to pursue research for social justice endeavors. However, cultural knowledge is only a starting point for fostering rapport with research participants and communities. If we recognize that participants (as well as ourselves) live intersectional lives, then we must recognize that there will be other identities that mediate our lives and how we develop trust and rapport.

See Black feminist researcher Johnson-Bailey (1999) for a full discussion on the conceptualization of insider/outsider statuses and racial essentialism. Johnson-Bailey directly engages with the issue of racial essentialism as she discusses the challenges she faced as a Black woman interviewing other Black women. She argued that tensions occurred, despite a shared racial identity (Blackness) and gender identity (woman) because of differences in socioeconomic status as well as skin color. The lesson learned here is that as qualitative researchers, we cannot assume that any real or perceived identities will suddenly or absolutely grant us unmitigated access to individuals or groups. As individuals, we must never overlook the power of social stratification, individual agency, or human dynamism.

In short, there is no research involving human participants that does not involve some kind of power dynamic. Early feminist research sought to disrupt what was presumed to be (and was) a hierarchical relationship between the researcher and the researched. Reflexivity was initially used in research as a way to create nonhierarchical research practices (Josselson, 1996), and some feminist researchers attempted to befriend their participants. Ultimately, Behar (1993) remarked on how tragic this was:

> Feminist ethnographers have found themselves caught inside webs of betrayal they themselves have spun; with stark clarity, they realize that they are seeking out intimacy and friendship with subjects on whose backs, ultimately, the books will be written upon which their productivity as scholars in the marketplace will be assessed. (p. 297)

The desire to create research relationships that were nonhierarchical raised problems for researchers who came to understand that no matter how hard one tries for the researched–researcher relationship to be equitable, there might still be strains on these relationships and the potential for exploitation as well as outright betrayal. We think the best way to ensure that you are not abusing power (or ignoring it) in a research relationship is to continually disclose who you are as the researcher and how your decisions influence the research process and any outcomes. As a reminder of the importance of reflexivity to an equitable relationship, Reinharz (1992) reminds us that "researchers who self-disclose are reformulating the researcher's role in a way that maximizes engagement of the self but also increases the researcher's vulnerability to criticism, both for what is revealed and for the very act of self-disclosure" (p. 34). Now that we have thoroughly discussed the role you play as researcher and data collector, let's turn to how you go about collecting data in the form of interviews.

Interviews

The purpose of any research interview is to better understand how the participant thinks or feels about a subject, event, text, relationship, and so on. As qualitative researchers, we are interested in our participants' perspectives and interpretations of the social world. What is meant by *perspective* in scientific inquiry? Quite simply, qualitative researchers are interested in gathering a participant's sentiments and ideas as grounded in and contextualized within the participant's life experiences (Schutz, 1967). Further, we are interested in how participants came to hold their views of the world. The notion of *perspective*, of documenting lived experiences in qualitative research (see Van Manen, 1990), is derived from phenomenology. As researchers interested in a person's perspective or lived experiences, you must philosophically believe that people's stories—and how they come to share those stories—matter. If you are only interested in getting a person's opinion and gathering it quickly, it is much easier and more time efficient to complete a survey. But if you are truly willing to ask a set of questions to come to an understanding about how a person's shared experiences have shaped their opinions and beliefs, then an interview is one of the most efficient and effective data collection methods in scientific inquiry.

Generally, interviews are categorized in three ways: structured, semi-structured, and unstructured (Roulston, 2010). A structured interview may be the most common interview in program evaluation. The questions are the same for every participant and they are intended to get at breadth instead of depth. In other words, structured interviews tend to be short and precise, with the goal of receiving a direct response from the interviewee. In structured interviews, the interviewer typically asks a handful of questions and will not probe more deeply. We might view the structured interview as an oral survey of sorts. Today, it is more common to find these types of structured interviews delivered as an online survey in which the researchers ask participants the same standardized but open-ended questions, as opposed to taking the time to meet, record, and then transcribe the short answers interviewees provide.

Semi-structured interviews are similar to structured interviews in that researchers will come to the interview prepared with a list of questions (or sometimes topics) to ask a participant. However, the interviewer understands that the questions or topics are a loose guide and that the participant may veer off on other topics. The questions or interview topics will allow the researcher to cover the most important ground and have a way to steer the discussion. This allows for some flexibility but, overall, most of the intended questions get answered.

Unstructured interviews are more similar to guided conversations. A researcher will have a general topic in mind but may not have prepared specific questions to ask. These types of interviews are the most flexible and open ended. You cannot anticipate what type of responses or data you will end up with nor will you be able to predict which topics of conversation get explored in the most depth. Success in this data collection method is really based on your conversational style and previous experience with interviewing. It has been our experience that unstructured interviews can take the research down a long, winding road, and it will take a skilled researcher to bring the research participant back to the topic at hand. Furthermore, when the researcher reviews the conversation for data analysis purposes, they will also have to be skilled at knowing how to connect some of the disjointed information in more ethical ways. Ultimately, the researcher will have to decide which parts of the conversation in the unstructured interview to keep and which to leave out. We have experienced firsthand that the unstructured interview may go longer than two or three hours! Definitely consult with your research committee about this type of interview structure, because you want to be sure that you address the research questions and topics your dissertation committee approved.

Because we value lived experience and culturally rich stories, especially from those living at the margins, it is important before deciding on the type of interview structure to first decide which method (1) is respectful of your participants' time, (2) honors the dignity of the person, (3) is more culturally appropriate and aligned with the customs of your participants and the cultural context, and (4) is more feasible as it relates to resources (i.e., time, physical location, supplies needed, etc.). For example, if you know that you will be interviewing five youth participants in a detention center and you are only allotted 60 minutes with each participant, it may not be feasible or appropriate to ask them to take you down memory lane about their childhood starting with preschool. You would want to collect as much information as possible from them while respecting the time frame and any issues of privacy, as well as giving them enough time to process (i.e., feelings of ease or discomfort, memories, discernment, etc.) any information shared.

To become more skilled at interviewing, you should practice interviewing people you know, such as your classmates, to learn how to transition between questions, probe an interviewee, or even fine-tune the research protocols. In traditional research coursework, we were told that it was best to complete interviews with people we did not know very well. We assumed that our level of familiarity with participants would grow deeper as the study persisted. However, as research becomes more culturally responsive and social justice–oriented, of course there will be times when we know (or think we know) our research participants or the community context under study.

For example, we sometimes engage youth participants in research studies (Youth Participatory Action Research) at their school sites, in their own neighborhoods, or at youth groups. At other times, people who are a part of an organization want to learn how a program or policy impacts the people that they serve. Obviously, they will know their participants without necessarily knowing their opinions, perspectives, or experiences as it relates to the topic at hand. Again, intersectional research acknowledges that not all research is conducted by a cultural outsider or stranger to the community.

Sometimes researchers do have an investment in the topic under study. However, when researching as an outsider of a community or talking to participants that you have no previous relationship with, you are entering the study with a fresh set of eyes, so to speak. This outsider perspective will help you not take the research relationship, information and stories shared, or access to people and communities for granted. With someone you are comfortable with, we tend to rely on presumed shared assumptions; thus, we can wrongfully assume that we know what the other person means or how they think (Bogdan & Taylor, 1975; Spradley, 1979).

In a research interview, you cannot take for granted that you understand what the other person means or what they are trying to convey in a statement. Depending on your chosen interview structure and larger research question, you might continually probe deeper to collect explicit examples that will illustrate to you and others what the participant means. Your role as the interviewer will really be dependent upon what type of interview you are conducting. For example, in conversational interviews, you are participating in the interview as both a listener and as an engager as well as a talker.

This means that you may decide to share as much as the participant does, but you definitely must be mindful of your role in the study, the participant's role in the study, and power dynamics. Do not speak so much in the study that you overshadow the participant's presence or story. Also, keep in mind that the research participant is not bound to the same code of ethics as you are as the researcher. For instance, you are bound by confidentiality while the participant is free to share whatever parts of the study or your shared experiences with whomever they want whenever they want! With this in mind, a general rule is to only share with participants whatever you feel comfortable sharing, stick to the scope of the study, and do not share any information that you might be embarrassed or ashamed of if the information got shared out of context one day.

Similarly, with intersectionality in mind, you might want to consider this: Do not ask your research participants any questions that you yourself would not be comfortable answering. Due to power dynamics in research, there are times that white, educated, and middle-class researchers feel comfortable probing into the affairs and thinking of those with less social status (e.g., Black, Indigenous, and people of color [BIPOC]; poor people; women; immigrants; detained people; minors; etc.) but disclose little about themselves, their histories, or their circumstances. Further, those with status also have the privilege of asking those with less status and prestige about taboo topics: "How do you cope with racism at school?" "Talk about your experiences as a survivor of sexual assault." "As a first-generation immigrant, how do you feel about a president who talks about building a wall?" Researchers from a more privileged background might take for granted or assume that any one of these questions are harmless; they may not understand the embodied pain of the experience or the potential vulnerability that it takes to respond to such questions asked by someone who may be a member of the group that caused the harm. Thus, knowing *who to ask, when to ask it,* and *how to ask it* are equally as important as *what to ask*!

Focus on the Participant

In both structured and semi-structured interviews, it is best for the research participant to do most of the talking during the interview. The focus should be on what the participant says and less about what you think or what you think about what the participant has told you. It is important for us to note here that our recommendations regarding interviews are mainly for a U.S. context. As Kvale (1996) reminds us, norms and social customs regarding directness and openness are different, depending upon your global location. Furthermore, intersectional research strives to center the cultural views and worldviews of the research participants, so be sure to adjust your research questions, interview, or conversational styles, and consider what should be shared or not shared based on the cultural contexts and mores of the local setting.

The Number of Interviews

Many novice researchers wonder about how many interviews they should complete in order to have a full understanding of a person's perspective on a given topic. The number of interviews partially depends upon what type of interview you conduct, what your research questions are, and how long each interview will be. Also, the number of interviews to conduct with each participant is really based on how many interviews it will take for you to reach an in-depth understanding of the research topic. How many interviews will you need to conduct with each participant or group of participants to answer your research question(s)? You want to have a complete understanding of a social phenomenon, and there is no guarantee that one interview will be enough or that more than one would be too many. To be clear, it is nearly impossible to gain a complete understanding of any subject/ topic or a person/group. The goal of social science research is to *better understand* a particular social phenomenon or cultural group based on multiple interactions and observations, but we accept that partial knowledge is what we usually achieve.

With the aforementioned in mind, Seidman (2013) recommends a three-interview series. According to this approach, the first interview should establish the participant's life history and personal context. The second interview would focus on the reconstruction of detailed life experiences while the third interview would allow participants a chance to reflect on the meaning of their experiences. In this approach, it is recommended that each interview be at least 90 minutes in length. We would not suggest holding an interview for less than 60 minutes. When other researchers report that they held a 30-minute interview, we immediately wonder what could have been discussed in such a short amount of time beyond initial greetings to establish rapport. In fact, we prefer interviews that range from 90–120 minutes. Across and within cultural groups, time itself is a social construct. Therefore, it is important in advance of the interview to know some cultural attributes of the individuals or groups of people whom you will interview: (1) How long does it typically take to establish rapport? (2) How does the interviewee view time (i.e., linear, circular, etc.)? (3) Generally, is it acceptable to ask personal questions during the first meeting? (4) How much time is expected or appropriate for the researcher to share information about herself/himself/themselves? For example, in some cultures, it may be inappropriate to ask personal questions during the first meeting. Also, amongst some cultural groups, people tell stories instead of answering a question directly, then circle back around to the original question. In other cultures, pleasantries are spoken first, then people get down to business. Another example related to interviewing is related to age: In some cultural groups, age differences between the researcher (asker) and participant (respondent) may make it difficult for the younger researcher to ask a direct question to an elder. The elder may feel compelled or expected to direct the questioning. Either way, you should plan in advance how you might account for cultural norms and expectations during the interview process. These cultural norms and expectations will certainly influence how you will plan for time during the interview process.

Interview Questions

Many novice researchers will be developing interview questions for the first time. Below, we present a simple template as you develop your interview protocol for your intersectional research project (Figure 5.1).

Interviewing with intersectionality in mind is a skill that you will develop over time. However, we can share some tips with you that should enable you to complete interviews that yield richer data. Some of these tips seem like common sense, but you will be surprised at how often researchers overlook many of the practicalities of interviewing people.

Initial Contact

How one makes initial contact with research participants and establishes relationships with narrators and community members is an important aspect of the

Figure 5.1   Creating Interview Questions

Primary Research Question(s)	What Do You Want to Know About the Topic?	What Questions Could Generate the Information You Want to Know?
What are school social workers' (who work in predominately under-resourced, high-poverty school communities) experiences with reports of suspected child abuse and neglect?	I am interested in understanding • how cases are reported to school social workers, • how often they follow up (if at all) after a report of suspected abuse or neglect, and • when and how they make decisions to involve the department of child and family services.	1. In your school or school district, who is ultimately responsible for investigating child abuse or neglect? 2. What process is used to alert others regarding a teacher's suspicion of abuse or neglect? 3. Walk me through the last time you dealt with a suspicion that a child was being neglected or abused. 4. In situations where you or others have suspicions, what do you do to investigate these suspicions? 5. At what point in a case of suspected abuse do you involve the state department or one of your direct supervisors?
How were school social workers trained regarding district, state, and national child abuse reporting policies and/or laws? Did any of these trainings include culturally responsive prevention or intervention methods? How does social work training account for sociocultural differences in reporting and who gets reported?	I am interested in understanding what trainings and professional development tools school social workers in under-resourced communities receive regarding reports of suspected child abuse or neglect and the role of race, class, and gender in prevention and intervention efforts and reporting procedures. • How does district-level training differ from what school social workers learn in formal coursework about following up on allegations of child abuse and neglect with a culturally sensitive approach? • How up-to-date is their training with contemporary societal norms? • How prepared do they actually feel to handle suspected reports of child abuse or neglect at their school, especially when working with families from different racial or class groups?	1. Since coursework in your social work major, what other culturally sensitive trainings and/or preparations have you received regarding child abuse or neglect? 2. Reflecting on this cultural competence training, what did you learn that was left out of your undergrad or master's program? 3. What do you think of the cultural competence training or preparation you had as it relates to investigating suspected child abuse or neglect? 4. How prepared do you feel to handle the cases you have investigated? 5. Reflecting on the times you have dealt with child abuse or neglect, what information do you think you lacked? What would have prepared you to be a more culturally competent practitioner in these cases? 6. What are the differences between the local and state policies/laws and how they are actually enacted in practice and in your particular sociocultural context?

research process. The first suggestion we have is regarding your initial contact with the participant. First and foremost, you cannot begin to formally collect data until your study has been approved by the institutional review board (IRB). Once you have IRB approval, you should contact the potential participant, introduce yourself and any institutional affiliation, and briefly explain the purpose of your study. It would be helpful for the participant to understand what it is you are interested in knowing and what it is that you believe you can learn from them. It might be helpful at this time to express that there cannot be right or wrong answers and that you are genuinely interested in the participant's perspective on the topic at hand. You should set up a convenient time for you both to meet in a quiet place that offers some semblance of privacy. If you are a student, be sure to provide the participant with your contact information, including email and a contact phone number, the contact information of your research advisor (i.e., the principal investigator), and the contact information for your institution's IRB office, in case participants have questions or concerns about the study.

Interview Setting

Your formal interview should take place in a quiet setting with little or no potential for distractions. Although a public place might seem like the safest location for two strangers to meet, it is not the best for recording. Coffee shops where glasses are clinking, coffee is percolating, and people are talking will be distracting to the thought-provoking conversation taking place and may cause unnecessary background noise on the recorder. If appropriate, you may want to consider offering to meet in the participant's office or home. If you must conduct the interview in a public place, you may want to invest in a high-quality microphone that might be able to silence extraneous background noise. When selecting the interview setting, be mindful of the participant's comfort. Do not choose a place where they can easily be overheard discussing sensitive topics. Also, remember that they are doing you a favor. Thus, you should be the one meeting them on their terms and at their convenience. Once again, consider power dynamics such as gender or age differences or cultural norms when deciding when and where to meet.

Given the COVID-19 global pandemic, more research interviews are being conducted virtually. This is okay, assuming your institution's IRB approves the data collection modality. There are some benefits to conducting online interviews, such as scheduling convenience, built-in transcribing software on certain programs, lack of geographical boundaries (i.e., you can interview participants outside of your geographic area). Of course, along with advantages come some disadvantages to conducting virtual interviews. For one, it is much harder to build rapport and develop trust with someone. Second, because the participant may be at home or work while conducting the interview, they may not be able to provide undivided attention to the interview. Additionally, some may not be in a completely private space and, thus, may not be comfortable divulging personal information. Finally, not everyone has reliable and strong internet connectivity and, as such, you may end up with a skewed sampled of participants.

Recording Equipment

Both authors collected their dissertation data in the late 1990s, when people still used tape recorders. Jennifer remembers clearly losing two interviews due to malfunctioning equipment. In one instance, she had not checked the batteries of the recorder and, sure enough, the batteries died during the interview. She did not even realize this until it was too late, and the interview was over. Another time, Venus experienced a faulty tape. The tape became stuck in the recorder, unraveled, and was destroyed. Venus also remembers the time when she wanted to be technologically savvy and upgraded to her first digital recorder, only to find out later, after an hour-and-a-half interview, that the digital recorder captured nothing but the sound of air! Jennifer, in using her first digital recorder, remembers that with the push of one button, she accidentally deleted an entire interview. Times have changed; thus, the recording equipment you will use will most likely be digital, such as an iPad or cell phone. Needless to say, you must be careful about transferring and storing digital files or audio. As mentioned earlier, depending on the device you use to record, you may want to invest in a microphone that will better record voices without distractions in the background. Part of this decision will depend on how much background noise will be present during your interviews, whether the device you record with is compatible with microphones, and who will be doing the transcribing. Here is an old-fashioned tip: Even if you are using a digital recording device, continue to take notes of the interview by hand. Those notes or jottings can save your study!

Poker Face

You are asking someone to open up and share aspects of their life story with you. This puts them in a vulnerable situation as they entrust you with their stories. You should strive to be as nonjudgemental as possible as they recapture a moment in their life or share their beliefs. If you want people to share honestly and open up to you, then you must refrain from making negative judgements about what they say. Sometimes we do not verbally express our disgust, but our discomfort or disagreement might show through our facial expressions if we aren't careful. Be mindful of your facial expressions and avoid eye rolling, side eyes, frowning, and other looks of disgust. Cultivate a look of natural curiosity or, if you can't do that, then muster a blank look or a poker face so it is not immediately clear what you are thinking.

Active Listening

You want to be an active listener during a formal interview. Show that you are listening by nodding your head, leaning forward, smiling, and asking probing questions. Also allow participants to talk with you and actively listen and engage the conversation while keeping in mind that they are the experts of their lives. But at the same time, don't be afraid to politely guide the interview and keep the interview on track. Most people who agree to be interviewed enjoy telling their stories and sharing their opinions on a subject matter. You have to strike a balance between letting them do the telling of their stories and facilitating a dialogue (based on your research protocol) that will be most beneficial to your project by ensuring that they discuss the main research questions you have prepared in advance. In other words, listen tentatively, but do not allow the research participant to derail the purpose of the interview—to answer relevant interview questions to meet the objectives of the study. When it comes to the formal research process and the techniques of interviewing, there is nothing wrong with redirecting someone back to the task at hand as needed. However, during the interview or observation, you don't want to be too rigid or inflexible because otherwise the participant will have trouble telling you their story in the way they want to tell it. And *how* they want to tell it is really important in the intersectional qualitative research process.

Be Observant

Pay close attention to what you hear and also to the participant's nonverbal cues. If the participant looks uncomfortable or upset, it is a good time to reflect on how to proceed. If ethically you should not do harm to a participant, that would include forcing them or expecting them to continue talking if they are upset. You can always end the interview and reschedule it for a different time. It also may be appropriate to inquire about their emotions in the moment. For example, you might state, "I noticed that you began to get teary-eyed when responding to that question. What about the question made you get emotional?" or "I noticed that you changed the subject on that particular question. Can you tell me a little bit more about why you skipped that discussion?" In short, being a good interviewer requires one to pay attention to the obvious and not-so-obvious and know when it is relevant to the research topic to address the subtle and not-so-subtle. But always respect your research participants' physical and emotional boundaries. You should also observe your own emotional or physical reactions and verbal or nonverbal cues during an interview. Intersectional research calls for us to give attention to our own intuition and emotive states, too. How we respond to the participant is an important part of the research.

Probe, Probe, Probe

Never assume that you know what your participant means. Always explore broad descriptors such as *good, bad, same, different, us, them, diverse, inner-city, suburban, positive, negative*, and so on. If a participant told me their work setting was *diverse*, I would immediately ask, "What do you mean by *diverse*?" I would ask them to explain what this term looks like to them because the descriptor *diverse* means different things to different people. The point of the interview is to understand what things mean for your participant. Along these same lines, look for specific examples so you can better understand what things mean. For example, if a participant says, "I am a strict counselor," ask for examples of strictness. You might say, "So, when you say that you are strict, can you give some examples of what this looks like?" or "Tell me about a time when you think you were being strict." An important skill of interviewing is knowing how and when to probe further or to delve deeper into participants' meanings. You should follow up on topics by asking specific questions that encourage participants to describe experiences in more detail. Some important probes are *What do you mean? Can you give me an example of that? Can you tell me a story about that?* or *What does that look like?*

Be Careful How You Phrase Questions

Ask only one question at a time. If you ask multiple questions, the participant will not be able to remember them all and will usually answer the last question asked. Ask open-ended questions that begin with *how*, *what*, or *why*. Avoid asking close-ended questions that could be answered with *yes* or *no*; instead of "Do you enjoy talking with patients before their examination?" ask, "What have your experiences of talking to patients before an examination been like?" Also, avoid setting up a binary question. Instead of asking "Is your overall demeanor friendly or stand-offish?" ask, "How would you describe your overall demeanor?" Finally, avoid leading questions. People who agree to be interviewed generally want to help out. They are looking to make you happy and often want to know what you want them to say in order for you to be successful. Avoid this situation by wording questions carefully. A leading question directs them to the answer you want to hear. It actually puts words in their mouth. Often, in a desire to please the interviewer, a participant will spin off a leading question even if they never thought of it before.

Don't Ask Your Research Questions

For the most part, your main research questions are broad and theoretical. They are simply your guide or, stated differently, your script. And no actor stands on stage and reads verbatim from their script! In fact, at times, we like to consider research as a performance. The research context is the setting and you are the lead actor interacting with other characters in the (research) scene or study. Like any good actor, you must rehearse your protocol in a way to get at the questions without asking them in a monotone scripted speech. Reflect on your research questions, write interview questions to help answer the research questions, and raise your inquiries with participants in ways that provoke conversations and dialogue.

Another thing to consider is related to the types of questions you will ask. For example, what broad areas of knowledge are needed to answer your research questions? Once you can answer this important methodological question, then you can develop interview questions that focus on these areas. Remember that in intersectional research, you want to ask about their experiences and how those experiences are shaped by their race and gender and other overlapping social identities, not simply close-ended yes/no questions. Also, try to avoid too many theoretical questions. If you ask theoretical questions, you will get theoretical answers. *How do you understand your racial/cultural identity? How do you understand your sexuality?* These are theoretical questions. Academics think and live theoretically but not everyone else does. Don't ask your participant a question that requires them to do your analysis. Instead, raise questions that elicit stories and encourage your participants to share parts of their stories in their own voice and as a first-person witness to their life. How can you ask questions about race, class, gender, sexuality, and other social identities to get at specific stories? It is *your* job as the researcher to then theorize those stories.

Let's return to an example from a previous chapter. In Chapter 4, we proposed a narrative inquiry (interview-based study). Here are the research questions for that study:

1. How do adult refugees and/or asylum seekers who were forcibly separated from their children navigate the application process?

2. What sources of support did they draw upon through the process?

3. How are their stories impacted by trauma, despair, hope, and resilience?

Let's try to write some interview questions.

Personal Questions

Don't assume that someone will be too embarrassed or afraid to tell you something. The boundary you anticipate or create in your head might be *your* issue, not

Table 5.1 Interview Questions		
Primary Research Question(s)	What Do You Want to Know About the Topic?	What Questions Could Generate the Information You Want to Know?
1. How do adult refugees and/or asylum seekers who were forcibly separated from their children navigate the application process?	I am interested in the events in people's lives that led them to this harrowing journey and whether they knew about the U.S. policy before they crossed the border. Also, once they were separated from their child/children, what was life like in the detention center or once they were released?	• What were your reasons for leaving your home country and trying to enter the U.S.? • How did you cross the border? • What happened once you crossed? • What do you know about where your children are and how they are doing? • Who explained to you what was going on? • If you had known in advance that your children would be taken from you, would you have still crossed? Why or why not?

Primary Research Question(s)	What Do You Want to Know About the Topic?	What Questions Could Generate the Information You Want to Know?
2. What sources of support did they draw upon through the process?	I would like to know what types of help are available to people who were in this situation. Who is advocating for them? How easy is it to find advocates? How are other detainees helping (or not)?	• Who assisted you once you crossed the border? • How have you learned information about where your child/children are? • What type of advocates have provided you with help? • What is your relationship with other parents who are detained? • What is your relationship like with the family and/or friends you have in this country?
3. How are their stories impacted by trauma, despair, hope, and resilience?	I can't imagine the horror and pain these parents are dealing with. How do they navigate this? How do they stay sane despite the loss of their child/children and potentially not knowing where or how they are?	• What do you do when you feel like giving up? • Who or what helps to keep you fighting to get your child/children back? • What has been your lowest moment so far? • What are the thoughts you've had since your child/children were taken from you?

theirs. Ask the questions and see if they answer. Also, you don't have to preface things with "You should answer only if you are comfortable doing so." They are completing the interview as a favor for you. They know they don't have to answer your questions. Ask the questions and see what happens.

Interviewing Children

Interviewing children can be frustrating, as they are often unable to discuss topics in the abstract way adults do. For instance, if a researcher is studying Indigenous girls' early experiences with math, they might ask a first grader, "Tell me about math class." The young student might respond, "I like it" or even ask, "What do you want to know?" You may have to be more specific in your questioning of children. Instead of asking more general questions about her experience in class, you may have to ask, "What happened yesterday in class?" This may prompt a memory or story she can share that will help you glean what her experiences are like. You could also ask the child to take you on a tour of her classroom. During this tour, you might naturally be able to ask her questions. Another helpful strategy is to ask the child to draw a picture of the classroom for you. Once they have drawn the picture, you can ask them questions about it.

Focus Groups

Focus groups are group interviews. A group interview may allow you to get multiple perspectives in a shorter period of time than interviewing each individual, though you would not go as in depth as you would in an individual interview. Focus groups also allow you to hear research participants feed off of each other's perceptions, so they are a good method if you want ideas to emerge from a group. You also may want to conduct focus groups if you are interested in different stakeholders' perceptions on a topic. For example, you might be researching a topic in education and want to understand the perspectives of students, teachers, parents, and administrators. It might be helpful to hold separate focus groups with each stakeholder group. This will allow you to see a range of perspectives on the single topic. Focus groups can be especially helpful for middle or high school students who may be reluctant to open up with an adult. Being in a group situation may put less pressure on them and encourage them to speak more openly, since there is safety in numbers.

An ideal focus group would have 6–8 participants. A group smaller than that might not allow you to get a range of perspectives. Anything larger might be difficult to manage and you would not have time to hear everyone's perspective. There are some researchers who believe it is best to create homogenous groups in terms of participants' race and gender, while others believe mixing a group facilitates a more interesting conversation.

Your role as the facilitator of the group is an important one. The first step is to develop personalized contact with your potential participants. It is more difficult to get participants for focus groups than it is for interviews. It will be your job to interact with the participant in such a way that they will want to come. Personalize your invitations. Why do you want this particular person to come to the group? Set up a convenient location and time. Offer food and drinks during the focus group as a slight encouragement or payment for their time.

During the focus group, you want to stay alert. Be sure that everyone has a chance to talk and that one or two participants are not dominating the discussion. Be sure your questions are clear and easy to understand. Shorter open-ended questions are best. You may want to set a time limit for each question in order to cover your topics.

You should set ground rules at the beginning. You want to set the tone for a respectful atmosphere. All participants should feel as if their opinion is valued. Remind participants that what is said in the room should remain confidential. Unlike an interview, you cannot guarantee confidentiality in a focus group. This is because others (not only you) will hear what is said. Confidentiality means that everyone in the focus group must keep what was said confidential.

You may want to have a co-facilitator or an assistant to help you run the focus group. As the researcher, your task will be to ask questions and try to manage the discussion. You don't want to worry about replenishing paper plates or showing someone where the restroom is in the middle of the discussion. If you have an assistant, you can delineate roles beforehand and ask that your assistant help in getting what participants need or want. That way, you can stay focused.

When we teach about focus groups in class, we assign students mock roles. We ask two students to volunteer as the facilitator and co-facilitator of the focus group and we provide them with a hypothetical topic as well as some focus group questions. Then, we ask for other volunteers and we assign each of them a role to play as a focus group participant. While these roles tend to be overly exaggerated for the purposes of the role play and lesson, it allows students the chance to see different personality archetypes that might show up in a focus group. We assign one student to be the "dominant talker." This person is generally uncomfortable with silence and enjoys talking. The dominant talker will try to speak frequently, even if it means others are interrupted or silenced. Tips for dealing with a dominant talker include ignoring the person by avoiding eye contact, turning your body away from the person, reminding the group that everyone needs to speak, and letting the person know directly that you appreciate their perspective but you would like to hear from other people as well. Because research shows that members of the dominant group are less tolerant of the tones of speech and voices of those from marginalized groups and that those from the dominant group tend to perceive minorities and women as speaking too long or longer than they actually spoke, it is important to pay attention to why you think someone is dominating a conversation or speaking too long. Be conscious of issues of race and gender.

The opposite end of the spectrum is the "shy or quiet" person. We will never understand why someone who does not enjoy public speaking would agree to participate in a focus group. However, you will see this person there. They will not volunteer information and, when called upon, might even say they "don't know" or "aren't sure what to say." Tips for dealing with a shy/quiet participant might be to remind everyone that all perspectives are important and that your goal is to hear and learn from everybody. You might turn your body toward the person. You might call on them specifically with a question. If they don't have an answer right away, let them know that they can think about it and you will circle back to them—and then do so.

The "rambler" is the next archetype you may see. This person does not stay on topic and instead rambles on tangents that are not helpful to your research. You might need to keep this person focused by asking short one-part questions. You will need to interrupt them if they go off too far on a tangent. In one-on-one interviews, there can be more leeway for tangents. But because focus groups involve so many other people, you want to keep tangential comments to a minimum and keep everyone on topic and on task.

Another archetype we have seen in focus groups is who we call the "inflammatory" person. This person says things that are racist, sexist, homophobic, or that are contrary to the overall politics of the group. Let's say you are studying a contentious issue such as creating a union. It could be that the majority of the people in the group have strong opinions one way or another. The inflammatory person will say whatever they want without much thought as to how the group will receive it. You will have to make a quick decision about this. You should not allow someone to say things that could potentially traumatize others. They are there to do a favor for you and should not have to put up with inflammatory discourse. We recommend interrupting the person and letting them know that we are trying to create a respectful community. If the person continues, you may have to ask them to leave in order to protect your other participants. Also, you may want to lay out the rules and expectations of the group at the beginning of the focus group meeting.

There are some ways you might get the discussion going without asking questions initially. You might use icebreakers or introductory activities. For instance, you can ask your participants to draw a picture (using paper and markers or crayons) to describe your topic. If you were studying unions, what does a union look like? Then have each participant hold up their picture and describe it. After everyone has shared, you might ask what participants noticed regarding the pictures. What was similar or different? Another possibility is that, in advance of the focus group, you ask participants to bring in three things that represent the topic. Let's say you are studying mentoring. Ask them to bring three objects or pictures that remind them of or represent mentoring. Each person can share their things and describe why they were selected.

Toward the end of the focus group, you might want to have the group clarify or summarize discussions. What did they learn? How was the overall process? What are some key takeaways? Focus groups can be challenging to run but they do garner a variety of perspectives at once. They also might be used at the stage of member checking. After you have conducted and analyzed individual interviews with participants, you might consider bringing some together in a focus group to discuss your findings thus far. You could also use focus groups as a sampling tool. Perhaps you are interested in recruiting participants with a range of opinions about a topic; a focus group might be one way to narrow it down.

Observations

One of the hallmark data collection methods in qualitative research (observation) hails from anthropology. Observation is a method in which the researcher engages in a systematic process of looking at a culture or group in their natural environment. That sounds quite scientific, as if you should be wearing a white lab coat and goggles. The key words here are *systematic* and *natural*. By conducting field research, you are engaging in scientific inquiry. You are not merely "hanging out" with participants. You are there to systematically study people and their activities within a given context. Thus, you must be focused on observing and not doing anything else. You are also in your participants' natural environment. Thus, you don't have to wear a lab coat and stick out as an outsider. While you are an intruder to the natural setting, if you engage appropriately, people will eventually forget that you are an outsider and they will behave as if you aren't really there to observe. Observational research is generally referred to as "naturalistic inquiry because it does not require people in the setting of interest to deviate from their daily routines during research" (Bailey, 2007, p. 2). To shift from traditional ways of engaging communities of color or other marginalized communities, think of how interlocking systems of oppression shape how they engage in their environments, think about their environments and choices, and construct their realities in ways that serve to make a way out of no way. Your observations and analysis should focus on both resilience and resistance, vulnerability and agency.

Moreover, you may hear others use the terms *participant observation* and *nonparticipant observation*. Participant observation presumes that the researcher will take part in daily activities while observing whereas a nonparticipant observer is presumed to sit quietly and observe. We disagree with these mutually exclusive designations. Your mere presence in the room (regardless of what you do) makes you a participant. Your presence will shape the setting to some degree whether you sit quietly or not. However, in the interest of observing what is really happening in the setting, we think you should sit quietly and observe. Let's use an example. Suppose you are observing teacher–student relationships in a third-grade classroom. Your plan is to sit in the back of the room and quietly watch what occurs. If students are engaged in group activities and the teacher is walking around, you may get up to listen to what is happening. However, your focus is on observing teacher–student interactions. If the teacher asks you to, for example, help a child one-on-one at the back of the room, you are no longer able to be a persistent observer; now you are a tutor, a teacher's aide, or even a volunteer. But you do not cease being a researcher. Because we attempt to not solely take from our research participants, we also set out to give back or at least make sure that our research is of service to the communities we are collecting data from. It is important that you learn quickly how to observe, document, and record at the same time that you are being of service in that space (see Emerson et al., 2011, on jotting field notes). If you are not very good at multitasking or observing and later recollecting what you saw, then you might want to make a deal with the teacher: For every hour of observation, you can volunteer another hour to help out. That way, you are still able to collect fieldnotes, your presence in the research setting is increased, and you are able to give back to your participants in some small way.

What you observe will depend on your research questions. Some researchers go into a setting with only a very loose idea of what they might observe. They watch everything initially until they narrow down their topic. Spradley (1980) offers useful suggestions for when you are engaged in initial observations and have yet to narrow down a topic. He recommends the following:

1. Spaces: the physical places

2. Objects: the physical things that are present

3. Actors: the people involved

4. Act: single actions that people do

5. Activity: a set of related acts people do

6. Event: a set of related activities that people carry out

7. Time: the sequencing that takes place over time

8. Goals: the things people are trying to accomplish

9. Feelings: the emotions felt and expressed (p. 78)

You may also wonder how long you should observe. Lincoln and Guba (1985) suggest "prolonged engagement" in the field. There is not a hard-and-fast rule about the number of hours, days, months, or years you should observe. However, you should have observed long enough that you are treated as an insider. People in the setting should recognize you as part of the cultural group and not only as a researcher who is studying them. One way of determining if you've been in the field for long enough is an older term called *data saturation*. Are your observations yielding the same information? If you aren't able to glean any new information about your topic after a few observations in a row, you probably have reached saturation.

Some researchers may conduct observations alongside other types of data collection, such as interviews. In that instance, they might be using observations to further understand a topic. If observations will be used as supplemental data alongside structured interviews, you may not have to do as many. You still, of course, want a feel for what is happening in the setting. This may take a while, so be sure you factor in time as you design a study that includes observations.

You should also document your observations in field notes. As you write up your observation notes, it is important that you keep separate what you observed versus what you think about those observations. Of course, the boundaries between what you see and what you think about what you see are permeable; what you think shapes how you see. However, you can do your best to try to separate your judgements from the actions occurring in the room. Imagine that you are a fly on the wall in a room. Everything you see and hear can be written down in your notes. When you make judgements about what you see and hear, those should be noted as *observer comments* (*OC*). They are your reflections on what you think is going on in the setting. Let's look at an example:

Suppose you are observing in the back of the classroom. You see a woman and child walk in the room and the woman hugs the child goodbye. You might write,

A mother and daughter walked into the room and the mother hugged her daughter goodbye before she left the classroom.

Do you actually know that the woman is the child's mother? If not, refrain from making that assumption and stating that in the notes. Instead, you might write,

> A middle-aged person (appearing as a woman) and a girl student walked into the classroom. The woman gave the girl a hug and waved goodbye. She then left the classroom as the girl put her coat on a hook. OC: It seems that the woman was the girl's mother; both were wearing jackets as if they had just come inside, even though school was already in session. The woman gave the girl a hug and the girl hugged her back before they waved goodbye to each other.

We suggest either bolding or using a different color font for your OCs so that they are easily distinguishable from your general observation notes. Your OCs will eventually be the beginning of your analysis of observation notes. The more you observe, the more you will be able to address some of your guesses about who people are in the setting and what their relationship is to each other.

We recommend either video recording or audio recording what is happening in the room as you observe. In this way, you can get a more complete picture of dialogue and what people are saying.

Document Analysis

Many researchers triangulate or crystallize their interview and observation data with document analysis. A document is a social text and, as such, should be interpreted by the researcher within its social context. Prior (2003) makes the point that documents are products of social life; thus, the researcher cannot analyze only the document's contents. Instead, the researcher must examine the contents, process of production, and consumption of the text.

Your analysis of a document should be thorough and systematic. You want to trace the evolution of your thinking about each document. In order to do so, you should be systematic in your record keeping as you analyze each document. We suggest you fully answer the following questions before you begin to analyze a document:

1. Provide a detailed description of the project's purpose. What are the questions the analysis will answer? How is intersectionality accounted for in the analysis? Why did you select this document?

2. Provide detailed context regarding the document as well as the document's scope and coverage. How did you acquire the document? What is its significance? What type of document is it? Who was the author? What was the author's motive or purpose for creating the

document? What is the author's identity and is it relevant to the study? When was the document written and for what purpose? What does the document say?

3. Explain your positionality in relationship to the document. Who are you in relationship to the document? Why did you select this document?

4. Contextualize the document within a larger cultural, historical, and political moment. How does this document fit? Why was it written? Who is the audience for this document? What has been the response, if any?

5. Provide a framework for how you will approach the document analysis. How does this framework fit in light of the research purpose and the type of document analyzed?

6. Specify a data analysis method and explain how you will utilize it for the analysis.

We will discuss analysis in Chapters 6 and 7. You will need to choose a way to analyze the documents alongside your theoretical framework. In the actual analysis of the documents, you should include relevant data excerpts from the documents to show how you arrived at the analysis. These excerpts should be interspersed with your actual commentary, interpretation, and/or analysis. You can do this by making comments directly on a hard copy of the document or by using software that will enable you to comment on the electronic version of the document. It is important that you analyze every aspect of the document. Don't neglect visuals at the expense of written narrative. These documents and/or relevant visuals may also be considered artifacts of the study.

Other Data Collection Methods

We have only discussed four methods of data collection: interviews, focus groups, observations, and analysis of documents. There are other methods you may want to investigate, such as surveys or photo voice (visual research method where participants document their lives with a camera or videorecorder). We do not have the space to cover all data collection methods in detail, but the methods describe here are mostly aligned with intersectional research projects. We suggest you study, from a methodological standpoint, what methods of data collection are being utilized in studies similar to your own. You can then research those particular topics in more detail. Be sure to select a method that will allow you rich access to data and methods that are reflective of your personality, skills (i.e., previous preparation), talents, and resources. In order to obtain rich data, an open-ended survey should be used in conjunction with interviews or observations. In critical qualitative studies, context is crucial and you may only discover that context through watching and/or listening.

Summary

We think data collection is the fun part of your study. You will have the most interaction with your participants at this stage and it is during data collection that your study will really take shape. We have outlined different data collection methods, such as interviews, focus groups, participant observations, and document analysis. Each method has its own pros and cons. What will be important for you is to figure out what information you need to answer your research questions as well as what the best methods are to get that information. Be prepared to make mistakes in the collection of data and to be flexible! Stay close to a trusted research mentor who may be able to help you develop better interview or observational skills. Most of us were not born with good research skills and habits. These develop over time and only after careful reflection and trial and error.

DISCUSSION QUESTIONS

1. The authors state, "Thus, intersectional qualitative researchers intentionally utilize research processes to expose how research perpetuates deficit perspectives of racialized minorities and women of color and to explore how research can interrupt stereotypes." How will your research intentionally utilize research processes to achieve intersectional goals?

2. How will you navigate mandates in your field regarding objectivity? How is subjectivity an intersectional concern? What does it mean to be a critically aware researcher and how will you push yourself to become one?

3. The authors state, "Because we value lived experience and culturally rich stories, especially from those living at the margins, it is important before deciding on the type of interview structure to first decide which method (1) is respectful of your participants'

time, (2) honors the dignity of the person, (3) is more culturally appropriate and aligned with the customs of your participants and the cultural context, and (4) is more feasible as it relates to resources (i.e., time, physical location, supplies needed, etc.)." As you think about your potential sample of participants, how will you negotiate this in your research?

4. Take another look at Table 5.1. Using your research questions, complete your own table. Fill in the following items: What do you want to know about your topic? What interview questions could generate the information you want to know?

5. What documents might you analyze to help you answer your research questions? How will you use your theoretical framework in this process?

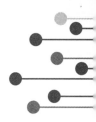

CHAPTER 6

Data Analysis, Part 1

Alonzo has been collecting observations and interviews for a yearlong ethnography. He is studying how high school teachers use culturally relevant pedagogy in their classrooms. After almost the entire school year has been completed, Alonzo knows he must start the process of analysis. Unfortunately, his data are all over the place. He has a field notebook that he takes with him on certain days to write down notes. Some of these notes have been incorporated into the field notes he writes after each visit, but some have not. He also uses a researcher journal at home to capture reflections. This is a handwritten journal that chronicles Alonzo's thoughts about the study. He also has field notes and transcripts at various stages on his laptop (i.e., some are audio recordings while some have been transcribed). He has avoided data analysis because he is completely overwhelmed at the thought of what to do with all the data. Instead of beginning analysis, Alonzo continues to collect data in the field, only adding to his data woes. What Alonzo needs, before he can even begin analysis, is a better data management system.

As a beginning qualitative researcher, one of the biggest struggles you will face is how to analyze your data. In fact, qualitative data analysis is the most mysterious part of the research study (Thorne, 2000, p. 68). Knowing this, we have written two chapters regarding data analysis to help you face this challenge. However, we also understand that two chapters may not feel like enough to you. No matter how much attention is given to analysis in a qualitative text, it may never be enough for some students (Bogdan & Biklen, 2007). That is normal to think and we will do our best to include as much information as we can to help you feel less anxious about data analysis.

Analysis is a mysterious process. Many researchers, in discussing their analysis, will say "My themes emerged." But wait . . . you may be wondering: Where did your themes emerge from? How did this magical process happen? When did it happen? And can it happen for me? We want to assure you that themes do not magically appear. In fact, we wish researchers would not say that *themes emerged* because this is not a passive process. Themes do not simply emerge from some liminal space. We, as researchers and data analysts, construct themes out of our relationships to the data and to our thoughts/reflections about the data. We will discuss this in much further detail, but for now, we want you to understand that in order to analyze your data, you will need to put in the work as the researcher. Your themes will not appear before you one day and announce themselves as such.

Data Management

Before we begin to discuss analysis, we must first discuss data management. Bhattacharya (2017) makes the important distinction between *data analysis* and *data management*. Data management encompasses the tools and strategies a researcher uses to manage what is, typically in qualitative studies, a large volume of data. Strategies for data management should be decided on at the beginning of data collection. Questions the researcher must answer include the following: Where will data be stored? How will I organize data files? How will I most easily access data when I need to begin analysis? Data management is especially important because of the sheer amount of data you will have. Patton (1987) notes:

> The data generated by qualitative methods are usually voluminous. I have found no way of preparing students for the sheer mass of information which they will find themselves confronted with when data collection has ended. Sitting down to make sense out of pages of interviews and whole files of field notes can be overwhelming (p. 146)

Patton is correct. The task can seem overwhelming, but with the right amount of preparation, analysis is something you can complete. We suggest keeping your data as organized as possible *before* you begin analysis. In fact, we suggest developing a management plan *before* you collect the data. If you are organized and consistent in your management plan throughout the collection process, you will find it much easier to find and retrieve the data you need for analysis.

There is no right or wrong way to organize and manage your data, but we do want you to understand that organizing your data is just as important as analyzing them. Most researchers will use some form of electronic means to store their data (usually on their computer's hard drive). Qualitative data are generally in the form of audio/video recordings that have been transcribed or descriptions of observations. Some researchers may use handwritten notes or reflections while out in the field, since it is easier to carry around a small notebook in the field than it is a laptop. If that is your preference, be sure you then transfer that handwritten data to an electronic medium. That way you will have all of your data in one form.

Electronic Storage

Given that your data will be stored electronically, we cannot stress enough that you should back up your files. That means do not only have a copy of your data on your computer's hard drive. Your computer can be lost, stolen, or damaged. You want to have more than one copy of your data in this instance. Maybe your university has a drive that you can save to that is backed up every day? Or, with the right security settings, you can put things in your cloud or in some storage system outside of your hard drive. We have all lost data, files, and/or completed manuscripts due to technological problems or hardware malfunctions. It is not pretty.

We wrote our dissertations in the late 1990s and early 2000s. We luckily had the use of word processing systems, but we certainly did not have as much electronic storage as we have today. Jennifer remembers being instructed to store a copy of her data and dissertation on a floppy disk that she placed in the freezer. Why, you may ask? Because, supposedly, in a potential house fire, a freezer might help protect the data from melting or being burnt/lost in the fire. Luckily, her dissertation survived any major catastrophe but, throughout her career, Jennifer has lost data. In fact, her university once switched drives. The IT (information technology) staff imported files over on the new drive, but it was each faculty member's responsibility to double-check that all of their files were there. Jennifer did not check. Thus, when she went to access 50 transcriptions that had been saved on the old drive, she realized they were not there. And, to make matters worse, it was too late for anyone from IT to recover the files. She managed to recover some from her Dropbox and some from emails between her research assistants and the transcriber, but recovering the data was an arduous process. In the end, about 20 of the 50 interviews were forever lost. Think of how much time and resources were lost with that much data loss. We share this story to remind you of how important it is to have multiple copies of your data in the event of technological problems. Now that we have stressed the importance of backing up your data, we encourage you to develop a consistent plan of nomenclature for the multiple files.

To help manage and retrieve data easily, we suggest creating a naming system that is consistent across the project. Begin with a folder on your computer that is named Research Project. Within this main folder, you can include subfolders. For example, if your project includes participant observations and interviews, you might have a subfolder for your interview transcripts and a subfolder for your observations. You would name your observation files as Observation 1 or Observation 12/22/20 (to signify the date). The interviews might be named with the pseudonym of each participant and the interview number (Erica 1, Erica 2, Denise 1, Denise 2, etc.). Figure 6.1 shows a potential way of organizing.

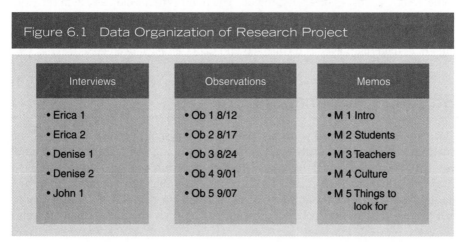

Figure 6.1   Data Organization of Research Project

Interviews	Observations	Memos
• Erica 1	• Ob 1 8/12	• M 1 Intro
• Erica 2	• Ob 2 8/17	• M 2 Students
• Denise 1	• Ob 3 8/24	• M 3 Teachers
• Denise 2	• Ob 4 9/01	• M 4 Culture
• John 1	• Ob 5 9/07	• M 5 Things to look for

Figure 6.2   Data Organization Continued

Interviews	Observations	Memos
• Erica 1	• Obs 1 8/12	• M1 Intro
• Erica 2	• Obs 2 8/17	• M2 Teachers
• Denise 1	• Obs 3 8/24	• M3 Students
• Denise 2	• Obs 4 9/02	• M4 Culture
• John 1	• Obs 5 9/04	
• Erica 1 Coded	• Obs 1 Coded	• M1 Coded
• John 1 Coded	• Obs 2 Coded	• M2 Coded

Things get more complicated once you have coded the data. You should have a subfolder for coded data as well. So, once Erica 1 has been coded, it can be included in a coded file folder as Coded Erica 1. You will have lots of memos to keep track of as well. We suggest you have a memo subfolder. Some people prefer to designate the purpose of the memo (i.e., is it a methodological memo in which you reflected on data collection or is it a memo that discusses data analysis?). If that organizational structure makes sense for you, then use it. Otherwise, you can label your memos with the date to keep progressive track of your thinking or in some other way that makes sense to you. The point is to develop a system early on and to be consistent. And, as a friendly reminder, make multiple copies of this data retrievable by some other means besides your hard drive. See Figure 6.2, which illustrates data that have been collected and data that have been coded.

Starting Data Analysis

Once you have developed your data management system, you are ready to begin analysis. We believe that analysis is best learned by doing. We again want to remind you that "there is no quick fix, no easy set of procedures to apply to all projects" (Bogdan & Biklen, 2007, p. 160). As is common in qualitative research, there are no hard-and-fast rules about how best to analyze your data. We also know that it is a process that intimidates many researchers. In their chapter on data analysis,

Bogdan and Biklen (2007) discussed the very real fears novice researchers have when it comes time to analyze data. They say that some people extend their time in the field collecting data to avoid beginning analysis. Alonzo, the student in our chapter vignette, was guilty of this. He continued to collect data in the field despite having already collected what he needed. We agree that this feeling of dread about the analysis process is common even in experienced researchers. In fact, both of us have extended time in the field to procrastinate beginning analysis. Why? It is fun in the field. As qualitative researchers, most of us are natural voyeurs. We are curious and attentive (some might even say nosey). In the field, we can focus on other people's lives and be all up in their business. When it comes time to begin analysis, it is only us, alone with our data. That is definitely not as fun! We share this to let you know that anxiety about how to analyze your data or how to "get it right" is common.

Up until this point, we have been using the term *analysis* and assuming your familiarity with the word. It might be helpful for us to explain what analysis is and compare it to *interpretation*. Bhattacharya (2017) says that "data analysis involves creating processes that would allow for deep insights that reflect how the researcher integrated theoretical and analytical frameworks, previous understanding of literature, and the focus of the research purpose and questions" (pp. 149–150). Other researchers mark a distinction between interpretation and analysis. We like Bogdan and Biklen's (2007) distinction between interpretation and analysis. They state that *interpretation* is when you develop ideas about findings and relate them to the literature whereas *analysis* involves organizing data, breaking data into smaller pieces, coding, and synthesizing them.

Based on the Bogdan and Biklen (2007) distinction, interpretation can be done throughout the study. As you collect data, you can relate the ideas that emerge to current literature on the topic. This is a process that you, as the researcher, engage with and it is a process that you must keep track of as your thinking progresses. This thinking is broad in scope and is always situated in outside literature. Analytic procedures or methods, on the other hand, involve your raw data. This is where you situate yourself deep within the data and conduct whatever form of analysis you have chosen to do. It involves marking up and, sometimes, moving data around. While we will discuss coding (which is a method of analysis) in this chapter, we will discuss other methods of analysis in Chapter 7. We see the processes of data interpretation and analysis as being in sync with each other. These processes will help move you from a description of your data to a finished product, such as a manuscript (LeCompte & Schensul, 1999).

Often in qualitative research, we make the distinction between *inductive* and *deductive* analysis. Deductive analysis often occurs in quantitative studies. Researchers make analytic decisions based on previously defined criteria or accepted models and formulas. In contrast, qualitative research often involves inductive analysis, which assumes the researcher is not beginning analysis with preconceptions or any type of theoretical model that will be placed on the data. You will often hear researchers say that their theory emerged from the data through a bottom-up approach instead of top down. Inductive research involves looking at the raw data with an open mind and keeping track of the researcher's thoughts as they progress through the analysis.

One of the most complicated things to accept about qualitative data analysis is that it is iterative and emerging (similar to data collection). There are no hard-and-fast rules about much of it and it is not a neat, linear process that a researcher can complete one step at a time. The first thing any researcher must do is familiarize themselves with the data. This means reading and rereading the data and thinking about them constantly. This means while you cook, take a shower, and drive, you can be imagining the data and allowing your mind to start making connections with them. Bhattacharya (2017) offers practical suggestions about how to begin an inductive analysis and, after every suggestion in the process, she suggests the researcher write about it. We agree and cannot stress enough how important capturing your thoughts and processes are during this time. Keep an analysis journal to write reflexively about how you are thinking about the data and why you are thinking in this way. Given that themes do not emerge out of some mystical land as you analyze, you will have to describe the process of how you created data-based arguments with your data. We will discuss in more detail about moving through the process of inductive analysis but, for right now, it will be important to remember that you will benefit tremendously from keeping track of your thoughts and actions during analysis.

When do you begin analysis of your data? Bogdan and Biklen (2007) discuss the two ways qualitative researchers conduct analysis—some begin analysis while they are collecting data; others wait until after they collect data to begin. Bogdan and Biklen recommend that novice researchers wait until data collection has ended before beginning analysis. This is because novice researchers may still be trying to master data collection techniques; thus, their attention should not be diverted while they are in the field. Yet, once you are comfortable with analysis, you might begin it while still collecting data. The benefit of this way is that you begin to narrow your focus on data collection sooner rather than later. You might have an area of focus that emerges from a close analysis of data already collected. This approach also allows you to engage in theoretical sampling (discussed in Chapter 2), where you make sampling decisions based on previously collected data. Yet, Bogdan and Biklen (2017) remind us that there is not a clear boundary regarding when analysis begins because qualitative researchers are always reflecting about their findings and making decisions regarding next steps throughout the study, even if systematic analysis has not yet begun. As we mentioned previously, that constant thinking about the data is part of interpretation and interpretation can occur throughout the study. You will have to determine what you are comfortable with if you are a novice researcher; you might want to wait until data collection has ended before you begin analysis. The point to remember here is that data analysis is a process. It can be iterative (cyclical) whereby the researcher collects data, analyzes, collects more data, analyzes, and so on. See Figure 6.3 for a visual of this process.

Figure 6.3   Cycle of Data Collection and Analysis

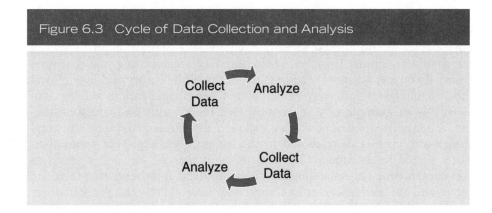

It can also be iterative in the sense that you move back and forth between analytic methods and interpretation. Figure 6.4 shows an example of this.

As your thinking about your data deepens, so too will your methods of analysis. You may be asking where and how your theoretical framework fits into the analysis. We told you that you would return to it often as you conducted analysis. As you start interpreting and analyzing your data, you should revisit your theoretical framework often. Examine your framework(s) so that you create a lens from which to view the data. Once we begin showing you data examples, you will see how the framework is integrated.

Finding Your Place

In thinking about data analysis, you will have to decide somewhat early on which method(s) you would like to use. In Chapter 7, we discuss some of the more common methods, especially those that fit with critical theory and critical research. Keep in mind that not all approaches will fit with a critical approach. For example, post-structural analysis has been critiqued for ignoring the materiality

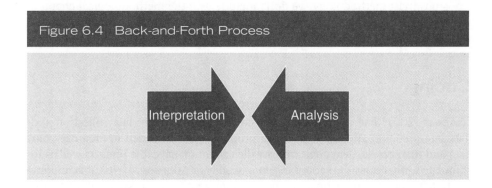

Figure 6.4   Back-and-Forth Process

of identities and the body. This means that race and gender have material consequences (racism and sexism) that continue to oppress some while privileging others. If we get rid of these identity categories, the oppression/privilege does not simply disappear. Thus, we would only recommend using post-structural theory if you can adequately address the limits of the theory and how critical theory could be put into conversation with it. See Happel-Parkins and Esposito (2018) as an example of using critical race theory with post-structural theory. You may be wondering why we include a disclaimer about post-structural theory and whether there should be disclaimers regarding other approaches. There should be disclaimers for all methods of analysis. You will discover as you deepen your understandings of methodological approaches that there are camps and/or cheerleaders for each approach. Some of these camps are in direct conflict with each other. Part of your job as a researcher is figuring out where you fit in and who you will follow in terms of methods. Johnny Saldaña (2018) says it best:

> Being a qualitative researcher means finding your methodological tribes. In this eclectic field of inquiry, there are some approaches we may find more appealing to our personal interests, and we socialize and bond with those who share those same affinities. We invest ourselves in selected research genres or styles because they feel right as forums for our creative investigation. (p. 2044)

While we do not want to engage in any battles among the camps, we do stress that you must figure out which camp(s) you claim and why. It is worth noting that one of the methods we value, coding, is often criticized as being too reductionist. While we can understand some of the concerns coming out of the post-structuralist camps, we would also note that all approaches have their strengths and weaknesses. We believe coding is quite useful, especially for the novice researcher because it forces you to get down and dirty with your data. We will use many grounded theory methods of data analysis. Some of you might be familiar with grounded theory as a methodology. Because it is more of a postpositivist methodology, we don't include it in the methodological chapter. However, grounded theory methods of data analysis such as coding and memo writing will be discussed here.

Coding

Charmaz (2001) has called coding the critical link between data collection and data interpretation and analysis. It is a process that is intended to organize your data and then break them apart into smaller, more manageable units as well as to stimulate further questions about the data (Coffey & Atkinson, 1996). It is important to note that coding is only one way to analyze your data. We think coding is helpful to begin the process of analysis, but coding should not be the only thing you do to generate arguments about your data.

In order to engage in coding, it might be helpful to know what a code is. Saldaña (2016) says that "a code in qualitative inquiry is most often a word or short phrase that symbolically assigns a summative, salient, essence-capturing, and/or evocative attribute for a portion of language-based or visual data" (p. 4). Saldaña's *The Coding Manual* will be an invaluable asset to you as you begin the coding process. Another way to think about coding is how Charmaz (2006) describes it: "Coding is more than a beginning; it shapes an analytic frame from which you build the analysis" (p. 45). She also says that "coding is the pivotal link between collecting data and developing an emergent theory about these data" (p. 46). We will discuss coding in this chapter, but we do not have the space to illustrate all of the types of codes you could use to analyze your data.

Saldaña breaks coding up into two cycles (the first and second). Grounded theorists discuss two types of coding, *substantive* and *theoretical* (Glaser, 1998), while Charmaz (2006) calls the stages *initial* and *focused*. You can choose who you would like to read, learn from, and cite before you code because when you write up your methods, you will use particular language that originates with the theorists/methodologists you read.

It is important to remember that coding is a process that is not completed after one attempt. Saldaña (2016) calls it a cyclical act:

> Rarely is the first cycle of coding data perfectly attempted. The second cycle (and possibly the third and fourth, etc.) of recoding further manages, filters, highlights, and focuses the salient features of the qualitative data record for generating categories, themes, and concepts, grasping meaning, and/or building theory. (p. 9)

Coding does not happen independently, and we cannot stress this enough. Along with coding, you should be reflecting on your codes through memoing. We will get to this but, first, let's talk more about the process of coding and show you some examples of how to do it.

Coding Cycles

Your first coding cycle method should happen during initial stages of data analysis. The first coding cycle could be your first attempt at analyzing the data. There are a variety of first coding cycle methods but probably the most common is descriptive coding. Grounded theorists will sometimes call descriptive coding *open coding* or *line-by-line coding*. It is a method that allows you to describe what is going on in your data. You read your data literally line by line and try to write down a code for each line or groups of lines. Saldaña cautions that too many researchers use descriptive coding as a default method. We will be honest with you: Descriptive coding is pretty easy to do. It is important to note, however, that by *easy* we do not mean you can do it quickly or mechanistically (Coffey & Atkinson, 1996). There are no right or wrong ways to complete it and all you are doing is reading and rereading the data and writing down one, two, or a few words that jump out at you. It is a line-by-line process and, thus, can be time-consuming. However, not too much analytical processing has to occur for you to be able to do this method. You do, of course, have to make decisions about what parts of the data you label with codes. Still, Saldaña (2016) cautions that descriptive coding offers the researcher a list of subtopics (or subcodes) but does not always offer insight into what is really going on with the data. Thus, open coding breaks your data up into smaller units but may not always provide you with a deeper engagement into the data. Knowing this, then, should you use the time to do descriptive coding? We say, "Yes!" Especially for novice researchers, descriptive coding forces you to read and reread the data and it allows you a chance to make sense of how things are said and described. As you code descriptively, there are questions you should ask of the data: *What are this data a study of? What category does this incident indicate? What is actually happening in the data? What is the main concern being faced by the participants? What accounts for the continual resolving of this concern?* (Glaser, 1998, p. 140). The detail you will pay to your data allows you to unveil explicit statements as well as implicit concerns (Charmaz, 2006). To assist with this task, Charmaz recommends these strategies while coding:

- Breaking the data up into their component parts or properties
- Defining the actions on which they rest
- Looking for tacit assumptions
- Explicating implicit actions and meanings
- Crystallizing the significance of the points
- Comparing data with data
- Identifying gaps in the data (p. 50)

The point of coding is to generate themes (or theories) about your data from the ground up. You want to stick closely to your data so that the arguments you make can and will be supported by the raw data.

You can be fancy and use a variety of coding techniques in the first cycle. Descriptive coding does not have to be conducted by itself. Another useful coding method is *in vivo coding*. In vivo coding allows you to describe what is going on in your data with your participant's words and frames of references. In descriptive coding, you as the researcher can name a data passage with any word or phrase you choose. The participants did not have to use the language that you use in order to code. In in vivo coding, however, you would describe the data using the language of the participants. Thus, all of your in vivo codes would be words or phrases that a participant has used. Charmaz (2006) cautions researchers to "take participants' usage as problematic rather than reproducing it. Hence, we look for their implicit meanings and attend to how they construct and act upon these meanings" (p. 55).

A famous example of not taking participants' words for granted comes from Howard Becker's essay, "How I Learned What A Crock Was." Becker was an ethnographer and, in 1955 under the supervision of Everett Hughes, studied medical school culture at the University of Kansas medical school. Becker had very little direction and, in keeping with traditional ethnography, did not have any theories or even a specific topic in mind. He explained

> With no problem to orient myself to, no theoretically defined puzzle I was trying to solve, I concentrated on finding out what the hell was going on, who all these people were, what they were doing, what they were talking about (Becker, 1993, p. 29)

Becker (1993) soon noticed that the medical students labeled particular patients as *crocks* (i.e., *crock of shit* meaning someone who is not being truthful). He went through different theorizing in order to discover the full definition that his participants used for a crock. While the students took the word and its meaning for granted, Becker sensed that there was something important about this labeling of patients and how frustrated students were when they encountered a crock. Becker states, "My discovery of what the word 'crock' meant was not a lightning bolt of intuition. On the contrary, it was guided by sociological theorizing every step of the way" (p. 29). Becker described his search for the meaning of the word *crock*. At first, it appeared as if a crock was a patient with psychosomatic symptoms. Yet, when Becker checked his understanding of the term after one of the medical students did his assessment of a patient, Becker was told that no, that patient was not a crock because even though he had a psychosomatic illness, he actually had an ulcer. Thus, Becker updated his definition that a crock was "a patient who had multiple complaints but no discernible physical pathology" (p. 32). Becker then explored why medical students devalued crocks and eventually developed the main theory in his book, *Boys in White*. Medical students valued experiential learning over book learning. They enjoyed assessing patients and diagnosing them. Because crocks had no discernible physical pathology, all the students could do was talk to them. The medical students felt that their time was wasted with crocks because they did not gain experiential knowledge. We share this story to help you see the importance of in vivo codes but also to illustrate that meanings of the words participants use cannot be taken for granted and should be explored in all of their complexities. It is important to note that in Becker's case, he was analyzing while still collecting data; thus, he had an easier time of following leads and developing his theory.

Example of Coding

It is time to show you an example of coding (Figure 6.5). We will use both descriptive and in vivo coding in our example and will use the theoretical framework of critical race theory to guide our thinking. These data come from a study about how

Figure 6.5 Coding Example

Excerpt from Interview with Jo	Coder Comments
I think the Latino kids here are just very different in the sense that they expect you to belong to a certain group, the Latino group.	Group(s) on campus (descriptive code)
I was telling S. how I was interested in joining a Black sorority	
So, upon people hearing of me being interested in Black sororities, I've noticed that some Latino friend I've had, they just kind of like. Well, they're kind of like, "Oh? Okay. Well, she decided to go *that* route."	Black sorority vs Latina sorority (descriptive code)
You know?	
And, it's because the Latino culture here is even smaller than the African Americans here so it seems like they expect all of us to stick together.	Numbers of Latinos vs African Americans (descriptive code)
	Does she feel marginalized (asking questions of the data)
And, um, I have white friends, very good white friends, and Black friends.	
And, that's just not me.	"That's just not me" definition for how she sees race relations (in vivo code)
I don't like confining myself.	"Confining" (in vivo code)
So, I thought to myself, maybe it's because it's a college campus.	
When I get out into corporate America, I will meet people from all different, from all over. Not all Latino people are the same way but it's hard you know?	Diversity (descriptive code)
	"Into corporate America" (asking questions of the data)
It's like my community, where I live back home. Washington Heights is a predominately Latino community. I'm starting to understand that I want something more than we have.	Home reality vs desire upon graduation. (Is she torn between life in Washington Heights vs the possibilities of something more? Different?)

women of color undergraduates negotiated studying at a predominantly white institution. In this particular excerpt, Jo, who identified as Latinx (Dominican) discusses her decision to join a Black sorority on campus:

> I think the Latino kids here are just very different in the sense that they expect you to belong to a certain group, the Latino group. I was telling S. how I was interested in joining a Black sorority. So, upon people hearing of me being interested in Black sororities, I've noticed that some Latino friend I've had, they just kind of like. Well, they're kind of like, "Oh?

Okay. Well, she decided to go *that* route." You know? And, it's because the Latino culture here is even smaller than the African Americans here so it seems like they expect all of us to stick together. And, um, I have white friends, very good white friends, and Black friends. And, that's just not me. I don't like confining myself. So, I thought to myself, maybe it's because it's a college campus. When I get out into corporate America, I will meet people from all different, from all over. Not all Latino people are the same way but it's hard you know? It's like my community, where I live back home. Washington Heights is a predominately Latino community. I'm starting to understand that I want something more than we have.

The descriptive codes, for the most part, summarize or describe in one word or short phrases what the data excerpt contains. The in vivo codes also describe the data but use the participant's same language. In this example, Jo used the term "confining" which ultimately became an important code. Other women of color felt as if the racial/ethnic group they belonged to was confining them to spend their time within that group for protection and solidarity. Other participants used the same word or variations of it ("constraining"). In addition to writing down codes, we also began asking questions of the data. Before Jo trailed off in her response, she spoke of how she imagined corporate America as including people from all different racial/ethnic backgrounds. Then, she imagines Washington Heights, where she grew up and says, "It's hard. . . . I want something more than I have." At this point, she has not explicitly said that she is torn between her community back home and the life she imagines for herself upon graduation. But we note this here as a possibility because we anticipate this as important and may see this story come up again in her narrative.

Up to this point, we have not mentioned the term *subcodes*. Codes can be broken into even smaller units of subcodes. We see a subcode as a more descriptive term to describe a piece of data within a larger code. Let's look at an example of subcodes using the same data excerpt from earlier (Figure 6.6).

You can see that not every code has to have a subcode. For the "That's just not me" code, we are not sure, at this point in analysis, what this means and if it is important. We cannot break it down any further so there are no subcodes for it. The codes "Group(s) on campus" and "Confining" have the subcode of "Expectations." This might be a later clue, as we condense codes, that these codes are similar and might become categories. But, for now, we will use the same subcode for each of those code groups because it signifies something different (i.e., for "Group(s) on campus," *expectations* signifies that students from the same racial/ethnic group expect other students to hang out in solidarity, while for "confining," *expectations* signifies that the participant does not want to limit herself to only social interactions with peers from the same racial/ethnic group). Eventually, our coding schema will include larger categories. We initially break the data into smaller units and then we try to condense those units into a larger category that contains multiple codes. In order to create categories, you should revisit your

Figure 6.6 Subcoding Example

Excerpt from Interview with Jo	Coder Comments
I think the Latino kids here are just very different in the sense that they expect you to belong to a certain group, the Latino group. I was telling S. how I was interested in joining a Black sorority. So, upon people hearing of me being interested in Black sororities, I've noticed that some Latino friend I've had, they just kind of like. Well, they're kind of like, "Oh? Okay. Well, she decided to go that route." You know? And, it's because the Latino culture here is even smaller than the African Americans here so it seems like they expect all of us to stick together. And, um, I have white friends, very good white friends, and Black friends. And, that's just not me. I don't like confining myself. So, I thought to myself, maybe it's because it's a college campus. When I get out into corporate America, I will meet people from all different, from all over. Not all Latino people are the same way but it's hard you know? It's like my community, where I live back home. Washington Heights is a predominately Latino community. I'm starting to understand that I want something more than we have.	Group(s) on campus (descriptive code) Racial categories (subcode of group[s] on campus) Latinx group (subcode of group[s] on campus) Expectations (subcode of group[s] on campus) Black sorority vs. Latina sorority (descriptive code) Choices (subcode of Black sorority vs. Latina sorority) Numbers of Latinos vs. African Americans (descriptive code) Sticking together (subcode of numbers) "That's just not me" definition for how she sees race relations (in vivo code) "Confining" (in vivo code) Racial expectations (subcode of confining) Diversity (descriptive code) Corporate (subcode of diversity) Difference (subcode of diversity)

theoretical framework to be sure your coding schema is informed by it. Let's create categories for the data excerpt we coded.

You can see from Figure 6.7 that our many codes and subcodes from this data excerpt have been moved into a larger category of "Race structures choices." This category encapsulates a variety of smaller codes and subcodes that were related. We also were able to use our theoretical framework as we thought about a larger category. Is a category a theme? No, but you are getting closer. We will discuss generating themes in the next chapter.

Saldaña makes the point that coding is not a "precise science; it is primarily an interpretive act" (2016, p. 5). He continues, "Coding requires that you wear your researcher's analytic lens. But how you perceive and interpret what is happening in the data depends on what type of filter covers that lens and from which angle you view the phenomenon" (pp. 7–8).

To provide direction and an analytic lens as you code, the process should be aligned with your research questions and your theoretical framework. It is helpful

Figure 6.7 Moving toward Categories

Codes	Subcodes	Relation to Theoretical Framework	Categories
Group(s) on campus	Racial categories Latinx group Expectations	A question we returned to with these excerpts was whether Jo felt "different" on campus. One of the tenets of critical race theory (CRT) is recognizing that race and racism is endemic to society. Here, race structures the groups on campus.	Race structures choices. The larger category that seems to scream out between many of these codes, such as "Group(s) on campus" (expectations) and "Confining" (expectations) is that race structures Jo's choices.
Black sorority vs Latina sorority	Choices	Race also structures Jo's choices. She is torn between groups with clear boundaries.	Race structures choices. While race structures who Jo aligned herself with, it also determined what sorority she would join. She could not make a decision without accounting for race.
Numbers of Latinos vs African Americans	Sticking together	Being marginalized within a larger marginalized group shows the ways privilege and oppression shape the choices Jo makes.	Race structures choices. Jo made choices based on how much support (or lack thereof) she would have as a racial minority on a predominately white campus. As Latina, she was a minority within a minority group and that mattered.
Confining	Racial expectations	Jo feels confined because she perceives pressure from the Latinx students to hang out with them in solidarity.	Race structures choices. Jo can't decide what group to hang out with or focus on without coming to terms with how she identifies racially and who she wants to align with. She feels immense pressure to be in solidarity with Latinx people, but she also feels drawn to other racial groups and the possibilities of learning about them.
Diversity	Corporate	Jo imagines a racially diverse world and craves practice at interacting with different or diverse people.	Race structures choices. Jo is looking into the future and understands that in order to be successful in corporate America, she will need to be able to deal with and understand different races.

to have your research questions and a description of your theoretical framework in front of you while you code your data. Both will guide you in recognizing what might be important. Below, you will see an example of the same piece of data coded two different ways based on theoretical framework.

Coding an Interview Two Ways

This interview excerpt was taken from a study on how urban educators negotiate their beliefs about culturally relevant pedagogy with their school district's prescribed school reform. We will use this brief excerpt to show you how data may be analyzed differently depending upon the theoretical framework or lens through which the data are viewed.

Interviewer: Tell me more about that decision-making process.

Star: It's tough, I mean, I want my kids to learn and to excel and I also want to do what my principal expects of me. But, sometimes I pull out the script and it is just so boring and *not* relevant to my kids. I mean, why do Black kids always have to learn about whiteness? Why can't they ever see their faces or hear stories related to their lives? It gets frustrating and then it becomes up to me to change it. But, dang, sometimes I don't want to have to put in all this extra work. So, I have a choice: Do I run around town trying to go to libraries and bookstores to find books that reflect my students' lives and then spend the time trying to figure out how to incorporate the books into the scripted lesson? Do I find the books, scrap the script, close my classroom door, and go with my gut as far as teaching these kids the content the way I want to? Or do I just do the easy thing but the thing that won't let me sleep at night.

Interviewer: What is that?

Star: Use the lesson as is. No add-ons, no cultural relevance.

So, now that you have read the excerpt, let's code it in a few different ways. The first way is through a critical race lens, where we would be interested in how race and racism impact the student. In Figure 6.8, we are using critical race theory as a theoretical framework.

In this excerpt, the primacy of codes center around culturally relevant pedagogy (a race-based approach) and, in relationship to that, teacher decisions around this race- and culture-centered pedagogy. You can see that the main code of "Culturally relevant pedagogy" includes multiple subcodes, such as "Cultural irrelevance," "Scripted lesson," and "Incorporation." Questions you might ask of the data at this point include the following: How much time do teachers invest in

Figure 6.8 Coding an Interview Through Critical Race Theory

Excerpt from Interview with Jo	Coder Comments
Interviewer: Tell me more about that decision-making process.	
Star: It's tough, I mean, I want my kids to learn and to excel and I also want to do what my principal expects of me. But, sometimes I pull out the script and it is just so boring and not relevant to my kids. I mean, why do Black kids always have to learn about whiteness? Why can't they ever see their faces or hear stories related to their lives? It gets frustrating and then it becomes up to me to change it. But, dang, sometimes I don't want to have to put in all this extra work.	Expectations Culturally relevant pedagogy Cultural irrelevance Whiteness as the norm Race: whiteness, Blackness
So, I have a choice: Do I run around town trying to go to libraries and bookstores to find books that reflect my students' lives and then spend the time trying to figure out how to incorporate the books into the scripted lesson? Do I find the books, scrap the script, close my classroom door, and go with my gut as far as teaching these kids the content the way I want to? Or do I just do the easy thing but the thing that won't let me sleep at night.	Culturally relevant pedagogy Books, incorporation, scripted lesson Culturally relevant pedagogy Scripted lesson Teacher choice Teacher ethics
Interviewer: What is that?	Culturally relevant pedagogy
Star: Use the lesson as is. No add-ons, no cultural relevance.	Cultural irrelevance, scripted lesson

ensuring their lessons are culturally relevant? Where do teachers find culturally relevant materials? How do they make decisions about what counts as a culturally relevant material?

Recoding

Now, let's code the same data excerpt using a different framework or lens. In Figure 6.9, we use teacher and learner autonomy, a lens that shapes our coding around ideas related to choices and practices that promote autonomy in the classroom.

Given that our frame was teacher and student autonomy, the codes we developed are closely related to the frame. We coded the data with an eye for the choices teachers and students get to make. We used "Autonomy" as a main code and noted the types of autonomy in the subcodes. Questions you might ask of the data at this

Figure 6.9 Coding an Interview Through Teacher and Learner Autonomy

Excerpt from Interview with Jo	Coder Comments
Interviewer: Tell me more about that decision-making process.	
Star: It's tough, I mean, I want my kids to learn and to excel and I also want to do what my principal expects of me. But, sometimes I pull out the script and it is just so boring and not relevant to my kids. I mean, why do Black kids always have to learn about whiteness? Why can't they ever see their faces or hear stories related to their lives? It gets frustrating and then it becomes up to me to change it. But, dang, sometimes I don't want to have to put in all this extra work.	Autonomy (teacher, lack of) Scripted curriculum Autonomy (student, lack of) Autonomy (teacher) Frustration Making change Extra work
So, I have a choice: Do I run around town trying to go to libraries and bookstores to find books that reflect my students' lives and then spend the time trying to figure out how to incorporate the books into the scripted lesson? Do I find the books, scrap the script, close my classroom door, and go with my gut as far as teaching these kids the content the way I want to? Or do I just do the easy thing but the thing that won't let me sleep at night.	Autonomy To decide Choices
Interviewer: What is that?	
Star: Use the lesson as is. No add-ons, no cultural relevance.	Autonomy (lack of) Cultural relevance Scripted curriculum

point include the following: How do teachers make decisions in regard to following orders and doing what they think is ethical? When teachers become frustrated, what do they do? How do teachers understand the lack of cultural relevance on students?

In both instances, we will eventually answer the same research question of how urban educators negotiate their beliefs about culturally relevant pedagogy with their school district's prescribed school reform. But the critical race frame would encourage us to see the data through a race and culture lens whereas the autonomy lens would push us to focus more on what type of decision making is happening in the classroom. Both coding approaches will allow us to categorize the data and break them apart into smaller segments.

Code Lists

You should keep track of your codes in a code list, complete with each code's definitions. So, for the above example, our code list would look like this:

Code List/Definitions

Autonomy: How much freedom for decision making is there?

    Teacher: How much freedom a teacher has to decide
    Student: How much freedom a student has in their learning
    Lack of: Autonomy has been stifled
    To decide: When teachers decide

Scripted curriculum: Script for class

Frustration: Becoming frustrated with administration

Making change: How much can teachers really change things?

Extra work: Captures the extra stuff teachers do (buy supplies, plan, etc.)

Choices: Even with proscribed reforms, do teachers have choices?

Cultural relevance: Teaching/curriculum/materials that are culture based

    Add-ons: Adding culturally relevant materials to scripted curriculum

You can see that a short definition was added to each code and subcode. This will help us keep track of codes as well as help us be consistent as we code further data. The code list will also be key in helping us to decide how to collapse codes (i.e., decide which codes are similar to each other).

Is there any limit to how many codes you should develop? Not really. The point of the first cycle of coding is to break your data apart into chunks. In the second cycle of coding, you will reorganize those chunks and, perhaps, collapse codes. Saldaña (2016) uses a technique in the second-round cycle called "splitting and lumping"; see page 229 in *The Coding Manual* for further information.

For grounded theorists, the second stage of coding involves focused or axial coding. One of the goals of focused coding is to determine the adequacy of your initial codes (Charmaz, 2006). This involves closer readings of your data with an eye to determine whether code categories can be collapsed into each other. Axial coding occurs in a similar vein. The point is to bring your now-fractured data back into an integrated whole. Axial coding, according to Strauss and Corbin (1998), answers the questions, "When, where, why, who, how, and with what consequences?" Axial coding will link codes with subcodes in an attempt to create larger chunks of data that have a fresh frame. The frame is developed by the researcher as they pare down codes and subcodes.

Another second-round coding cycle method that Saldaña discusses includes creating conceptual maps and charts to help you visualize how codes are related to each other. These visuals may also help summarize your codes and compare coding schemas. You can do these by hand or find software that allows you to create visual maps. None of the second coding cycle methods should be done without much writing and reflecting on your part. Again, this is because coding (both first and second cycle methods) is only the first step.

Moving from Codes to Themes

One of the more difficult things for students is knowing how to move from codes to themes. This is why coding is never enough in analysis. You must transform your coding schema into some data-based arguments. A code and a theme are *not* the same thing. Eventually, you have to let readers know what can be learned from your study. This is why it is helpful to think of a theme as an argument. Researchers are fond of saying, "My themes emerged." But a big mystery is how this happened. Themes will not drop onto your computer screen and announce themselves. And yes, while our analysis is emergent, we are the ones helping it emerge. What you need to learn is how to take the codes you have developed into themes that reflect them.

Saldaña (2016) provides a few strategies that you might find useful. Most of us code with one or two words or short phrases. Saldaña recommends trying to expand those codes into longer phrases. This technique might prompt you to see how you can develop an argument in relation to that code group. Saldaña also recommends another technique of adding the verbs *is* or *means* to a code. Let's say your code is "Performing masculinity." You can say "Performing masculinity *is* . . ." and then fill in the blanks from your data. So, in the study of Black masculinity, we might add "Performing masculinity is a process learned by watching male figures throughout a boy's life" or "Performing masculinity means drawing upon accumulated knowledge about learned examples of masculinity in order to act like a man or exude traditional characteristics of masculinity that would allow the performer to be accepted as a man." This is quite a theoretical definition and will need many examples to illustrate how this works in a practical sense. But this is a nice way of moving from a short code to a larger idea about that code.

Another good strategy is what Saldaña (2016) calls "shop talking." Holding conversations about your data with trusted colleagues or your advisor is a great way of moving your thinking ahead. Let someone else put their eyes on your study and tell you what they see. There are no easy ways to move from your coding system. It will involve work and a lot of writing and reflecting on your part. We will return to the idea of moving from codes or beginning analysis to themes in the next chapter.

The important thing to remember while you code is to be open to new ideas and to try not to impose your preconceptions upon the data. Charmaz (2006) has cautioned researchers:

> Be careful about applying a language of intention, motivation, or strategies *unless the data support your assertions*. You cannot assume what is in someone's mind—particularly if he or she does not tell you. If people tell you what they "think," remember that they provide enacted accounts reflecting social context, time, place, biography, and audience. Participants' unstated purposes in telling you what they "think" may be more significant than their stated thoughts. If you reframe participants' statements to fit a language of intention, you are forcing the data into preconceived categories—yours, not theirs. Making comparisons between data about what people say and do, however, strengthens your assertions about implicit meanings. (p. 68)

This is, unfortunately, not as cut and dry as Charmaz assumes. We share with you an excerpt from Jennifer's dissertation interviews. The interview was conducted when she was a graduate student and still a novice researcher. It is flawed, of course, in that the interviewer might be seen as leading the participant into what was, up until that point, more of an implicit understanding. The research study aimed to understand how college women made sense of femininity intersected by race and class. In this particular interview, the researcher asked Kiesha, a Black female chemistry major at a predominately white institution (PWI), to talk further about her experiences in a particular class where she expressed that she was the "minority."

Jennifer:	What is it like being a minority in class?
Kiesha:	There aren't too many people of color in my major. I don't know, sometimes, I just feel intimidated by him.
Jennifer:	Is he a white guy?
Kiesha:	Yeah. With these piercing blue eyes. Sometimes I'm scared he's looking at me funny.

We do not share this excerpt as an exemplar of data collection. Certainly, the researcher could have asked a more open-ended probing question besides "Is he a white guy?" But we share this excerpt with you because, when Jennifer submitted an article containing it to journals, reviewers again and again flagged this excerpt as an example of the author making assumptions about what was in the participant's mind. Reviewers found this excerpt especially problematic because they believed that the researcher forced the issue of race by naming the professor as "a white guy." It became such a frequent comment that eventually, she addressed reviewer's questions about the excerpt directly. (This author was set on including these data because it encapsulated what so many women of color felt as they sat in classrooms with white male professors.) When the article was published (Esposito, 2011), this is how the author explained her thoughts:

> Kiesha was not sure how the professor was "reading" her. Did he find her to be an incapable student? Did he wish he were not teaching chemistry to a young Black female? Kiesha wanted to be recognized as a smart and capable student, but she feared her professor was misrecognizing her. . . . This data excerpt might raise questions for readers because Kiesha does not explicitly say that the professor is "looking at her funny" because of her race. I argue, however, that given that she was answering the question "What is it like being a minority in class?" Kiesha was coding her language to talk about race (Castagno, 2008). I asked Kiesha a question regarding her experience as a Black woman at a PWI and she responded with an example of a professor who looks at her in a strange manner. In an attempt to encourage her to explicitly name race or due to, perhaps, my racialized assumption, I asked Kiesha if the professor to whom she referred was white. She affirmed and then detailed the color of his eyes (blue eyes are a racial attribute). As the interviewer, this was enough for me to connect her fear of his perceptions of her to his race. It does not matter, in this instance, what the professor really thought. What matters is that Kiesha had to, at the minimum, confront issues of race in all areas of her higher education experience. (pp. 149–150)

We share this write up of the data excerpt and the author's explanation of it as an example of how you might have to explain your thoughts regarding analysis and interpretation. Your job as a writer is to convince readers that how you made sense of the data is the "correct" way. Of course, there is not really a correct way, but there is a way that will allow your readers to trust your judgements. When readers with limited knowledge about race and racism try to make sense of something through a critical lens, they may need further guidance on how you, as the researcher, have conceptualized it. In some instances, you may want to anticipate a reader's struggle with a particular interpretation and be more specific in regard to your description of your process.

Computer-Assisted Qualitative Data Analysis Software (CAQDAS)

Jennifer and Venus attended graduate school over twenty years ago. At that time, researchers generally hand-coded using sticky notes and colorful pencils or pens. There were some data analysis programs but they were not yet widely in use. We remember hoping that someone would develop a software program that would actually conduct the analysis for us. We were jealous of our quantitative colleagues who could, at the push of a button, receive statistical analysis results without the hours of intense belaboring over every word of a transcript, field note, or memo. Yet, twenty years later, no one has quite developed a software program that would actually conduct qualitative data analysis. At best, CAQDAS will help you with data management and organization as well as help you situate your coding schema. Popular programs that exist include NVivo, Dedoose, and ATLAS.ti.

ATLAS.ti first came out about 20 years ago. It is known for being able to handle very large data sets. It can handle both qualitative and some quantitative data. You can upload your textual data in multiple formats and also upload sound or video files. There are multiple tools and features that will enable you to code and categorize your data. We especially like that ATLAS.ti can help you conduct word counts, which is important for content analysis. There is also a feature (the interactive margin) that reminds us of our hand-coding days. We would handwrite notes, comments, and codes in the margins. ATLAS.ti allows you to do this virtually.

Many of our graduate students use Dedoose because the software does not have to be purchased. With Dedoose, you pay for the service per month. Dedoose is capable of handling all types of data, including some mixed-methods data types, such as spreadsheets. You are also able to integrate some quantitative data, such as test scores. It is web based, so unlike ATLAS.ti or Nvivo, you will need an internet connection to use it. You are able to share your work with other people who can access what you've done.

Nvivo has grown increasingly more intuitive with each version. It has become so popular that many colleges and universities will provide access to it on their computers. Our graduate students are able to purchase it through special student pricing. The intention of Nvivo is to help you store, manage, and analyze your data in a deeper way. Nvivo offers matrix coding queries and other visualizations that will help you think in a more complex way about your data.

There are many other analysis programs that you may want to check out, including Transana, CAT (Coding Analysis Toolkit), and QDA Miner. Just remember that none of these programs will actually do the analysis for you. It will be up to you to do the hard work of analyzing the data but CAQDAS will make things easier for you once you get the hang of it.

Conclusion

In an effort to wrap up this chapter, let's examine a few other issues that may arise as you first start to analyze your data. Remember that we continue our discussion of data analysis in the next chapter as well.

Transcribing

If you record the audio of participant interviews, you must transcribe them. Transcribing is a process in which you capture word for word what was said in the interview. As of this writing, there are no software programs that automatically take an audio file and transcribe it, but there are voice-to-text software programs (such as DragonNaturallySpeaking) that could aid you in the process. We recommend that you do your own transcribing because there is some level of judgement on the part of the researcher. Certain voice inflections or patterns may be difficult for an outsider to understand. Also, unless given specific instructions, a transcriber may not capture the interviewee's pauses, struggles, laughter, sighs, and so on. These utterances help the researcher understand the context of the words and are important to include. If you pay someone else to transcribe, you should, at the very least, listen to the audio recordings as you read the transcripts and edit for understanding or mistakes made by the transcriber. Many students want to know if there is a proper form for transcriptions. There is not necessarily a proper form, but you do want to be sure everything is labeled correctly, especially regarding who said what. Some researchers prefer line numbers on their transcriptions because it assists them in keeping everything organized during the analysis. Both authors are distracted quite easily, so we prefer not to include line numbers. Of course, we do include page numbers.

Negotiating Subjectivities during Analysis

Prominent Cuban author, Anaïs Nin, once said, "We don't see things as they are, we see them as we are." This is true as we reflect on moments in our lives and it will also be true as we think about and analyze our data. Who we are will shape our interpretations and thus our analysis of the data. This is not something you have to be afraid of or hide. In fact, it is important to be up-front and direct about this. You can reflect on how who you are shapes the research project. In fact, intersectional research demands this because it recognizes the ways that research is an embodied act.

Schwandt (1997) reminds us that good research has gone through the process of "examining one's personal and theoretical commitments to see how they serve as resources for generating particular data, for behaving in particular ways . . . and for developing particular interpretations" (p. 136). We call this process *reflexivity* and have discussed it at length in an earlier chapter. Of course, reflexivity is prominent throughout the study and not only at the analysis stage. As a reminder, Guba and Lincoln (2008) state,

> Reflexivity forces us to come to terms not only with our choice of research problem and with those with whom we engage in the research process, but with ourselves and with the multiple identities that represent the fluid self in the research setting. (p. 278)

This is true during data collection, but it is also something we must be cognizant of during analysis. In Chapter 7, we will discuss memoing and, when we do, we will return to the notion of reflexivity as it is best explored through memoing.

Disconfirming Data

In data analysis, we search for patterns. Because life is complex, we may not always see consistent patterns across the data. What happens when you have some data that seem to disconfirm your other findings? In quantitative research, researchers are allowed (even encouraged) to get rid of what they term *outliers*—data that are so far from the mean that they would otherwise skew the results if included. Are there such things as outliers in qualitative data? Yes and no. We may not have, as stated before, consistent patterns across the data. Sometimes, if you can further explore data that stand out, conflict with other data, or are in some way contradictory, you may end up with some very rich and important understandings of social life. This, of course, would involve you discovering the contradictions during data analysis and then going back to the field to investigate further. If you are unable to go back to the field or if you are unable to come to a full understanding of the contradictory data, you have a few choices. You can be honest in your write-up that, for reasons unknown to you, these data were contradictory. You can suggest that this might be an area of future research for yourself or others. You can also consider the data as an anomaly and not report them in your final report. Of course, this assumes that it is a small amount of data (for example, one participant out of 20 or two observations based on 25 total). While there are no hard-and-fast rules about not reporting data, you will have to use your best judgement. Qualitative researchers generally collect way more data than we report anyway so you are not being unethical by not reporting, as long as you aren't purposefully trying to hide something.

DISCUSSION QUESTIONS ●

1. What will your data management system be? What factors should you consider as you develop a long-term data management and storage plan?

2. What is data analysis? How does it differ from interpretation?

3. Johnny Saldaña (2018) states, "Being a qualitative researcher means finding your methodological tribes. In this eclectic field of inquiry, there are some approaches we may find more appealing to our personal interests, and we socialize and bond with those who share those same affinities. We invest ourselves in selected research genres or styles because they feel right as forums for our creative investigation" (p. 2044). Who is part of the methodological and analytical groups you claim? Who is not? Why?

4. Describe the process of coding. How does one code data and why? What are the strengths and weaknesses of coding data?

5. How are themes generated (i.e., themes do not simply "emerge")?

Data Analysis, Part 2

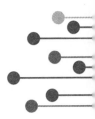

A team of researchers had been investigating undergraduate women's understanding of gender. They were at the analysis stage and had spent hours poring through hundreds of pages of interview and focus group transcripts. All 50 of the participants had been asked what it was like in their respective majors. The following are some examples from the data:

Interviewer: What is it like being a woman and an education major?

Respondent: Well, I am surrounded mostly by other women. That makes it easy for me. There are maybe one or two men in every education class, so.

Interviewer: What is it like being a woman and a chemistry major?

Respondent: There are not many of us. Sometimes I am the only woman in a class.

Interviewer: What is it like being a woman and an engineering major?

Respondent: There are almost no female engineering professors. I can count one, maybe two, but I think she is a graduate student who teaches a class.

In the above three interview excerpts, the research team noticed something. When we asked undergraduate women what it was like to be a woman in their majors, they all responded with numbers. They started counting, either how many women were present in their major or how many men. While not every participant did this, there were enough who did to make it catch our attention. We started to code instances of this as "Enumeration." We found over 100 instances of this enumeration. Yet, it was not enough, in terms of analysis, for us to say that women started counting in response to this question. We had to come up with potential reasons for why they might enumerate in response to this question regarding gender.

We had many conversations about this code and the cultural, social, and historical context in which the participants lived. Finally, the PI [principal investigator] suggested that given second wave feminism's focus on equity and, in many cases, increasing the numbers of women in the workforce, perhaps that is why the participants equated gender with counting. The participants had been born in the 1980s and this was a time when *the feminist movement had made some headway in terms of shattering glass ceilings. While things were far from equal (especially in terms of women of color), there had been strides made in securing positions in politics and the corporate world for (mostly white) women. Thus, we hypothesized that these college-age women associated gender with the feminist movement, which, to them, meant equity and increasing numbers of women in traditionally male-dominated fields.*

In the process of member checking, we asked a few participants what they thought of our analysis. Most were surprised that they responded to the question in such similar ways. While they remained surprised, they also thought there was truth to our theory regarding their understandings of gender.

There has been, throughout history, a battle over the superiority of knowledge— that is, whose histories, epistemologies, traditions, and methodologies get recognized, shared, and validated? We mentioned in an earlier chapter that positivism holds more weight in the field of research not because it is a better paradigm but because it has been the tradition that has circulated within academic spaces. It is the research paradigm that many are comfortable with. But, just as there are many comfortable with positivism, there are many, like us, who find it problematic. Delgado Bernal and Villalpando (2002) have used the term *apartheid of knowledge* in academia to denote the ways that academic knowledge continues to value and perpetuate Eurocentric epistemologies at the expense of others. This has created legitimate and illegitimate forms of knowledge, ways of knowing, and methods/ methodologies. Positivism has consistently been deemed legitimate to the extent that when researchers, especially researchers of color, draw from knowledge that falls outside of positivism, it is often critiqued in harsher ways—if not outright rejected as valid. To counter this, we aim to center ways of knowing and researching that may make some people (those most familiar with and reliant upon positivism) uncomfortable. This is not our intent, but it is important to remind you that if you feel uncomfortable by the data analysis methods we center, you must ask yourself why. Why should positivist and postpositivist methods be centered uncritically? Why is it that research that may challenge or disrupt dominant epistemologies is subjugated? As researchers, we should be aware of how research methods and methodologies have historically been used to "other" people of color (Fine, 1994) as well as the many ways traditional research has been utilized as a colonial project.

The vignette above is an example of using a more subjugated theory (feminist theory) to examine the complexity of people's lives. Without interrogating participants' responses through the lens of feminist theory, the research team might not have made sense of the ways college women understood gender. While the research team conceptualized gender as a process, a construction, and an identity, for many of the younger women participants, gender was about feminism and feminism was about equity. By applying a feminist lens to the analysis, the research team was able to say more than the obvious. What was obvious was that women counted when asked about gender. What was not obvious, until the team applied a feminist lens, was why.

While there are different theories you may draw from in your analysis, we see critical race theory, critical race feminism, and intersectionality as useful tools in analysis. The commitment to not continuing to tell majoritarian stories should be front and center in a researcher's analysis. In addition, the basic recognition that systemic oppression (in multiple forms) shapes every aspect of our lives is important. These theories allow researchers the ability to examine their data in relation to the messy context in which lives are situated. And, by *messy context*, we mean the specific historical, cultural, political, economic, and social moments that undergird peoples' decisions, outcomes, and processes. Again, we want students to embrace theory as they analyze their data, and there is not a set way to do this. We will discuss some ways of incorporating theory into analysis, but first, let's further examine the position of theorizing data.

Theorizing Data

There have been some criticisms of qualitative research: that it is pretty much common sense or that you might know what the outcome of a study is before you undertake it. There are such things as descriptive studies whereby researchers merely describe what is occurring in classrooms, for example. Most of us have been in classrooms at some part of our lives as students, instructors, or parents. We have a sense of what occurs in classrooms based on our own experiences. Thus, if a researcher is merely describing what happens in classrooms and the classroom looks quite similar to classrooms we have been in previously, we won't learn much from the study, other than thinking that our experience might have been normal or common.

There are qualitative researchers who claim that it is their job to describe what they see and not to make interpretations about it. We do not advocate this position; in fact, we think it is a dangerous position to claim. There are all types of interpretations that comprise someone's description. For example, a researcher might describe a female teacher as warm, nurturing, and fair. Another researcher might describe this same teacher as cold and unjust. It is possible that both researchers saw the exact same situation but interpreted the experience differently. Let's be more specific about what we mean.

Suppose you are observing a third-grade classroom taught by a white female teacher. You may observe her smiling and reassuring a group of white students who are seated in close proximity to her work area. These repeated interactions lead you to believe that the teacher is warm and nurturing. Another researcher observing this same classroom might notice that the kids who are seated closest to the teacher are all white, whereas kids of color are seated along the outer perimeter of the classroom. The researcher rarely sees this teacher smile or interact with the students of color unless it is to tell them to stay on task or focus. Based on her interactions with students of color, the researcher may conclude that the teacher is actually very cold and attempts to manage and control students rather than teach. Could both researchers be correct? Did both really see what they think they saw? These are larger philosophical questions about the nature of reality and how we come to know what we know. But, as we have mentioned in various chapters in this book, who we are does and should shape every aspect of the research process. As a reminder, Schwandt (1997) suggests that we must engage in the process of "examining one's personal and theoretical commitments to see how they serve as resources for generating particular data, for behaving in particular ways . . . and for developing particular interpretations" (p. 136). Our point in raising the observation example is to remind you that description is not unfettered by our subjectivities and, therefore, analysis will be mediated as well. We cannot say that we have merely described something. We now understand that there is no such thing as simple description; all description involves layers of interpretation. We think it would be careless of researchers to pretend as if their study is only description. It is not, nor should it be. Willig (2014) expresses this sentiment below:

> In this sense, every qualitative study, irrespective of which specific method is used, interprets its data because the data never speak for itself. It is always processed and interrogated in order to obtain answers to particular questions, to shed light on a particular dimension of human experience and/or to clarify a particular aspect of an experience or a situation. (p. 147)

We encourage researchers to embrace theorization of data. Dive deeper into what the data show you. By doing so, you may realize that the situation in the classroom example is not, literally, black and white. You will have to situate your analysis of your field notes within the literature and use your theoretical framework to better interrogate the data. Hopefully, after reading the remainder of this chapter, you will have a better idea of how to proceed.

Memoing

We spent a lot of time in Chapter 6 explaining how to code. We also mentioned that moving from codes to themes would involve reflection and memo writing. In this section, we will explain in further detail how to write memos that will push and expand your thinking about your data. Moving from codes to themes to arguments that are data based can be a tricky process, given that many researchers have not been descriptive about what this process looks like. We mentioned in Chapter 6 how often we hear researchers say, "My themes emerged." While we wish it were that easy (themes could simply drop from the sky or magically appear on the page), you must go through the hard work of theorizing your data. There are different approaches to how you do this, but all of the approaches involve thinking, reflecting, and writing about your thoughts. Some people use the term *researcher journal* while others use *analytic memos* or *reflective memos*. Basically, you are capturing your thoughts about the data as you press forward to develop larger arguments. The important thing to remember is that "you identify themes out of your own analytical thinking. As you work closely with your data, you begin to see patterns, which inform the way you identify themes" (Bhattacharya, 2017, p. 151). This means, then, that the themes that emerge are closely connected to your data. Just as a reminder, themes are connected to coding in that they are outcomes of categorization and analytic reflection, but themes are *not* codes themselves. We suggest that the number of themes you develop be kept to a minimum in order to keep your analysis coherent. And, as we will show you, your analysis will be quite dependent upon the theoretical framework. Thus, by using a different framework, you can always recode the data and generate different themes.

Memoing is one way you can write to encourage deeper reflection on your data. Charmaz (2006) states that memos

catch your thoughts, capture the comparisons and connections you make, and crystallize questions and directions for you to pursue. Through conversing with yourself while memo-writing, new ideas and insights arise during the act of writing. Putting things down on paper makes the work concrete and manageable—and exciting. (p. 72)

Memos do not have to follow academic conventions. They can be letters to yourself, to your dissertation advisor, to your participants, and so on. No one even needs to read your memos except you, so you can feel free to play with ideas and test out theories in your memos. Try to quiet your inner critic and simply write. In fact, sometimes you might even want to address a memo to the critic that encourages you to doubt yourself or doubt your thoughts about the data. Part of memo writing is trying out ideas about your data that you might not want to share with others yet. Your memos are a private place for you to discuss ideas, tease out concepts, and play with theories.

Schatzman and Strauss (1973) catalogued different types of analytic writing that may be useful in overall analysis: observational notes, methodological notes, theoretical notes, and analytic memos. Observational and methodological notes are similar to what we called *observer comments (OCs)* in Chapter 5. We encouraged you to reflect on methodological choices as well as to discuss what you see in the data while you write up your field notes or transcribe your interviews. OCs are the beginning stages of you theorizing your data. Given that they are initial thoughts you have about the data, OCs can easily turn into a longer memo in which you flesh out your thoughts. Theoretical memos are longer reflections about the data, and these are often contextualized within your theoretical frame. Analytic memos are the place you would further discuss the beginning stages of analysis, your coding schemes, and any emerging themes. While the boundaries among these different memos may not always be steadfast and clear, the point is that you should encourage yourself to think about your data in different ways in order to fully theorize them.

At this point, you might be wondering what you write memos about more specifically. This will be up to you and what you think is important to your data and your study. Don't feel pressure to label your memos as one of the memo types we referred to above. We included those different categories to give you a sense of the possibilities for memo writing. While there are different topics you may want to explore, Saldaña (2016) provides some specific ideas for memos:

- How you personally relate to the participants and/or the phenomenon

- Your code choices and their operational definitions

- The participants' routines, rituals, rules, roles, and relationships

- Emergent patterns, categories, themes, concepts, and assertions

- The possible networks and processes (links, connections, overlaps, flows) among the codes, patterns, categories, themes, concepts, and assertions

- An emergent or related existent theory

- Any problems with the study

- Any personal or ethical dilemmas with the study

- Future directions for the study

- The analytic memos generated thus far (metamemos)

- Tentative answers to your study's research questions

- The final report for the study (p. 53)

We cannot stress enough how important it is to write a wide variety of memos. As examples, we will use the memos of Dr. Rosalyn Washington, who recently completed an interview study of the practice of academic redshirting (delaying a child's entry into kindergarten despite being of legal age). She has graciously provided us with a few memos to help illustrate the variety of topics researchers can write memos about.

In this first memo, Washington takes up the issue of what a "good school" means to her participants. As the parents discussed, the notion of what good schooling means kept coming up in interviews about their reasons for delaying their child's entrance into kindergarten. As a former teacher, Washington found herself troubled by the ways the definition of a good school is entangled by socioeconomic status and race. She tried to work out her thoughts about it in Example 7.1.

In the next memo, Washington clarifies her plan to continue sampling participants. Securing participants who meet your sampling criteria and who want to participate in interviews is often time intensive and frustrating. Washington outlines her next steps to help her stay focused and motivated in Example 7.2.

Chasing a "good school": This notion of a "good school" I admit grates on my nerves. I believe now that it is part of American Utopian Fantasy. Part of the American dream, and as American as apple pie. Just as we long for good middle-class jobs with health insurance, vacation time, and a pension, Americans carry a view of a "good school" with a multicultural or low minority school, clean and new or historic and well-preserved, in a tidy neighborhood with lots of parental involvement, grandmas who come in to read, active PTAs [parent–teacher associations] with bake sales, smiling young multicultural (or again, low minority) teachers whose children attend the school, etc. I think that people speak commonly of "a good school," expecting the other person to nod and understand, just as we speak of "a good job" or a "good neighborhood." And we can tell a "good school" when we see it, often by the neighborhood or address. Never do we make a person qualify or quantify these things.

Source: Courtesy of Dr. Rosalyn Washington.

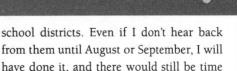

I was thinking about what I need to do so that I have completed my due diligence for my participant selection.

1. I decided to take the hold off of my research, remove all limitations. Remember that God wants to give me what I want, and I should live in a sense of expectancy. I'm going to put out lots and lots of pots and I'm sure that God will make things happen.

2. I am going to make a list of places I would like to pull participants from if there were no limitations, places like the food stamp office, places like [redacted] public schools and [redacted] public schools,

3. So, I am going to put in applications with both [redacted] schools, and [redacted] school districts. Even if I don't hear back from them until August or September, I will have done it, and there would still be time for me to find a few people from those sites.

4. I am going to set the goal of contacting at least 50 daycare sites, so that I get a significant amount of responses.

5. I just realized that I don't have to visit each and every site in order for a site manager to take me seriously. I am going to create first-, second-, and third-tier sites. Kind of like first choice, second choice, and third choice.

6. I will make it a priority to visit the first-tier sites, but I will simply send emails to all of the third-tier sites.

Source: Courtesy of Dr. Rosalyn Washington.

In the next memo, Example 7.3, Washington has coded her data and is asking herself questions about what she has found.

Example 7.3: Third Memo
Reflections

Topic: Reflecting on my interviews at large and my interview with the redshirt "mom/dad pastors."

- So many of my mothers held the public schooling to be distasteful, literally saying "I hated his teacher," although she loves him and although he loves her and kindergarten. I think the redshirt "mom first dibs" said that.

- "mom: my familiar" talked about hating her child's third-grade teacher; so many of the parents held the teachers in low regard for the educational experience.

- Even after they had paid rent in lieu of tuition, or had paid rent as an entry fee, as a fee for entrée. ***That's a good theme; I like that "rent as a fee for entrée" to these particular public schools

- I must remember that "my mom: my familiar" also paid rent as a form and a fee for entrée before she purchased this house.

- So, although they've been very selective as to the school their children go to, the parents remain unhappy.

- Right off, the only parents who expressed happiness with their child's school was the first "mom: DEK2006" and the "mom/dad: Cherokee." Both of whom are from a higher socioeconomic status, and both of the schools are probably very high-performing schools. This school is the zoned school for both families, and they do not appear to be paying rent in lieu of tuition.

- It seems that all the other moms have had very little positive experiences.

Source: **Courtesy of Dr. Rosalyn Washington.**

The next memo of Washington's that we share, Example 7.4, is one in which she reflects on her ethical and methodological responsibilities. She is troubled by researcher guilt, a common feeling when the research process is such that researchers take from their participants more than they give. She also wonders how best to

Example 7.4: Fourth Memo
Responsibilities

Topic: Reflexivity on my responsibilities as a researcher to these mothers

Again, I count it no small thing that they trusted me with the lives of their children, much in the way they are trusting me with their narrative now. And it's because of this trust that I have been called "mommy" (a sweet, sweet thing), mistakenly innumerable times in the six-and-a-half–hour days that I spent with them. It is because of this trust that I have felt the clinging of warm arms around my neck, tears on my shoulder or on my cheek, have been greeted with smiles and laughter and so much love that I cannot tell it here now. No small thing that they trusted me with their children and their children's very lives then, and it is no small things that they trust me with their narratives, true as they know them to be. I surely do owe them something. As Elie Wiesel said, I do not believe in collective guilt nor collective innocence and I attest, I will not brush them all with the same brush. Allowing some off the hook, and yet holding some of them culpable. I know that I owe these women something, these women who will sit down with me and tell me about their children and their decision making. Their insight and their fears, their dreams, their resources, and their lack of resources. I know that they will do it knowing full well that they are contributing to my dissertation research and allowing me to fulfill a large personal and profes-

sional goal. I cannot simply cluster them together as privileged or underprivileged women who are leveraging capital or making decisions based on lack of capital. The experience I imagine will no doubt remind me of the countless conversations I had with mommies about preschool experiences and kindergarten expectations. These conversations will be largely past tense, whereas the conversations I held were largely present tense. But it is no small thing that these women will sit and talk with me and tell me their story. And they will do it largely for me, as I have very little to offer them. Telling the story itself may or may not be cathartic. This is not therapy, and I have no resolutions to offer them. Yet they will offer me a voice, and I will measure the use of capital and parental negotiation, and yes, fulfill my personal and professional goal of finishing my PhD. So I certainly owe them something. They are not unlike the women I have known very personally over the last 18 years. Although I am a childless woman I feel kinship with (and honestly some degree longing aimed at) the mothers of young children, because of the hundreds of intimate relationships I have had with mothers of young children. And yes, I begin to feel some guilt.

Source: Courtesy of Dr. Rosalyn Washington.

represent the women who have shared their stories. She does not want to reduce them down to a one-dimensional portrait and yet, given the limits of language, she may have to.

The last memo we will share from Washington's project is one in which she teases out definitions for her codes in Example 7.5.

As you can see from the example of Washington's many memos, a memo can serve a variety of functions. It can be a to-do list as you move forward. Or you can use it as a chance to reflect on thoughts and hunches you have as you complete data analysis. Memos are really the fuel by which you will feed the analytic fire you will need to create. In memos, you will tease out your thoughts and hunches about the data. Eventually, the memos will serve as a road map to how your thinking

Example 7.5: Fifth Memo

Notes from Interviewing AN.

Code "Guilt"

She did express some mommy guilt, maybe this is something that I can explicate on other opportunities. She said "I stayed at home with him. He did not go to school until age 3"

She used some words and phrases that I think is indicative of mommy guilt.

Code "Public Schooling"

She talked about the decision to delay kindergarten going out of the window after they got into the lottery. I think being drawn into the public-school lottery represents two things. It represents the resources and large-scale support of the public schools, all that has to offer, maybe setting children on a fixed path. And even to a family of means, it represents a year of free schooling that would have otherwise cost money.

Code "Boy"

She made lots of references to her son being a boy, and seems to have bought into the notion that boys are less mature, she seemed to make at least three references to his being a boy. She does have an older son, and an older stepdaughter to which I assume she compares him regularly. Again, I would have liked to have asked how their journeys went.

I just listened to the audio tape of my interview with AN and I think the interview went well, even though it was short. The mother was as open as she knew how to be.

Several things came up in the interview.

Code "Struggle"

The mother repeatedly used several synonyms for the word *struggle*. She actually used the word *struggle*, used the words *trudging along*.

Code "Catch Up"

She also used several phrases for comparative speech comparing her son's journey to other children's journeys. Things like *catch up, stay on course, getting ahead, fall behind*. She illustrated this comparative sense by saying that she did not want to modify his work, I believe this is related to a fear that he would fall behind, even on mundane things like spelling words. I am always surprised by the importance parents place on things like weekly spelling tests. Perhaps because they seem easily understood, easily controlled.

Code "Fluent"

She was very fluent in the educational process and how to seek out resources. This is illustrated by the ease with which she talked about the process. The fact that she used so many abbreviations such as ESY, IEP, 504 plan, OT. This makes sense because she is a member of the public school community and is a public school nurse.

Code "Hung the Moon"/"Lots of Support"

She said several times that her child is receiving lots of support. This is illustrated in the fact that he began receiving speech in prekindergarten, without a 504 plan in place, with no IEP filed in the public schools to support it. He also has been given a diagnosis of a processing delay, he receives pull out I believe it's 3 hours a day, he receives occupational therapy, and his work is modified.

She also talked about the fact that in the school that he is currently in everyone has "hung the moon," and spoke repeatedly about how much support she has received.

Even with all of the support, she still used the *struggle* language. She did make reference to other siblings, I forgot to ask what their journey was like.

Future interviews: I added the question about other siblings' journeys so that it could be included in future interviews if it was appropriate.

Source: Courtesy of Dr. Rosalyn Washington.

about the data progressed or changed over time. Just as you can use coding with multiple other forms of analysis, we suggest that you use memo writing with all analytic methods.

Methods of Analysis

We discussed coding in Chapter 6 and would like to introduce you to a few other methods of analysis. This is not a comprehensive examination of data analysis and, to truly do it correctly, you will have to read much more and practice techniques. We hope our chapter will be a springboard for you so that you may identify an analysis method of interest and pursue it further. Some methods for analysis include content, conversation, discourse, narrative, phenomenological, semiotic, and thematic. See Table 7.1 for a summary of each of these methods. We will examine a few of these in more detail but encourage you, regardless of the method

Table 7.1 Data Analysis Methods

Data Analysis Method	Description	Further Reading
Content Analysis	Emerges from a positivist tradition; involves counting data to uncover frequencies and patterns	Altheide, D. L., & Schneider, C. J. (2013). *Qualitative media analysis* (2nd ed.). SAGE. Berelson, B. (1952). *Content analysis in communication research.* The Free Press. Schreier, M. (2012). *Qualitative content analysis in practice.* SAGE.
Conversation Analysis	Emerges from ethnomethodology; focuses on understanding the systematic structure and organization of talk and social interaction	Silverman, D. (2006). *Interpreting qualitative data: Methods for analyzing talk, text, and interaction* (3rd ed.). SAGE. ten Have, P. (2007). *Doing conversation analysis: A practical guide* (2nd ed.). SAGE. Wooffitt, R. (2005). *Conversation analysis and discourse analysis.* SAGE.

(Continued)

Table 7.1   (Continued)

Data Analysis Method	Description	Further Reading
Discourse Analysis	Studies language and power; examines how language is used to convey particular meanings	Gee, J. P. (2011). *How to do discourse analysis: A toolkit.* Routledge. Gee, J. P. (2014). *An introduction to discourse analysis: Theory and method* (4th ed.). Routledge. Speer, S. (2005). *Gender talk: Feminism, discourse and conversation analysis.* Routledge.
Narrative Analysis	Examines participants' stories in terms of their narrative structure and content	Clandinin, D. J. (2020). *Journeys in narrative inquiry: The selected works of D. Jean Clandinin.* Routledge. Polkinghorne, D. (1988). *Narrative knowing and the human sciences.* SUNY Press. Riessman. C. K. (2008). *Narrative methods for the human sciences.* SAGE.
Phenomenological Analysis	Emerges from a philosophical tradition; examines how a participant experiences and later describes a particular phenomenon	Moustakas, C. E. (1994). *Phenomenological research methods.* SAGE. Van Manen, M. (2016). *Phenomenology of practice.* Routledge.
Semiotic Analysis	Attempts to standardize the process of meaning within a text; generally used for images (or signs); seeks to understand how individual signs form systems of signs that create thought patterns	Aiello, G. (2020). *Visual semiotics: Key concepts and new directions.* SAGE. Manning, P. K. (1987). *Semiotics and fieldwork: Some examples.* SAGE. Peirce, C. (Author). Hartshorne, C., Weiss, P., & Burks, A. W. (Eds.). (1931–58). *Collected Writings* (8 Vols.). Harvard University Press.
Coding/Thematic Analysis	Contextualized within a theoretical framework, looks for overall patterns in the data	Grbich, C. (2007). *Qualitative data analysis: An introduction.* SAGE. Miles, M. B., Huberman, A. M., & Saldana, J. (2014). *Qualitative data analysis: A methods sourcebook.* SAGE.
Intersectional analysis	Examines data through the frame of intersectionality; a culturally situated method for interrogating knowledge projects	Edwards, E. and Esposito, J. (2019). *Intersectional analysis as a method to analyze popular culture: Clarity in the matrix. New York:* Routledge. Edwards, E. B. and Esposito, J. (2018). Reading the Black woman's body via Instagram fame. *Communication, Culture, and Critique, 11(3),* 341–358.

type, to engage in further reading and practice of the methods. Also, it is important to note that we did not include grounded theory in this table only because we spent the bulk of Chapter 6 detailing ways to code. The specifics of coding originated with grounded theory. In addition, as we explore memo writing, we return to grounded theory methods.

There are a variety of types of data analysis and we certainly cannot do them all justice in one textbook. Thus, we will provide comprehensive information on a few methods to show you how you might implement them in your analysis, but we encourage you to read research studies from your content area to assist you in pinpointing the important analysis methods in your field. The methods we have selected to include stem from our content area (sociology of education) and are more common than some others, such as phenomenological analysis, which you might be more likely to see in nursing or psychology. The methods we elaborate on are also methods that merge well with intersectionality. For example, though content analysis is quite useful to uncover patterns in data, we prefer narrative analysis because it allows data to be better contextualized. As an example, content analysis might be extremely useful in uncovering how many times a school district mentions race or diversity on its website. But a discourse analysis of that same website would allow the researcher to better explain the way that race and/or diversity were discussed and represented. Thus, in this chapter, we privilege narrative analysis and discourse analysis. Regardless of what analytic method(s) you select for your study, we encourage you to read much more about the method. Data analysis is the most challenging part of qualitative research. It is sometimes made more challenging in intersectional qualitative research because positivists will accuse you of having an agenda or finding only what you expected to or wanted to find. At the end of the chapter, we discuss the trust-worthiness of data analysis. However, we want you to know up front that you will have to learn to silence those who accuse intersectional research of somehow being less valuable to other forms of research. We, for one, won't play the game of using positivist language or of adopting positivist frameworks for studies to make the haters happy. Instead, we continue to push for culturally situated and embodied research.

Thematic Analysis

Thematic analysis is a generic form of analysis, but it is tightly aligned with your theoretical framework. Generally, your themes will come directly from your coding schema. We say thematic analysis is generic because it is not tied tightly to a methodological framework in the same way other analytic methods are. You will see below that narrative analysis and discourse analysis have methodological traditions that would structure how you collect data while thematic analysis can be completed on any qualitative data. If we return to the data excerpt about Jo in Chapter 6, we left off with the category of "Race Structures Choices." If we were to continually reflect on that category throughout the data, we would be able to develop a larger argument regarding this category. Keep in mind that in order to illustrate how to code, we used very small excerpts of data. The data from Jo's interview came from a much larger qualitative study that included thousands of pages of data. When we reflect on multiple interviews with participants from all different races, it became easy for us to turn this category into an argument. We relied on the first tenet of our critical race theoretical framework, which states that race is endemic and racism is permanent. If this tenet is true, then it follows that all of our participants, regardless of race, would make choices necessarily structured by race. Our theme became this argument: College students, regardless of race, must negotiate what race is and what race means and the ways race structures their choices as they navigate college life. Race constrained some choices and had material consequences on students' lives. We developed this theme after careful consideration of the data and how we thought about the data. If you follow our thinking from codes to subcodes to categories (presented in Chapter 6), you can see how our theme directly emerged from how we coded. In other words, our theme did not simply emerge by falling out of the sky. We helped it along through a continual reflection and application of the theoretical framework and our developing coding schema.

Narrative Analysis

We are fond of narrative analysis because of its story element. Who doesn't love a good story? Narrative analysis often takes two approaches in its analysis of stories. The first recognizes that participants construct stories about their lives (that are then conveyed to researchers) and these stories often follow particular formats. Interested researchers might then examine the structure of the story in terms of its beginning, middle, and end or how characters are positioned (i.e., who is the hero, the villain, etc.). Davis (2008) conducted a narrative analysis of eleven documents produced by the National Cancer Institute on the topic of breast cancer. The narrative around breast cancer is commonly that the patient is the victim, the hero is the doctor, and the villain is the cancer itself. The documents follow this narrative structure and, therefore, contribute to medical discourse in specific ways.

Another way of analyzing narratives is to examine the ways people make sense of their lives through stories. How have participants come to understand the study topic? How do they communicate this to you as the researcher? Along these lines, Gubruim and Holstein (2009) make the case that understanding narrative context is as important as understanding the narrative's structure. They encourage researchers to pay as much attention to the process of narrating and collecting stories as to the story itself. Gubruim and Holstein suggest researchers consider specific questions:

> Who produces particular kinds of stories, where are they likely to be encountered, what are their purposes and consequences, who are the listeners, under what circumstances are particular narratives more or less accountable, how do they gain acceptance, and how are they challenged? (p. 23)

In this vein, researchers would be interested in the ways stories are put together, communicated, and disseminated. Thus, when the researcher begins the analysis, they would work beyond the interview or focus group transcript and might also consider notes regarding the story collection process. In addition, paying attention to the story's context means situating it within particular political, social, historical, and economic contexts. That means that you can't make sense of stories outside of the context in which they are situated. How does this context bear witness and shape the story? These are questions you should ponder as you analyze the data.

Catherine Riessman (2008) discusses different types of narrative analysis more fully in her text, *Narrative Methods for the Human Sciences*. She notes that thematic narrative analysis is different from the thematic analysis that originated in grounded theory. The most obvious difference is that narrative analysts use theory to guide their analysis while also trying to remain open to new ways of seeing the data. We take this approach with almost any analysis we do, and we encourage you to do so as well. We cannot separate our previous knowledge and understandings of theory. Just as we live "storied lives" (Clandinin & Connelly, 2000), we live theoretical lives. That means our lives are structured by theories whether we recognize them or not. Souto-Manning and Ray (2007) conducted a narrative analysis of their lives as women professors of color in the academy. They were particularly interested in understanding how each constructed their story and made meaning of it. They ended up with a dialogue about their experiences that shows readers the commonalities in their stories as well as the differences. Another difference in thematic narrative analysis and grounded theory methods is that a true narrative analysis attempts to keep the story intact. Often, when researchers develop themes in their data, they might take data excerpts (or parts of stories) from a variety of different participants to illustrate how the theme is true across the different cases. For example, Galuska, Hahn, Polifroni, and Crow (2018) completed a narrative analysis of 27 nurses' understandings of joy and meaning. They developed four themes that cut across all of the participants' narratives. In this particular manuscript, the authors spent time illustrating how the themes were consistent among the different participants. You may also complete a narrative analysis that spends more time delving deeply into each story while also showing how each individual story relates to the theme being discussed.

As we have tried to communicate in the previous chapter, there is not an easy way to analyze data. Narrative inquirers Clandinin and Connelly (2000) remind us that there is no easy transition from what they term "field texts" (*transcripts*) to "research texts" (*manuscripts*). "Field texts have a vast and rich research potential. We return to them again and again, bringing our own restoried lives as inquirers, bringing new research puzzles, and re-searching the texts," (p. 132). It is not uncommon for researchers to write multiple publications from their data because they see them in new ways or want to tell the stories using different frameworks.

Discourse Analysis

Conversational analysis is often linked to discourse analysis. Conversational analysis grew from the ethnomethodological work of Harold Garfinkel. Ethnomethodology aimed to study "the rational properties of indexical expressions and other practical actions as contingent ongoing accomplishments of organized artful practices of everyday life" (Garfinkel, 1967, p. 11). Ethnomethodologists were particularly interested in examining the ways people structured their actions, talk, and body language in order to accomplish a particular performance of identity. In order to be recognized in a particular way, social actors had to carefully manage their talk and actions (talk-in-interaction). The premise behind this work is that society is organized by a series of rules that we take for granted and follow without thinking. Ethnomethodologists were especially interested in moments when people broke the rules. Conversational analysts studied the way people communicated with one another and how those communications followed (or not) accepted social patterns and rules. While there are similarities between conversational analysis and discourse analysis, conversational analysis tends to focus more on what is actually said in conversation and less on the social/political impact of and context in which it was said.

Discourse analysis is most commonly associated with Michael Foucault, despite the fact they he didn't call himself a discourse analyst. Foucault (1975) was interested in how language (talk and written text) served ideological functions. In particular, discourse analysis is a critical examination of how language is used to perpetuate inequalities as well as how language and texts construct and maintain power relations. It is the intersection of language and the social that is of particular interest in discourse analysis (Fairclough, 1989). Discourses provide us with speaking positions (subject positions from which we speak). These positions are particularly interesting to critical researchers because these subject positions can be limiting and may constrain what can be said as well as who can say it (Esposito, 2009; Reay, 2001). Researchers who use discourse analysis recognize the ways in which discourses teach us how to function in the world and teach us who we are and who we can be. Gee (1990) calls discourses *identity kits* because they shape identities in powerful ways.

There are a variety of ways to conduct discourse analysis and it can be done on a variety of texts (i.e., interview transcripts, newspaper articles, blogs, television shows, curriculum, etc.). We encourage you to read James Paul Gee's (2011) *How to Do Discourse Analysis: A Toolkit.* He offers specific questions you can ask yourself of your data framed around what he calls "tools." As an example, let us use Tool #16 (The Identities Building Tool). In this tool, researchers are asked to determine what identities a speaker is trying to enact. In order to do this, the researcher must figure out what is being taken for granted or what assumptions are being made about the identities of both the speaker and the listener. In order to understand how to use this tool, let's return to a data excerpt shared in the previous chapter. Here, Jo, a Latinx undergraduate student, discusses her desire to join a Black sorority:

> I think the Latino kids here are just very different in the sense that they expect you to belong to a certain group, the Latino group. I was telling S. how I was interested in joining a Black sorority. So, upon people hearing of me being interested in Black sororities, I've noticed that some Latino friend I've had, they just kind of like. Well, they're kind of like, "Oh? Okay. Well, she decided to go *that* route." You know? And, it's because the Latino culture here is even smaller than the African Americans here so it seems like

they expect all of us to stick together. And, um, I have white friends, very good white friends, and Black friends. And, that's just not me. I don't like confining myself. So, I thought to myself, maybe it's because it's a college campus. When I get out into corporate America, I will meet people from all different, from all over. Not all Latino people are the same way but it's hard you know? It's like my community, where I live back home. Washington Heights is a predominately Latino community. I'm starting to understand that I want something more than we have.

In using the identities building tool, one of the first questions we have to ask ourselves is which socially recognizable identity the speaker is trying to enact or to get others to recognize. In the first line of Jo's response, she refers to the "Latino kids here" and she continues that they are very "different" because they expect her to belong to their group. In answering the question, I would say that Jo is juxtaposing Latino kids against unnamed white kids (she attended a predominately white institution [PWI]). She is creating an identity for Latino kids at the PWI that they want to stay in their own group and perhaps isolate themselves from others. Of course, Jo may not know *all* of the Latino students at the PWI she attends, but she is grouping them in such a way that they all appear to pressure her to remain isolated while Jo enacts an identity for herself that seeks more diversity. She says, in fact, that she craves more than what the people "back home" have. She is encouraging listeners to imagine her community back home, a community that is perhaps racially/ethnically isolated and that presumably has not experienced the types of privilege to which Jo now has access, given her attendance at a private institution of higher education.

There are other tools we may use to analyze the discourse in this small excerpt. The point is to be sure to look closely at what is being said, what is not being said, and how things are said or not said. By doing so, you will ultimately create a larger argument about what discourses are valued in a particular social space. In addition, you will be able to see who has access to and power to *construct* the discourses and who is being *constructed by* the discourses.

As we stated at the beginning of the chapter, we cannot discuss every type of data analysis available to you. However, we encourage you to look at Table 7.1 (of course, even this table is an incomplete list, as there are many methods of analysis) and check out the resources we suggest. Also, read studies that use the method you are leaning toward to see how others have conducted that particular type of analysis. With practice, you will become adept at making sense of your data and analyzing it in order to answer your research questions and make arguments about social life.

Subjectivity Statements

You cannot erase the importance of yourself in the data analysis process. Guba and Lincoln (2008) discuss how "reflexivity forces us to come to terms not only with our choice of research problem and with those with whom we engage in the research process, but with ourselves and with the multiple identities that represent the fluid self in the research setting" (p. 278). Who we are ultimately shapes the analysis that we complete. There is no need to pretend that it does not or that we can bracket our subjectivities out. While subjectivity statements in which the researcher reveals information about themselves are useful in allowing the reader to be mindful of how identities may have shaped analysis, the reality is that there is no real way of knowing the impact the researcher has had. We cannot and should not try to separate out who we are from what we do. Life is too complicated and messy for that. So, embrace how who you are shapes your study. Also, do not fall into the trap of thinking that if you are white, your analysis is not shaped by your racial position. Whiteness is a race and, as such, it shapes how you interpret and analyze data. We encourage all researchers to write subjectivity statements whereby they explore who they are and how they think about the topic under study. It should never be as simple as saying "I am a Black woman" or "I am Latina." Instead, we must interrogate our identities in relationship to the larger social context and how this relationship may impact our research study. The impact to the research study might be the way our participants trust (or don't trust) us. It impacts the types of questions we ask of the study, of our participants, and of ourselves. It certainly shapes the theoretical frameworks we choose. The other reason we encourage you to write a subjectivity statement is because it will provide a context from which the reader will make sense of you and how you made sense of the data.

Getting It Right

How do we know we have gotten it "right"? (How do we know that we have interpreted the data correctly? Ethically? Responsibly?) Although it may seem as if the researcher cannot be wrong if we take the stance that there are always multiple meanings and interpretations depending on theoretical and ideological lenses, we still must convince our readers that how we have theorized the data makes the most sense. Yet, the questions we asked at the beginning of this paragraph have different responses. How do we know we have interpreted the data correctly? For this, we can look to methods such as member checking, triangulation, crystallization, trustworthiness, and intercoder reliability. How do we know we have interpreted the data ethically and responsibly? This is a more philosophical question, and the answer may not be as straightforward. To answer this question, we must be mindful of questions regarding power.

How Do We Know We Have Interpreted the Data Correctly?

Lincoln and Guba (1985), in their approach to naturalistic inquiry, developed an alternative to the positivist notion of validity. *Trustworthiness*, or credibility of a qualitative research study, is comprised of a few different factors, including prolonged engagement, persistent observations, triangulation, member checking, and peer debriefing. Some of the criteria, such as prolonged engagement (how much time you spend in the field) and persistent observations (making sure that when you are in the field, you are focused on the specific perspectives under study), would be more relevant to data collection than to analysis. We will examine member checking and triangulation in further detail below. We also would encourage researchers to engage in peer debriefing. This process involves having trusted colleagues share their interpretations about how you analyzed the data. Do the colleagues trust your interpretations? Are there potential alternate interpretations you might have missed? There is no formulaic way to engage in peer debriefing and, sometimes, you might even share your raw data with a colleague in order for them to truly have a sense of how you may have developed your arguments about the data.

Member checking is a term used to describe the process of sharing analysis with participants. There are, of course, different levels to this process. In interview studies, many researchers choose to share transcripts of the interview with participants. This is a small form of member checking; it allows the participant the chance to see if what they said was accurately transcribed. It also allows the participant to redact sections of the interview that they may not want shared in the study. Researchers may also share their observation field notes or their notes of an analysis of documents to allow participants to provide feedback. More frequently, and at a higher level, researchers theorize the data and then share their sense of the data and/or the arguments they will make based on the data to see how participants respond. If you do this in a systematic way—in a focus group, perhaps—you will accomplish member checking while at the same time engage in further data collection. The focus group could be used as a method to help you explore some emerging themes or to collect more evidence to support or refute it. The point is, there is not one way to member check. However, there are ways that allow and encourage participants to more deeply engage with the researcher's interpretations. We take the stance that true member checking should allow for participants to talk back to the researcher's interpretations, if they so desire. Let's move on to another way of making sure your analysis is sound.

Triangulation

We mentioned triangulation when we discussed data collection. Triangulation was initially discussed by Lincoln and Guba (1985) as an indicator of trustworthiness when the researcher collected data in multiple forms (i.e., interviews, observations, documents, etc.). The point in triangulating data collection was to collect multiple sources of data that would allow for diverse perspectives and show the full story of what you were investigating. Guion (2002) expanded on triangulation and developed a typology of five types: data triangulation, investigator triangulation, theory triangulation, methodological triangulation, and environmental triangulation. Data triangulation is what has been previously discussed—collecting data sources in multiple ways. Investigator triangulation may not be appropriate for graduate students needing to conduct a dissertation on their own, as it requires multiple investigators. Theory triangulation entails the use of multiple theoretical perspectives, while methodological triangulation involves the use of different methods and environmental triangulation requires multiple sites for data collection. We would like to adapt this typology and include analytic triangulation. In this sense, multiple methods of analysis can be used to help ensure that the analysis is well rounded and there is a deep level of engagement with the data. Ravitch and Carl (2016) note that "analytic data triangulation" requires that researchers consider data from different angles. Instead of approaching the data chronologically, researchers should examine the data "within and across participants and other organizing constructs" (p. 227). In this sense, then, analytic triangulation involves the researcher going back, again and again, to the data to be sure that all angles have been considered. Of course, this process could be endless if you use multiple theoretical perspectives. But in this case, we mean using the one or two theoretical frameworks you have identified in the study and applying the lens in a variety of ways to create different possibilities for analysis.

In their discussion of analytic data triangulation, Ravitch and Carl (2016) pose useful questions for the researcher to consider:

- Have I subjected my data to methodological, data source, researcher, and theoretical triangulation?

- How do my data align or converge?

- How do my data differ or diverge?

- How am I making sense of the points of alignment and divergence?

- How do I need to revisit and challenge my interpretations based on what I am learning from my data? (p. 264)

These questions are not exhaustive as you attempt to triangulate analysis. However, the point to remember is that you should double- and triple-check your emerging interpretations to be sure you are not missing something and to help ensure that you are not rewriting the same old narrative with your data (i.e., is your analysis too scripted by familiarity or have you managed to think outside of the box, so to speak?).

Triangulation is a rather traditional notion and may not work for everyone. Thus, we would also like to introduce the notion of crystallization. It is sometimes referred to as the postmodern version of triangulation. Originally conceptualized by Richardson (1994, 2000), crystallization was founded on the belief that there are more than three ways to view an inquiry. Moving away from a triangle metaphor, Richardson introduced the concept of the crystal; there are multiple points in data that may converge, diverge, reflect, refract, bounce, and so on. Due to its complexity, there is not a quick and easy definition of crystallization, although we can say that it is an attempt at gaining a richer and deeper understanding of qualitative data than what triangulation might allow. In fact, through its process, the researcher is expected to explore competing ideas and assumptions (Denzin & Lincoln, 2011) in a way that reflects as many points as possible. We are discussing crystallization in a chapter on data analysis. However, we encourage those who are interested to read more about it because the method can be used at multiple points in the inquiry (not only during analysis). Ellingson (2009) lists the principles of crystallization as follows:

- Offers deep, thickly described, complexly rendered interpretations of meanings about a phenomenon or group.

- Represents ways of producing knowledge across multiple points of the qualitative continuum, generally including at least one middle-ground (constructivist or postpositivist) and one interpretive, artistic, performative, or otherwise creative analytic approach; crystallized texts often reflect several contrasting ways of knowing.

- Utilizes more than one genre of writing (e.g., poetry, narrative, report and/or other medium—video, painting, music).

- Includes a significant degree of reflexive consideration of the researcher's self and roles in the process of research design, data collection, and representation.

- Eschews positivist claims to objectivity and a singular, discoverable Truth in favor of embracing knowledge as situated, partial, constructed, multiple, embodied, and enmeshed in power relations. (p. 10)

Ellingson (2009) articulates crystallization as a way to interrupt positivist ways of telling stories and representing data. It aims for thick descriptions (Geertz, 1973) and multiple interpretations/representations while still maintaining systematic research methods.

How Do We Know We Have Interpreted the Data Ethically and Responsibly?

There is power involved in telling someone's story, even when the expressed goal is to "give someone voice." The idea of "giving voice" to the marginalized is a misguided one. Yes, it is important that researchers study the lives of those who have been traditionally marginalized. However, it would be irresponsible of researchers to believe that we are actually bestowing a voice upon these people. At most, we might be making space for perspectives that differ from what has been historically centered as "normal." As Limes-Taylor Henderson and Esposito (2018) note, many researchers discuss their research as if they have been asked to complete the research by relevant community stakeholders. This is often *not* the case, unless you are doing participatory research, in which your participants have a say (an actual voice) in what gets studied and how it gets studied. It is important to remember that when we conduct research on/with marginalized communities, we, regardless of whether we share a marginalized race/ethnic, class, gender, or sexual orientation position, still hold power as a researcher. The power imbalance between researcher and participant is such that the participant's voice gets interpreted through yours. That means that the researcher has the ultimate power to shape the narrative.

We agree with hooks (1990), who articulated that researchers who work with marginalized populations have a responsibility to use epistemological, theoretical, and methodological frameworks that do not distort the lives of participants and contribute to deficit narratives. There are many ways to do this, but underlying all the different ways is a requirement that you question yourself first and that you allow your participants to speak back to you. Dr. Martha Donovan is a white female researcher who studied Black female teachers during a yearlong ethnographic study of an urban school. Martha was committed to decolonizing methodologies and methods. As part of her stance, she shared her thoughts and writings with participants throughout the study to get their feedback. We will share an example of one of her memos (Figure 7.1) that includes comments from a participant who had the chance to challenge some of Martha's thoughts and assumptions. Martha explained the process:

> Because we worked this writing together, I came to understand Allecia better, I think, and differently. She also influenced the overall dissertation because after we discussed this, she steered me from thinking too much about myself as I was trying to understand the data. She put the mirror back on me, which I think helped me see the participants and the data with less of the "me" filter. (2018, personal conversation)

Allecia (whose real name is Xylecia Fynnaikins) was one of Martha's participants in the ethnography. She is a highly educated and knowledgeable teacher working in an urban elementary school. At the point when Martha wrote this memo, she was deep in her analysis of the findings and she was trying to tease out what "getting dirty" meant both as a researcher and as a person.

Take the time to read this memo written by the researcher Martha Donovan and responded to by the participant Xylecia (Allecia). In this memo, you can see Martha grappling with a phrase she heard at the beginning of her study. When she invited Xylecia to take part in the ethnography, Xylecia asked Martha if she "was willing to get dirty." Over one year later, Martha still was not clear whether she knew exactly what Xylecia had meant or if, in fact, Martha had actually gotten dirty during the research process. Xylecia calls Martha out on her assumptions and basically says that though her proposed definitions are courageous, she wonders if Martha knows if she "genuinely reconciled" Xylecia's meaning of getting dirty

Figure 7.1   Memo on Allecia

Findings: Allecia: the artistry of going beyond the curriculum	Comments from Xylecia G Fynnaikins
Allecia was a master teacher. She used song, voice, games, and critical pedagogy to engage students in heart connections. She had earned a Ph.D. in Educational Studies several years earlier and also had extensive research knowledge. She was a veteran elementary school teacher who told me she was "made" for teaching in inner-city schools. After I described the research and she agreed to work with me, she asked me if I was willing to "get dirty." She said that if I were going to do this, I would have to get dirty. So was I willing? I nodded (or something like that), affirming that I was cool with getting dirty- whatever that meant. Did she know I was not sure what she meant? To this day, I still am not sure exactly what getting dirty was. But I never stopped thinking about it, wondering, and trying to do it. I did this because I believed, from the way she said it, that doing it was going to be an essential key to unlock what drove Allecia's teaching meant. Also, and somewhat contradictorily, I never asked Allecia what it meant because I felt like the term warranted learning through experience. Like asking would have been like asking for a facelift or another plastic surgery. It felt wrong. So I approached the experience of the term as if it was something I had to grown into. Now in this way, Allecia's pedagogical craft worked itself on me as a researcher, so it is an observation that makes its way into the findings as part of the "Craft" code group. But it is also far more than a finding that verifies a research claim or a part of an answer to a research question. I evoked a larger question for me about what it means to teach in urban schools, perhaps what it means to teach altogether, but specifically what it means in the context of space in which policies oppress. It has become a fundamental question about what it means to teach, and for Allecia, what it means to teach in urban education, since it was this context in which she developed her craft and felt passionately committed to serving. It seems relevant to unearth my thinking about this concept of getting dirty as an aspect of craft that became so fundamental to this study, so here are some possible meanings of getting dirty. Some are based on what I learned about Allecia, and some are based on my own ideas. Also, I have included some answers. What does it mean to get dirty in urban educational research? Did I do it?	What is a heart connection? (you or research term) Did you ever ask her what she meant? If not, why? Do you think this is an understandable/ recognizable reference for others within in the urban teaching community? Why was it important for you to "try to get dirty" (esp. without even knowing the full meaning? Why did you even accept the notion of getting dirty? Was the teacher creditable, did you romanticize the idea, did you feel it inherently appropriate based on your own understanding of urban teaching? Did you already tease out the meaning of "pedagogical craft?" Does the meaning of teach change, contingent upon context? Is it a contextually relevant idea? Or. . . does the meaning remain unchanged but process, pedagogy, and "code" changes Specifically, what is the fundamental question? The development of craft or the development of a pedagogical code?
1. Entangling with others' lives is messy. You can't have intimacy without entanglement, and you can't have knowledge of others without intimacy. In this process, you are going to get some of their mess on you. If that is getting dirty, I did.	You courageously proposed meanings for getting dirty. Without getting clarity of the teacher of her meaning of getting dirty, how do you know if you genuinely reconciled her meaning with your own understanding? How does it affect your findings/interpretations of the research project if your understandings are based

(Continued)

Figure 7.1 (Continued)

Findings: Allecia: the artistry of going beyond the curriculum	Comments from Xylecia G Fynnaikins
2. Urban centers and therefore urban schools are also messy. People live stressful lives and kids bring those stresses into school. Some of the conditions kids are coping with are difficult, but some are unimaginable, even if your own past is full of mess. You have to be willing to hear people's stories without flinching and be open-minded. You have to absorb people's stories and let them be *their* stories, no matter how painful it seems. You cannot shut people's stories out because you can't handle their pain. You cannot silence people because you do not want to hear it or because you feel guilty because you do not have to experience it. If that is what she meant by getting dirty, I did.	"on your own ideas?" I think it is allowable, but does it enable you to tease out your goals and objectives of the overall study?

How do you know that you did it? You did it by doing what? Name the experience.

I enjoy reading this section, but it is noteworthy that you draw the conclusions about what the subject meant by getting dirty, and then you measure |
| 3. Teaching elementary school is busy. There are so many tasks it is impossible to truly keep up. You have to sort and prioritize and keep aiming for the goal. You have to manage your own life too and you have to try and stay healthy. Sometimes you have to do things that you do not agree with because your boss tells you to, but you are a contracted employee and you fulfill the terms of your contract. If this is what it meant to get dirty, I did not during this research, but I saw every one of my participants rolling around in that mess all the time, and in my own teaching position, I experience it daily. | Immediate boss or system higher up

Are you referencing ethics and moral integrity or differing views of practices and procedures |
4. People in the workplace encounter conflict. We collaborate as well as we can, until life interferes and our getting-along skills falter. Yet we persevere. We remain aware of the potential for drama. Relationships are messy. If this is getting dirty, in this work I really tried not to. Based on my observations, Allecia tried not to, too. I never observed her get caught up in other adults' messy dramas. Therefore this definition is probably not what she meant.	
5. Physical aspect of getting dirty. You should be physically dirty at the end of the day. You should have some dust on you. There should be some residue on you. But you also get to the point where you have to wash it off. What makes you clean? I come clean when they are smiling. We set goals and I see that those goals are being realized. It's in test data. It's in their abilities to perform. I see it when their confidence goes up.	
It's beyond the curriculum. At the end of the day for me, teaching is so much more than the scope and sequence. So much more than the standards. We want to be better people. There are a lot of people who've got great scores, but are they good people?	

She taught the children to feel good about themselves. Affirmation. Teaching them to be good people. Purpose. "You were born for a purpose, making life better for others." "The people we honor on holidays, they are people who made life better for others."

Which of these definitions is accurate? What did it mean to get dirty? When I began the project, I figured if I just threw myself into it head first, I would figure out how to get dirty in the process. Now, assuming Allecia's definition of getting dirty involves something she herself experienced, I imagine the definition lies somewhere in a combination of 1, 2, and 3. This combination is articulated theoretically in Goltz's (2013) discussion of the potential of stage performance:

> The unique strengths and potentials of performance are what make it dirty, messy, and dangerous. The co-mingling of multiple intersections of identity within a singular body, in a specific temporal and historical context, within specific relations is messy in ways our words try to, yet never can quite, organize. The intersubjective traveling and risk that performance potentializes are clumsy and dangerous for they ask that we travel on an unchartered journey to reexamine who we are and who we might be. The manner by which our stories, our lives, and our affinities and commitments cut across the clean, abstract language of the theoretical leaves us all dirty, grounded, and soiled in one another—or so we hope. (p. 23)

Allecia, whose pedagogical craft involved singing, preaching, praising, and oral performance of text as well as improvisational relationship-making and mothering discipline, was a performer who approached teaching as a performance craft. Goltz's phrases in this passage, "the co-mingling of multiple intersections of identity within a singular body" and "intersubjective traveling and risk" capture in theoretical terms what I witnessed in Allecia's classroom. She started each day with a 20-30 minute session in social-emotional learning that involved games, chants, and connections between children that brought their identities forth and led them to share deeply personal experiences and feelings as well as to own and to take responsibility for the shaping of their epistemological selves. She taught reading and social studies by the book, meaning she followed the curricula for reading and social studies the district handed to her, almost without complaint, and worked with her team to make decisions that all felt would help meet the goals for 4th grade, which involved a big dose of maximizing test-based achievement. She told her students stories about herself, her family, and her travels, and communicated her values, which included valuing multi-cultural experiences, travel to other countries, and learning other languages. She also upheld students' humanity and citizenship, and used the social studies curriculum, which for 4th grade was American history,

Comments from Xylecia G Fynnaikins:

Is the goal to figure out how you could get dirty? How your subject got dirty? How she qualified/ characterized that "getting dirty" in her views of her own practice.

Assumptions???? I would consider rephrasing

Goltz as ed. theorist

Are these your terms?

Does this performative nature hinder authentic relationship building? Is the performance translatable as "showmanship"? What is the purpose of her performative craft. . .does the performance obscure her true nature/subjectivities. How are her intersubjectivities revealed (in the midst of the performative nature that characterizes her practice)? What risks did she take? How might risk taking tie in to the theme of "getting messy"

Why is it important to note "without complaint?"

Is this a subtle assumption about whether it is commendable or uncommendable for a teacher, perhaps in an urban context, to teach the curricula handed down by the district?

(Continued)

Figure 7.1 (Continued)

Findings: Allecia: the artistry of going beyond the curriculum	Comments from Xylecia G Fynnaikins
to emphasize her students' rights to life, liberty, and the pursuit of happiness, per the ideals of the United States, her students' birthright. All of this took place in her classroom, all year. She was steady, consistent, and with the exception of the times when she was sick and her energy was low or when her kids got sick and she had to leave early to care for them, this was the Allecia I observed each week. She not only demonstrated pedagogical craft knowledge, Allecia had developed a methodology grounded in the belief in getting dirty that can be expressed as a combination of the first three definitions. She deliberately entangled her life with her students' lives (1), she made space to hear and reflect on all their stories, as well as their families' stories with an open mind and heart (2), and she referred to herself as a contracted employee who, no matter if the tasks assigned seemed unreasonable, strove to uphold the terms of the contract (3). These were all qualities I observed in Allecia's teaching, and if this is what "getting dirty" meant, this intersubjective, entangled performance of multiple identities, then in this project, getting dirty can be equated with constructing a classroom in which socially just teaching practices have transformative potential. (open space up for student voice to resonate. . . . Wants to be transformational. . . conversations about social justice) (trying to strike a balance). Persistently reflective "reflective to the point of nausea. I have to turn it off." Because students in Allecia's class opened up. They faced themselves and knew one another. They got to be themselves and they got to shape their own ideas. They also got to learn what it meant to be in community—in peaceful community—with one another. It was a messy classroom (transformational), yes, but it was grounded in nonviolence and in the respect and expression of human rights.	Does the teacher really teach without complaint,(verbal complaint)? AND/OR How might her "getting dirty," performative nature suggests an attempt to critically respond to the curricula and the district that handed it down. (Hmmm, critical compliance?????) But do #s 1, 2 and 3 really constitute getting dirty? Is the teacher simply finding balance and attempting to reconcile the entities at play in her practice? SELF NOTE-Transformation is messy because it often involves the erosion/deconstruction of one to make space for empowerment. Doing this without imposing or being offensive or overtly judgmental and displaying bias and stratification How does your characterization of getting dirty in 1-3 suggest the potential of transformative practice? According to the research what constitutes transformational teaching? Social justice teaching?
Constraints: contracted. Policy is necessary for holding us together. Building in some subversive measures that I can implement so that I am not oppressed and I don't have to suppress my children even as we meet the expectation of the policies. Multi-cultural sensitivities. Dirty means intermingling with low income people who some people think of as trash. It's dealing with the stench of school, the stench of policy, the stench of violated human rights. Multiple contexts multiple layers, multiple voices at work. You've got to go in and sift through all of that and do what's best for you and your kids. It can become profane, it can become sordid and chaotic. It means relinquishing your own biases and attitudes and how do I get so that I can help my kids lives better.	I enjoyed reading your work. Thank you for including the voices of me and my students. I think that deeper structuring/organizing of the work would make it more pivotal. As well, when you make claims about Allecia, perhaps follow up with an account or scenario that you observed. "Getting dirty" This is a loaded sentence and sounds remarkable, but it merits more explanation, esp. the part about human rights. To what degree was there activism, transformation, and the expression of human rights. Did you see full blossom or sowing and watering?

Findings: Allecia: the artistry of going beyond the curriculum	Comments from Xylecia G Fynnaikins

The room is chaotic, the room is messy, paint is flying, it is out of control, it is interactive, it is intentional. That's one point of the messy. You don't know what you're going to have to deal with day to day- you don't know who is going to cuss who out. Trying to find the right words. It's also good, when they have their own judgments. That gets messy. Power in our names- we're not calling each other names because that is disrespectful, that is wrong. Having a teacher's mind. Reconcile that your home culture is different than the culture. It's not my right as a teacher to judge what's going on at home, but it is my right to uphold expectations in my classroom. In my classroom we're only allowed to call each other by the names their parents gave them.

At the end of day we have to live in that classroom. That's our home.

Our society is not always clean. It is sordid, we're stratified, we're divided. It won't be easy, at the end of the day I want to make us better people.

Not all teachers are comfortable with these conversations.

All students' experiences are relevant to how they experience the classroom.

Sometimes you have to fight it out. . . in respectful ways.

Higher power, children are an inheritance. Some of my babies don't feel like they're an inheritance for anyone, so I figure that while I have you I have to do my best.

RQ#1

Navigation: understanding that I am contractual. The policies exist. But I'm still going to have relationships. That's not quantifiable. I am going to learn of my children, though I'm getting them ready for this test, I want them to have person. Affirmation, legitimation, human beings scholars. They are birthed out of traditions and norms, which may not be aligned, my job is to bridge that gap. I can talk about those biases.

Reconciliation of the contradictory moments that occur throughout the day.

Knowledge: knowing content so thoroughly that if we have those teachable moments in November, let's talk about it now even though I don't have to teach it till March.

Source: Courtesy of Martha Donovan.

with Martha's understanding of it. It's a fair and important question and one that Martha had to go back and explore. Xylecia provided multiple interpretations of what Martha wrote and pushed her to explore and engage topics more deeply. It is important to note that Xylecia had a PhD and, thus, was probably more comfortable questioning Martha as a researcher than someone without such a degree. In some senses, Martha had it a lot easier because Xylecia was already familiar with the research process and with data analysis. She may have felt like an authority on this exchange. The reality is that she *is* the authority on her life, regardless of whether she understood the research process and analysis. Having participants with PhDs will probably not be a common situation, so you, as the researcher, will have to figure out how to encourage your participants to speak back to you. You don't want them to do the hard work of theorizing your data—that is your job. But you do want them to feel comfortable challenging your assumptions and letting you know if they agree with your theorizations.

Conclusion

We have spent two chapters examining data analysis because it is so important in a study. In this chapter specifically, we discussed narrative analysis and discourse analysis in more detail. We encourage you to read other sources and practice analysis in order to feel more comfortable with a process that is not so cut and dry. We also addressed subjectivity statements and memoing. It is important that you write memos throughout your study in order to track the trajectory of your thinking (which becomes the crux of your analysis). Ultimately, your goal with analysis is to convince readers that your interpretations are data based, that they are correct and believable. You want to be sure that your analysis is trustworthy as well as ethical. We move on now to ways of writing up and (re)presenting your study.

DISCUSSION QUESTIONS

1. How are memos useful (or not) in a research project?

2. Write a short subjectivity statement (or, alternatively, discuss your subjectivities). How will this shape your research project?

3. In what ways are the featured data analysis methods more compatible with intersectional research?

4. Choose one of the featured data analysis methods and discuss its strengths and weaknesses. How will intersectionality be infused in your analysis?

5. The authors state, "We agree with hooks (1990), who articulated that researchers who work with marginalized populations have a responsibility to use epistemological, theoretical, and methodological frameworks that do not distort the lives of participants and contribute to deficit narratives." What do you think about this statement? How will you account for this in your research?

Authorial Voice

Intersectional Conversations

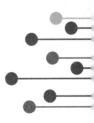

If there's a book that you want to read, but it hasn't been written yet, then you must write it.

— **Toni Morrison**

June is a graduate student at the writing stage of her dissertation. Her data have been collected and analyzed. Her advisor is waiting for June to write Chapters Four and Five (her results and conclusions). June is basically missing in action. She rarely responds to emails or calls inquiring about her progress. Her advisor knows she is at least trying to write; she has seen June's name signed up for writing workshops and retreats the university holds. Most likely, June is battling anxiety, which often comes in the form of writer's block. The pressure to write the perfect manuscript is too much for June to bear, so she ends up not writing much, thereby delaying her graduation.

Over the years, we have found that many of our students love collecting and analyzing data. They are happy to share with us their progress and discuss ways to strengthen or improve the process. But when it comes to writing up the study, many—like June—become anxious and avoid us. You may have heard the joke: *A dissertation advisor and her advisee walk into a bar. The advisor orders a rough draft and they sit in awkward silence for the next eight months.* This actually happens. We have had students who used to email or call frequently but suddenly disappear during dissertation prospectus/proposal writing time. Every once in a while, we might reach out and inquire about their well-being, only to be told all is well and they are writing. But definitions of *writing* vary. What does it mean to write? For some people, they may write pages each day in more of a free-flowing style but most of their words end up being cut out of a final manuscript. Others might belabor over each word so that after a few hours, they only have a few paragraphs—but those few paragraphs might be amazing. There is not a right or wrong way to write.

Writing Rituals

We all have experienced staring at a blank computer screen or a blank piece of paper and willing words to appear. Unfortunately, just as themes don't magically fall from the sky when you're analyzing data, words won't appear on your screen without you writing them. Writer's block is a real thing, and it can get in your way. We find it helpful to be proactive about it. Before you develop writer's block, it is helpful to understand your writing behavior. When we discuss writing in class with graduate students, we like to begin by talking about writing rituals and/or avoidance behaviors. Let's keep it real: Most of us have writing rituals and many of us procrastinate. For example, Jennifer prefers to write from home (a coffee shop is too distracting and her university office is too sterile). But, before she can commit to writing, the house must be spotlessly clean. Because the author understands that she needs to clean *before* she can start writing, she adjusts her schedule accordingly and allows for time to clean. This way, there will always be time to commit words to paper (or computer). She also knows that her best writing frame of mind is early morning (after she has had coffee and her children have left for school). Unless she has a deadline coming up, this author prefers to do most of her writing in daytime hours (preferably early morning through the early afternoon). Because of this, her cleaning happens the night before; thus, no writing time has been sacrificed.

Something that we have learned over time is how your personal environment can affect your writing process and possibly your voice. In advance, carve out writing time in your schedule, prepare your physical space for writing, remove yourself from distractions, and organize the items that you need to write. For some graduate students, finding the time to write and a positive stimulating environment to write in is a privilege. For instance, when Venus was preparing to defend her dissertation, she was a nursing mother of a newborn son! In between caring for her baby, she met with her research participants, conducted literature reviews, coded data, and presented chapter drafts to her research committee members.

Although she loved the smell and sound of her new baby boy, she also understood that it was difficult to think creatively while caring for a baby full-time. Therefore, Venus hired a neighbor's teenage daughter to care for her baby in a separate part of the house for short periods of time during the week. Venus also designated a small bedroom in the house to be dedicated to dissertation work. In the small bedroom, she spread on the floor scrawled fieldnotes, marked-up articles, sticky notes with jotted color-coded themes, handwritten transcripts, cognitive maps, and so on. Fortunately, Venus's doctoral studies were supported by a fully funded research fellowship that financially covered up to four years of tuition and fees and a stipend for personal needs, such as transportation, books, meals, and personal care. She utilized her time and created an environment that was conducive to dissertation preparation.

As professors now and as intersectional scholars, we are acutely aware of how privileged our writing rituals were and continue to be. The current global

COVID-19 pandemic has forced many graduate students to turn their homes into offices and everyday writing spaces. The pandemic and how it will impact all aspects of your life, including your writing time and space, are intersectional concerns that are important for us to note. Some students are essential workers and are risking their lives in the service of others. It appears that due to many mitigating factors, Black, Indigenous, and people of color (BIPOC) have more severe cases of COVID-19 and less desirable outcomes. Thus, it will be difficult to concentrate on writing a dissertation proposal or a journal article if you are in genuine fear for your life or the lives of your family members. Those who are parents and currently without childcare may find it increasingly difficult to find peace and quiet to write. Both Venus and Jennifer have high school children in the home and fielded many questions and/or assisted with virtual schooling during the revisions of this textbook. Our teenagers, however, are relatively self-sufficient and we do not have the added burden of preparing all their meals or sitting next to them as they navigate every aspect of virtual learning. We also recognize that many graduate students face financial, food, or housing insecurities—perhaps even further compounded by the pandemic. We say with much empathy that we know that sometimes, no matter how much you want to write or finish a writing project, there are situations that are simply not conducive to writing. In order for your brain to be creative enough to write, you need to feel safe and have your basic needs met. If you are currently struggling, please be kind to yourself and reach out to your advisor and university officials to see what assistance they might provide.

So, for those who are able to write, it is good to know that people have a variety of writing rituals that they must do before (and sometimes during) a writing session. Some people have a glass of wine or tea to relax them before writing. Others sit in a specific spot in their home, library, or other area. A graduate student we knew reserved the same writing desk in the university library for two semesters. She followed the same ritual of writing at the desk in the early evening hours and then treated herself to a meal after she was done. We found the notion of rewarding oneself to be a common strategy graduate students used to help with their writing. Some booked a massage after they wrote a chapter. Others would buy themselves something special. Again, these behaviors can be crafted on your own once you figure out what motivates you to write. It is important to point out that rewards that involve financial compensation are, of course, a privilege and not all people will be able to reward themselves in these ways. If money is tight, as it often is during graduate school and even more so during a pandemic, you could always reward yourself with a television show or time to read for pleasure (instead of for research) after writing. In fact, Jennifer has a novel waiting for her once book revisions have been completed!

Jennifer's final push to writing her dissertation involved a lot of writing in a short span of time. She had already collected and analyzed the data and also had the first few chapters written. She was awarded a fellowship (which meant she no longer had to be a teaching assistant or graduate assistant). She was literally paid for one year to sit at home and write her dissertation (and search for academic jobs). Her time was spent quite leisurely watching reality television and regretting that she didn't choose a different dissertation topic related to reality television. The year passed quickly, and she was offered a position. Of course, she was not able to defend in the spring semester because she hadn't written a thing. The position was dependent upon her having her PhD in hand. This meant that she had to defend at the end of the summer before she left for her new position. She had three months to write her last three chapters. She bought a book that used the premise of writing your dissertation in fifteen minutes per day (Bolker, 1998). This was before the days of Amazon Prime's free two-day shipping. While she waited for the book to arrive at the bookstore, she read through her thousands of pages of coded data and memos. She immediately read the book, and it suggested writing (even if it was nonsensical or stream of consciousness). Jennifer initially sat at her desk and wrote using the stream-of-consciousness approach. Her words were literal babble about data and her ideas about the data. She did this every day for a week. One morning, the babble started to make sense. The author saw how she could turn the babble into a theme. She wrote out her first theme (argument), and the rest is history. She sat at the desk every day at the same time each day and wrote until she couldn't anymore. Within those three months, she wrote and finalized three chapters. In order to accomplish this, of course, the 15 minutes per day turned into longer blocks of time. But the initial premise of being deliberate and consistent is what helped the author. Creating a writing routine that she relied on every day is what allowed her to finish the dissertation. We encourage you to craft a similar routine. Forcing yourself to sit at your computer for 30 minutes per day will eventually spark something on your screen as well.

Okay, so we started the writing chapter off by discussing ways to actually write. Most of us have anxiety about writing because we are perfectionists. Many BIPOC in academia struggle with imposter syndrome or the feeling that we don't really belong. This may be true for all women in male-dominated fields, regardless of race. In response, many of us are hypervigilant about our work. We know that we will be judged on different (harsher) standards than our white male counter-parts and, partially in response to this, we overwork ourselves and obsess over everything. An intersectional understanding of writing includes acknowledging some of the raced and gendered nature of perfectionism's roots. While there is no easy answer to overcome this type of perfectionism, it will be important for you to acknowledge it to yourself and, perhaps, to your advisor.

There is an upside to writing currently. The good thing is you are not writing during the days of typewriters. We have software that allows us to edit after we commit something to the screen. Write with the understanding that you can always change it. Just because you type it out does not mean it is forever committed to you. Revision is a necessity of writing. To be honest, revising work is something that both of us dread. We like to think of ourselves as careful writers, editing as we go. Thus, when we are forced to go back, changing words or editing is a painful process. But it is a necessity. We suggest you sleep on it or wait a few days before you return to your draft to edit. Looking at it with fresh eyes sometimes makes the process of editing less painful. When you are editing something based on reviewer feedback or dissertation committee feedback, that might be especially painful. We tell students, especially, to keep a "dream" copy of your manuscript on your computer. The dream copy is the one untouched by your dissertation committee or by the comments of Reviewer 2. It might help you emotionally to understand that this manuscript still exists in the form that you desire. But trust that your committee or reviewers know what is best for the manuscript and make the edits they suggest (within reason, of course). One of the authors used this approach for dissertation, since she was opposed to changing something her advisor wanted her to. The author went on to graduate and even published articles from the dissertation. And, along the way, she lost the copy of her dream dissertation!

Voice in Qualitative Inquiry

In this section, we will discuss qualitative inquiry and authorial voice. While reading this section of the chapter, keep in mind our previous point that every researcher has their own writing process. This process has been influenced by previous academic preparation, the researcher's personality, the environment in which she is writing, and the researcher's personal beliefs about writing, fears, and goals. For example, a graduate student researcher with an undergraduate major in nursing may have a different set of experiences with research writing than a graduate student researcher with an undergraduate degree in English language arts. Likewise, a doctoral student who holds a master's degree in art history may have a different approach to writing than someone who graduated from an MBA (master of business administration) program.

Again, previous academic training influences one's exposure to different types of writing and one's skill set in writing up research. No matter what type of writing you are accustomed to reading or writing in, take advantage of coursework and other writing opportunities to find your own writing style and a style that is appropriate for your dissertation's research topic and follows your department's guidelines for the dissertation. Also, when preparing for your dissertation, think about a writing style that is reflective of your personality. For authenticity to be portrayed in the written dissertation and to find a sense of gratification in the writing process and oral presentation of the dissertation research, it is imperative that the dissertation is reflective of your voice.

In the opening quote of this chapter, Toni Morrison advises that an aspiring writer must write the kind of book that she desires to read. Even more, the novelist and English professor's words hint that young authors of color will read dozens, if not hundreds, of books that do not reflect their taste, desires, wants, and reality. Whatever they feel is missing from those books, including the social realities not represented, they can use as their motivation to become a book author. We believe these same sentiments can apply to dissertation research. Student researchers might consider viewing the dissertation process as an opportunity to explore the kind of research topics that they desire to learn more about as students, scholars, and consumers of research.

Here are some questions to consider as you think about your personal interests when deciding upon a written dissertation presentation: What do you believe is missing from current research, curriculum, and/or policy discussions in your current coursework or research articles that you have come across as a student or in your professional career? What interested you or bored you to death as a reader of research texts? What type of research study do you wish to read that you have not read yet? Write that research study.

In addition to thinking about your own personal interests during the dissertation process, also think about the communities that you are a part of and/or those that you serve. Student researchers might decide to think about a research topic that benefits their respective cultural communities and choose to write up their research in ways that are more reflective of their own cultural norms. Of course, some student researchers will conduct research outside of their own cultural communities; therefore, it is really important to revisit the ethics chapter (Chapter 3) and previous discussions on researcher's positionality in this book. Most importantly, the best advice that we can give you based on years of experience as producers and consumers of research is to be sure to take a moment before sitting down to write your research proposal to reflect on your purpose for writing and your writer's voice. Many times in academia, we are taught to craft an academic voice, and this can seem foreign to those of us who have been historically excluded from academia. The academic voice is often rooted in white supremacist patriarchy and reflects ideas about objectivity. Thus far, you can see that we argue strenuously that research (and writing) is an embodied act; we therefore encourage you early on to develop a voice you are comfortable with. Hopefully, throughout graduate school, you've been exposed to a variety of voices instead of only the European canon. This will enable you to understand that there is room for you to develop your own style instead of being forced to mimic the "dead white men" who came before you.

Stepping into the dissertation writing process with "no voice" or a "foreign voice" can make you feel as if you are going crazy! Trust us, we have been there at some point as students or in our professional careers, but we quickly learned that discovering your own voice is not only wise but key to a dissertation that you will be proud to submit to your committee and share with the larger research community. To help get you to this point, we help save you time and keep your sanity by walking you through the writing process. As you read Chapter 8, think about the following questions, which attempt to combine your personal preferences and various communities that you are beholden to during the dissertation process:

- What are the types of dissertations that I would enjoy reading as a student or fellow researcher?

- What types of dissertations are members of my community more likely to relate to or read?

- Would members of my family be able to engage with my research presentation and/or final product?

- How might I meet the needs of my discipline and the needs of my community through my dissertation?

- How might I find pleasure in my dissertation research and writing the dissertation?

Besides finding the ideal times and places to write your dissertation, it is also important for graduate students to think about their personal beliefs, including anxiety, fears, and goals, about written research—or any kinds of writing, for that matter. If the reader recalls in Chapter 1, there is an activity that prompted you to reflect on how your personal values and previous socialization shaped your perspectives on scientific research. Review your responses to that activity to rediscover your enthusiasm or skepticism of written research. One's beliefs about research in general, or qualitative inquiry specifically, will certainly influence how one chooses to approach the written dissertation.

Furthermore, as previously hinted at in this chapter, one's personal beliefs about writing (and/or written research) are shaped by (1) how they were taught to write, including how they were rewarded or punished in the past for their writing; (2) what types of readings the student has been introduced to by their role models as "academic writing"; and (3) the curriculum that they have been exposed to in their studies, which shapes student researchers' beliefs about academic writing and says much about what kinds of writing are considered to be of value in their discipline or program of study. A student researcher's beliefs about writing will most definitely influence what they consider to be academic writing and, thus, their authorial voice in the dissertation process.

Lastly, for some racially, ethnically, or linguistically minoritized students, they may remember a time in their elder's history or their educational history where they (or someone they know) were punished for speaking or writing in their home language. Many people from Indigenous backgrounds, colonized people, and BIPOC in the United States (U.S.) and the diaspora were threatened with death, maimed, or killed to keep them from engaging in literacy practices. Further, research reveals that high-achieving students of color often reported educational experiences in which they received negative feedback from teachers or college professors on their written or oral language (Kubota & Okuda, 2016); received a poor grade outcome; or were labelled *slow* (Evans-Winters, 2016, 2019), *disabled*, or *mentally retarded* for their speech or writing style (Blanchett et al., 2009). In some cases, students were prohibited in the school environment from speaking their home language altogether (which was the case of Jennifer). Considering these social patterns in academic contexts, it is important, prior to the dissertation process and throughout the research experience, to reflect upon your beliefs about writing and engage in ongoing observation of your research voice. Decolonial and intersectional methodologies call for multiple representations of voice in our research performances.

From our perspective, it is typical for graduate students in the beginning of their academic careers to model the writing style of their favorite academic writers or university professors. Imitating the writing style of your academic role model is fine at first to get you started with writing. However, attempting to sound or write like a forty-year career veteran and highly published author may help provide a vision of your writing, but such high standards for a novice researcher can also hinder the writing process, if the borrowed style does not fit your habits of mind, research methodology, chosen theoretical framework, abilities, and talents—yet. During the process of discovering your authorial voice, take into consideration what it is you already know and what it is that you want to know to make the writing process more pleasurable and meaningful to you and others.

1. **Personal writing preferences**. A researcher's authorial voice develops as the person gets to know and becomes comfortable with himself or herself. As the writer becomes more intimate with the writing process and the variety of texts that they like to read, they will also know what kinds of writing feel familiar and reflective of who they are as a person and researcher.

2. **Research methodology.** The research methodology of the study—the explicitly stated intent by which one will collect data, the selected research site, and how one plans to interact with research participants—will also inform how the researcher will write up the study. The research methodology usually positions the researcher's authorial voice up front.

3. **Theoretical framework.** Dissertation research is framed by a set of interrelated concepts, a body of theories, and knowledge claims that situate a study within a larger context (i.e., field of study). The theoretical framework typically provides some indication of how the researcher views knowledge and the research issue. The selected framework will more than likely indicate the type of research product the investigator intends to produce. In most research projects, the theoretical framework is representative of the author's assumed or projected voice. The theoretical framework speaks volumes about who a researcher is or intends to become (as a scholar).

4. **Cultural ethos.** Culture plays a major role in how a researcher views, interprets, considers, and produces (written or oral) text. Cultural ethos refers to the dominated assumptions, dispositions, beliefs, practices, and essential character of an individual, community, or group of people. These codes of being make a group or community unique, and they influence how you view the written text and yourself as a writer/producer of text(s).

5. **Abilities and talents.** Every human being is uniquely talented and equipped with certain special abilities, skills, and talents. Throughout

our life span, we all will develop a special set of talents and abilities as writers and producers of written text. By practicing writing and—we cannot emphasize enough—reading for depth and breadth, the student of research will discover their own writing abilities. Writing is a skill set that takes practice, practice, practice! With much practice, one's research voice will emerge.

Your path to discovering your research voice begins with the doctoral dissertation. In most cases, a student begins to develop their research voice in previous coursework (all of those mini-research papers assigned throughout your course of study). Thus, the dissertation is merely a culmination of previous knowledge and experiences, which is why we recommend thinking of the dissertation simply as a showcase of everything, or almost everything, that you have learned throughout your doctoral journey. You already have what it takes to write the dissertation; now you must be confident in sharing your research ideas with an audience.

The Literature Review and Voice

Writing voice aside, your dissertation will be influenced by other factors as well, including the traditions of your discipline and your college or university requirements. Also, your dissertation chair and other committee members will advise you on the style and format of your dissertation, based on their own experiences advising graduate students, their own research, and the publication process. We recommend that students retrieve and review the dissertations or recently published articles of your dissertation chair and other committee members. Take note of (a) the type of research questions raised in their work, (b) the structure and tone of the literature review, (c) the explanation of selected theoretical framework, (d) the description of the methodology employed, (e) if/how they explain their positionality to the study, and (f) the authorial tone of the overall text.

After a review of the written dissertations or articles of committee members, how might their writing be classified? Is the writing style technical or descriptive? Poetic or persuasive? Are their presentations written verbatim as spoken by the research participant (or someone else who is a part of the context) or is the research written as an exposition narrative with detailed information about the historical context, setting, and so forth? Did the author's writing change over time (e.g., from a student researcher to a tenured professor) or across publication outlets (e.g., a policy brief versus a book chapter in an edited book or academic journal)? Of all the dissertations and articles written by your committee members, which one did you easily gravitate toward? As you ponder these questions, think about what aspects of each academic writing style you appreciate, and then consider how their approaches to writing might be integrated into your own writing style.

As will be explained below on writing the literature review, a review of the literature will also support the format and tone of your dissertation. In your dissertation, you will be expected to critique other research. As a part of the review of the research literature, you will consider the appropriateness of research questions for the selected topic, choice of research site, characterization of research contexts or participants, conclusions reached, and so on. As the review of the literature relates to research voice, you will discover how others talk about your research topic. Further, in your own dissertation, how you present your arguments or critiques of what was appropriately included or excluded from the studies you reviewed will capture readers' attention, and they too will develop an opinion about your research voice.

Yes, believe it or not, readers of research draw conclusions and make assumptions about the researcher all the time! In fact, we all make assumptions about an author. Think of your favorite book and think about how many times you imagined the narrator's or character's voice in your head! What conclusions did you draw about their personality or about their political or personal beliefs? None-theless, reviewing other people's research and other's feedback of your writing will assist in the development of your authorial voice. Hence, it is vital to your identity as a scholar to gain practice with the act of writing and read a diversity of texts to claim a voice that is more aligned with who you are as a cultural being and scholar.

The Research Proposal

Each institution and doctoral program has their own dissertation procedures and guidelines for graduate students. Be sure to check departmental and university guidelines before you start the dissertation proposal. Also, discuss necessary components with your dissertation advisor as well as peers who are ahead of you in the process. Next, we will guide you through the dissertation proposal. We will present a dissertation proposal outline that is typical of most university programs but, again, check on the standards of your university. The standard dissertation proposal consists of the first three chapters of the dissertation:

- Chapter One—Introduction to the Research

  In the introduction, you should let readers know what you are concerned about. This section should discuss the problem within its particular context and include a statement of the problem. In this section, you will provide a specific answer to the following question: What problem will you investigate? You will include your research questions in this section as well.

- Chapter Two—Review of the Literature

  The point of a literature review is to show how your project builds on existing knowledge. What studies have been done before yours? What can we learn from them? It is helpful to turn a methodological eye to the research to determine what methodologies and methods have been used previously and what the strengths and weaknesses are of each. You want to answer the following questions: What have I learned from these studies? Why is my study needed? The literature review might be the place you examine your theoretical framework as well. We say *might* because some writers will put it in the introduction. Your theoretical framework will guide every aspect of your study and will be especially helpful in data analysis.

- Chapter Three—Research Methodology

  This section is where you lay out your proposed plan. What exactly do you plan to do? What methodology will you use and why? Once you have introduced readers to your methodology, you will discuss methods. You need to draw a road map for others so they can follow your plans. It should be detailed enough that readers can visualize the different aspects of your project. You also will introduce your data analysis methods. Analysis, as we have stressed, should not be saved for the end of your project. Once you determine how you will collect data, you should also identify how you will analyze them. Once you know that, you will be better prepared to collect the data you need. In proposals, it is helpful to anticipate what the limitations of your study may be. There might be some problems that you can address, but others will remain as limitations. It is also good to provide a time line. If you are a novice researcher, a trusted mentor can let you know if the time line is realistic or not. Also, most proposals have appendices that include interview guides, observation protocols, institutional review board (IRB) consent forms, and other materials that allow readers to conceptualize the project as you envision it.

The dissertation proposal might be considered an opportunity for the advanced graduate student to prove to the research committee that they are prepared to conduct independent research—of course, while being advised along the way by their dissertation advisor. To guide the reader through the steps to writing the dissertation proposal, we will introduce you to Michelle. Like the students in the opening vignettes, Michelle is a fictitious character who represents the myriad students enrolled in our research courses or students we have advised as dissertation chairs over the years. Let us share some background information first about Michelle that might be relevant to her identity as a scholar and will possibly influence how she elects to write up her first three chapters.

Michelle's Story

Michelle is an African American graduate student. Prior to returning to graduate school, she served as a master's level social worker with five years of experience working in a nonprofit, faith-based community service agency. The agency was in a predominately working-class neighborhood and served mostly African American, first-generation Mexican, and white clients living in a mid-size city. Michelle lived and attended church not too far from the agency where she worked. In contrast, most of her white colleagues lived outside of the neighborhood where the agency was located. All the clients met the low-income requirements needed to participate in the social service programs offered at the agency. The agency provided social services such as GED and parenting classes, job placement services, life skills training, and individual and family counseling. Michelle started as a caseworker at the organization, then worked her way up to a supervisor position in the role of director of community programs. In this role, she developed a grant-supported program that provided court advocacy for parents involved with family court. Michelle deeply cared for her clients, but she felt frustrated with agency policies and court mandates that seemed to create more barriers than opportunities for her clients. After five years with the agency, Michelle decided to return to doctoral studies full-time in social work. Even though it was a sacrifice for Michelle and her family to leave her career and become a student again, Michelle felt an overwhelming desire to learn more about the relationship between her client's ethnic and cultural experiences and their contact with the child welfare system. She also felt that she could be a better advocate for her community if she worked outside the agency.

Introduction to the Study

Finally, Michelle has completed coursework and passed her comprehensive examination. She is now excited to draft Chapter One, the introduction to the study. After completion of the comprehensive examination, some students begin to feel nervous or unsure of how to narrow down their research topic. We suggest that graduate students look to their previous academic preparation and personal and professional experiences to decide on a research focus. Usually, graduate students have an area of interest, but they do not know how to focus the research interests to begin writing Chapter One.

To begin to narrow your topic for Chapter One and find your writing voice, first think about what makes you special or unique as a scholar. Stated differently, what set of experiences do you have that will help you provide more insight into a social problem or issue? What insights do you have about a specific cultural context or social environment that may inform previous conversations about a subject matter? Based on your preliminary review of the literature in other courses or in preparation for the comprehensive exam, what do you consider to be absent, ignored, or theoretically underdeveloped on a research topic? Michelle's story above gives some indication of her research interests, and below, we present an introduction to her first chapter.

In Chapter One, Michelle will inform the reader of the purpose of conducting the research for her dissertation. It is not enough to say that she is conducting research for the purposes of completing a dissertation. She will explain the purpose of her research, outline any questions that will be raised by the study, and operationalize relevant terms and concepts that are significant to the social phenomenon under study. The introduction chapter will also outline the layout for organization of the proposal. For the proposal, try to identify at least one major goal of your research study and a couple of related objectives of the study. Also, list three to five main questions that your dissertation will attempt to answer. Most people are interested in a research study because it will address or propose a solution to a problem that they confront in their personal life, the life of people they care for, or in their work environment. Inform the reader up front about what they will potentially learn from reading the research study.

In Chapter One, when predicting what questions will be addressed, it is also important to identify the audience(s) that might be interested in your study. Attempt to name a few interested groups that might benefit from your research, such as your prospective site participants, researchers of your respective discipline, policymakers, and so on. Your committee will want to know who (besides you) will be interested in the proposed study, and they, including the IRB, will also want to know who might benefit from the study. Tell the reader why these individuals or groups may be interested in the study and at this moment in history.

As you write Chapter One and use the literature to persuade your committee of the significance of the proposed research study to the scientific community at large and other beneficiaries, make sure to conceptualize disciplinary-specific terms and concepts specific to the study. Do not assume that readers understand the jargon of your discipline and understand a research concept in the same way that you do. Such an oversight can shift the meaning of a research project. Often, terms and concepts are culturally laden and/or specific to a disciplinary area. Now, we will revisit Michelle's story to see how she introduced her proposed dissertation study.

Michelle's Introduction to the Study

The purpose of this proposed dissertation research is to begin to locate Black mothers in discussions about criminal justice reform. In the proposed study, I purport that Black mothers have been overlooked in conversations about racial disparities in the child welfare system. For the purpose of this study, *Black mothers* are defined as women who self-identify as Black or African American and are primary caregivers of dependents under the age of seventeen living at home or in temporary state custody. The *child welfare system* refers to any voluntary or court-mandated social service programs mothers access to support their responsibilities as caregivers. A preliminary review of the literature indicates that Black children are more likely than other racial groups to have an encounter with child protective services, and Black mothers are judged unfit at higher rates than other mothers.

Borrowing from the tenets of critical race theory and Black feminist thought, the purpose of my study is to collect the stories of Black mothers who have been personally impacted by the disparities in the child welfare system. As a formally trained social worker, I know that many Black mothers are resilient in the face of adversity. Also, as a Black mother myself, I know that mothers rely on their family as a support and community organizations like the church and local social service agencies as sources of support. I am interested in studying how race, class, and gender influences female caregivers' perceptions of the child welfare system's support as they navigate allegations of neglect, abuse, or noncompliance with court mandates. In Chapter Two, I provide a review of the literature to demonstrate the short- and long-term social, emotional, and economic impact of race and gender inequity in society in general, and the child welfare system particularly, on low-income African American mothers, families, and communities. Chapter Three provides an overview of the proposed research methodology, social context where the study will take place, and procedures for the selection of research participants.

In this chapter (Chapter One), I will use research in social work and sociology to discuss the importance of this study for social work practice and policy. In the proposed study, I raise the following questions: (1) What are the experiences of Black mothers involved in family court and/or under state supervision, (2) How do historical and contemporary stereotypes of Black mothers and families affect the public's perceptions of Black mothers? (3) What are the ways in which Black mothers persist in the face of oppression and fight against the abuse of state power? The proposed study has implications for social work education, social work researchers, social welfare policy, and advocates of criminal justice reform. Social workers in child welfare, policymakers, and qualitative researchers in the social sciences may be interested in this study.

As you see from Michelle's introduction to the study, she sophisticatedly interweaved personal experiences, cultural insights, and previous work experiences into the proposed study. See if you can spot from the examples provided above how Michelle approached her study from an intersectional perspective. Pair up with others in your class or writing group and respond to the following statements and questions.

1. Identify Michelle's research statement. What is the purpose of her proposed research study? What social problem or issue does Michelle propose to address in the study?

2. Are you convinced of the proposed dissertation's importance? What did the author state or not state that convinced you?

3. Is it explicitly or implicitly stated who the proposed research study is important to and why?

4. What research questions does her research aim to raise and address? Are you convinced, based on the information presented here, that her proposed research study will be able to answer the questions raised in the dissertation? Why or why not?

5. What previous personal, professional, or academic experiences does Michelle have that may or may not help her approach the proposed research ethically and authentically? Is previous academic training or coursework preparation obvious?

6. Can you identify Michelle's theoretical framework? What is the theoretical framework?

7. Is it easy to identify the proposed methodology of Michelle's study? What is the proposed methodology? Do you believe it is befitting of the study's topic?

8. Is it obvious who will be a part of the research study?

9. Are research terms adequately defined or is Chapter One laden with jargon? Are you able to follow the discussion as someone inside her discipline? Are you able to follow the discussion as someone outside the discipline?

10. How would you describe Michelle's authorial voice? Is it persuasive? Technical? Argumentative? Descriptive of people, places, and things? Are you likely to continue to read the rest of the proposal? Are you curious about the development of her study? Why or why not?

Use Michelle's story presented above to draft Chapter One. Give attention to the purpose of the research, the questions raised by the research study, and how you propose to respond to the research questions. Most importantly, Chapter One must convince others that your research topic is worthy of further study and that you have the background knowledge, skills, and talents to implement the research responsibly. Moreover, a well-written Chapter One will help you stay monomaniacally focused on your topic; this chapter is your cognitive road map for the rest of the dissertation. It should tell you (and the reader) exactly (1) what you intend to investigate, (2) why you intend to investigate, and (3) who should be interested in what you will investigate. Chapter One and subsequent chapters should portray your researcher's voice and true commitment to the research topic at hand.

The Literature Review

Next, we discuss the literature review chapter (Chapter Two) from an intersectional perspective. The purpose of literature review is to give the student researcher an opportunity to gain in-depth knowledge about the historical, political, and social context of an issue, challenge, or problem of practice. You will read and assess the academic literature on the chosen research topic and then synthesize the information in a critical summary to be shared with a research audience. In the dissertation proposal, the literature review serves two purposes.

One purpose of the literature review in the dissertation proposal is to effectively demonstrate your knowledge of the literature to your committee members. You need to convince them that you know your stuff and that you are prepared to conduct thoughtful scientific research that is worth your time and the time of committee members and others who might be invested in the research study! Besides, professors still are intrigued by the curiosity, intellectual growth, and creativity of our graduate students. We learn much from our graduate students and their points of view of the social world. Believe it or not, we find great pleasure in witnessing our students' contributions to scientific knowledge, too.

Self-interests aside, university, faculty, and student resources (e.g., time, funds, facility space, etc.) are limited! Consequently, faculty and universities are obligated to consider the feasibility and relevance of a study. Hence, another purpose of the literature review is to confirm that there is enough evidence available to justify further examination of a research topic or cultural phenomenon and, additionally, to convince your audience that the subject will be investigated from a different perspective. Trust us, there is nothing like a student or veteran researcher recycling and regurgitating the same old research questions time and time again. Prove to your committee throughout the dissertation proposal that you have an alternative point of view and will be offering a different perspective on a research subject. Equally important—we cannot emphasize this point enough—be certain that the proposed research topic is relevant and thought-provoking to all who are devoted to your success as a doctoral student. You want your committee members to be enthusiastic about your topic—at least enough to be able to point you to more resources and useful literature!

Before we revisit Michelle's dissertation proposal, review the literature review process. Steps in the literature review process include the following:

1. Locate and record citations to books, academic articles, and documents that may contain useful information and ideas on your topic.

2. Thoroughly read or review the initially retrieved research. Select the most relevant sources.

3. Cite the most relevant book, article, or document using the appropriate citation style.

4. Write a concise annotation that summarizes the central theme and scope of the book or article and critiques it from a methodological standpoint.

5. Create a literature matrix that combines your summaries and critiques.

Without a doubt, the literature review process is not as linear as presented above. We review literature on our topic(s) of interest throughout the research process, consciously and subconsciously. The literature review, like all research, is ongoing. As you get started with the dissertation proposal, it may be helpful to review old course syllabi, assigned books, and lecture notes for ideas on how to begin the literature search for Chapter Two. You also may want to collaborate with other doctoral students and find out if they have recommended sources for your dissertation proposal.

Also, it is without saying that you should visit your institution's library research databases as a starting point, but if you get stumped in the review process, there are other places you can turn to for research sources. As you ponder what topics or research to cover in your proposal, it may be beneficial to recall any conference presentations you attended that were related to your research topic. Did you take extensive notes during the presentation? What did you find intriguing about the presentation or the research topic? You might consider retrieving the presenter's dissertation or published reports and/or requesting a copy of their conference paper.

Finally, once you locate relevant scholarly sources, include one or more sentences that (a) evaluate the authority or background of the author, (b) comment on the intended audience of the research presented, (c) compare or contrast the selection with another cited source you reviewed, and (d) explain how the cited research is relevant or useful to your proposed topic and why it is important to other researchers in your field of study. Be detailed and thorough in your literature review. Avoid the mistake that too many first-time student researchers make, knowingly or unknowingly: *Do not* copy and paste an article's abstract into your text! Avoid plagiarism by reviewing citation guidelines, scheduling uninterrupted reading time, and planning your organization of the literature in advance. Now, let's review how Michelle planned her Chapter Two and review of the literature.

Michelle's Approach to the Literature Review

Chapter Two Outline

Identify 45–60 scholarly sources (peer-reviewed articles from scholarly journals, books, or book chapters from edited volumes but *not* from blogs, internet/newspaper articles, or Wikipedia) related to my research interest in parental rights in the state where the study will take place. Reminder: See comprehensive exam! I will organize the literature into three areas: 10–25 sources focused on historical representations of Black women in the U.S.; 10–25 sources focused on current social, political, and economic trends influencing Black mother caregivers; and 10–25 sources focused on implicit bias in social welfare and the criminal justice system. Note to self: Use 7th edition APA citation style. In Chapter Two, I will provide a summary of the research findings, which synthesizes the sources gathered for the literature review.

The purpose of a draft of the literature review is to provide me with the opportunity to gain in-depth knowledge about the historical, political, and social context of parental rights in the U.S. I will read and assess the academic literature on this social work issue and then synthesize the information in a critical summary to be shared with other social workers and parental rights advocates. I will take the following steps to review the literature: First, I will locate and record citations to books, academic articles, and documents that offer useful information and ideas on my topic. Second, I will briefly examine and review the sources. I will narrow down the literature to the most useful sources for this dissertation proposal. My goal is to cite the most relevant book, article, or documents. Finally, I will summarize the central theme and scope of the book or article.

Literature Review (Draft)

I will engage in professional reflection based on the review of the research gathered. I raise the following question as I review the literature: What is my personal and professional experience with this important topic in social work? Who do I believe will benefit most by reviewing research on this particular topic? What are the expected outcomes at the university, national, or global front for addressing this social work issue and associated policies? How will I use this researched information to help transform my community or profession? I estimate that the first draft will include a review of approximately 45–60 sources, summary and synthesis of the research will be approximately 25–30 pages, and my personal and professional reflections of the research reviewed will be 3–5 pages. Two weeks before our scheduled meeting, I will email my professor a draft of Chapter Two.

Clearly, Michelle is a very organized and ambitious doctoral student! Her outline of Chapter Two provides much insight into the literature review. We know in advance how many sources she intends to cite in Chapter Two. We also can see how she plans to organize her sources, based on the themes of her research interests. The reader also knows in advance that Michelle's intended audience at this point is her dissertation chair and (later) social workers who serve Black women clients. Knowing and naming her audience helps the researcher identify relevant research and databases (e.g., social work policies, social work studies, legal journals, etc.).

As you draft your Chapter Two, there are other challenges to consider. For instance, as we have pointed out in previous chapters, there is a long-standing history of scientific racism and ethnocentrism in academic research (Kendi, 2017; Scheurich & Young, 1997; Washington, 2006). At times, novice researchers may feel compelled to cite research that does not necessarily align with their personal politics, experiential knowledge, or paradigmatic perspective of the social issue at hand. Sometimes research questions and conclusions are unostentatiously laden with racist, sexist, classist, or other ideals that demean certain behaviors or cultural groups. In your review of the literature, you may not right away be able to articulate your discomfort with a scientific theory or research study, but your intuition may inform you that something does not seem morally or ethically proper with the summations of the report.

Other times, a theory or research report is obviously peppered with deficit thinking or pathological assumptions about a particular social issue or cultural group. As a researcher, you will need to decide which literature should be included or excluded from Chapter Two of the dissertation, the review of the literature chapter. For some student researchers, decisions about what literature to include or omit can cause an ethical dilemma. In qualitative research, it is important to journal about whatever subtle or visceral responses that arise in your review of the literature, observations, or interactions with research participants or contexts. These reactions reveal who you are as a researcher and the problems inherent in our research epistemologies and scientific claims.

Nevertheless, it is up to you as the researcher to decide which previously published research you want to cite in your dissertation proposal. Be sure to go back to Chapter 2 in this textbook and review the politics of citations. You want to be sure that you are citing women and scholars of color who have been traditionally marginalized by the research canon. You do not have to continue to recreate the canon, given that it has historically privileged white men's scholarship. A well-written literature review will explain the reasons why or the process by which you selected a particular study to cite in the first place and, at times, why you excluded other relevant research reports from the review of the literature. In the literature review, you will also inform the reader of the relevance, accuracy, and quality of the source cited.

Think of the dissertation as your exit out of your degree program into the real world. It should be a concise representation of your expertise as a content specialist who has conducted research. The dissertation is different from a journal article because you have the room to show your knowledge. Indeed, the point of a dissertation is for you to prove that you are knowledgeable about your research topic. This means that your literature review will cover *all of the things*! In fact, in a journal article, your literature review is often only a few paragraphs or a few pages (depending on the journal and your discipline). Yet, in your dissertation, you should plan to cover as much literature as you can, including a review of the historical evolution of your topic.

Writing Up Your Findings

If you are conducting the research for a dissertation, you will most likely have a specific format to follow for the proposal and dissertation. The dissertation extends the components of the research proposal and includes further detail about how you analyzed data. It also includes your findings as well as a section or chapter that answers the question, "So what?" In other words, why should we care about your findings? What is important for us to know about the findings in relation to the problem under investigation? Dissertations are written in past tense because you have completed the work already. Past tense honors your participants and ensures that they will not be viewed as forever participants of a research study. Their participation is over, and the study is now in the past. The audience of your dissertation will obviously be, foremost, your dissertation committee. You will have to make individual members happy but, in general, their guidance and suggestions will improve your work. As academics now, we sometimes wish we had a trusted committee of mentors who worked together to improve our work! Instead, we have reviewers of academic journals who may or may not have our best interest at heart. When you find yourself frustrated by committee members, try to keep in mind that they want your work to be the best it can possibly be, since their names are attached. Finally, always refer to the most recent citation guidelines of your disciplinary area of study (for example, for this textbook, the authors are required to heed the 7th edition of American Psychological Association [APA] guidelines). Your graduate college will have guidelines for the recommended citation style for the dissertation. If you are writing a journal article, the journals will often clarify what style guidelines they prefer.

You also have an entire chapter (or multiple chapters) devoted to your findings. This means that you will have to determine how much raw data you should include in the chapters in order to support your arguments. When using raw data, there are multiple things to consider. Representation of your participants should be at the forefront. You will need to balance representing them in authentic ways with larger contextual issues: Will this representation perpetuate deficit narratives? If the answer to this question is yes, then you need to take a long and hard look into your own politics. Do you want to be a researcher who contributes to deficit narratives abut entire communities, especially when these deficit narratives are often rooted in racist and classist assumptions?

You should also ask yourself if the participant is okay with the way you have represented them. Imagine each of your participants reading your dissertation (or having someone read it aloud to them). Always ask yourself if your participants would like your portrayal of who they are. We certainly aren't suggesting that you change their personalities or major details, but if, for example, you mention that the person maintains a messy home, imagine that person confronting you about your opinion of the cleanliness or orderliness of said home. You must understand that whatever you write may get back to your original participants and, thus, you need to be prepared for whatever feelings that brings up. Carolyn Ellis (2007), in "Telling Secrets, Revealing Lies," reveals being forced to confront her participants' anger with how they were represented. Ellis notes that she hadn't expected them to read her findings; thus, she wasn't prepared to deal with what they thought of as a betrayal of friendship. Given the ways materials are disseminated electronically now, we think it is important that you actually imagine your participants reading your work because it is likely that they will. What would they think and feel about your descriptions? Use these images as a guide for how you write. It is no longer acceptable for you to believe that your writing will not have an impact on the people you are writing about.

Another question to ask yourself is if you should alter the language in any way. Many people use filler words such as *um*, *uh*, or *like* as they speak. Depending on the extent of this usage, these filler words can distract from real content. You need to make a decision (and be consistent) regarding whether you will edit out filler words for clarity. Your decision may depend on your choice of analysis. For example, filler words would be useful in content analysis because you can determine how and when such words are used. The increase of filler words or interrupted speech around particular topics, for example, might signal the speaker's discomfort. If you are not completing a content analysis, the excess words might simply be a distraction to the real meaning. Whatever you decide, you should be sure that you are consistent. If you edit one participant's speech, you should edit everyone's in the same way.

Raw data are excerpts from interview transcripts, observations, or documents. They are the crux of your study and what you have coded and analyzed. You might wonder how much raw data you should include in your write up. You certainly don't want to overdo it and bore your readers with long strings of direct quotations. However, you also want to show that your findings emerged from the raw data. It is your job as a researcher to tell a story with the data. You don't want to overwhelm readers so that they must make sense of everything. However, you also don't want to include so little data that readers doubt your findings. The best type of raw data to include would be the emotionally compelling excerpts. Sort through your data and label excerpts that are particularly powerful either because they drive home a point you make or because they draw readers in. You want to strike a balance of the usage of raw data with your own theorizing. Avoid plopping large amounts of raw data into the article or chapter. Instead, you want to walk readers through what is happening. Lead them into the excerpt and then lead them out of it. They wouldn't have access to these data if it weren't for you. Teach them how they should make sense of it and/or why it is important.

Your job as a writer is to convince others that what you are saying is true. Why should they believe you? Why should they trust your interpretations? It is helpful if you lay it out for them so that they don't have to do a lot of the work themselves. Use compelling examples so that they are hooked from the beginning and invested in the story you want to tell.

Summary

In this chapter, we covered quite a bit about writing, from writing rituals to developing a voice to writing a research proposal or manuscript. We paid particular attention to the literature review chapter, since students often struggle with writing. The important thing to remember is that you should own whatever voice you choose to develop. As a graduate student and/or novice researcher, try not to be afraid of making strong claims in your research.

As you review your dissertation proposal, ask yourself the following questions: Did you thoroughly provide evidence that there is a problem or issue that is worth writing about and of urgent concern for you and your prospective research participants and audiences? Did you discuss why you believe your research topic is a problem or challenge and why it should be of concern to others? Do you see this as a problem specific to your life (e.g., workplace, family, or neighborhood) or is it of specific concern to others around you (e.g., educators, men, parents, health professionals, teachers, policy makers, nonprofit organizations, etc.)? Is this an issue of interest to people locally, nationally, or internationally? Can you provide researchable evidence that the problem or challenge exists? Can you provide evidence that the topic is worthwhile to read and talk about before a (reading/print, visual, or social media) audience? Be sure to use the literature to define any key terms or concepts.

DISCUSSION QUESTIONS

1. What are your writing rituals? How are your rituals informed by race, class, or gender?

2. Does imposter syndrome play a role in how you think about and practice writing? Why or why not?

3. What is an academic voice? What has shaped your discipline's understanding of it? In what ways will you challenge the notion of an academic voice?

4. What are the components of a research proposal? How do these components compare to your university's requirements?

5. Revisit Michelle's writing. What can you learn from her process?

The Reimagining and Possibilities of Qualitative Inquiry

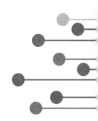

Almost twenty years ago, we sat in graduate classrooms, studied, and interrogated theories of qualitative research as well as practiced basic techniques such as interviewing, note-taking, and observations in public places. Neither of us were given the ultimate guidebook on the *dos* and *don'ts* of qualitative research (only because no such how-to manuals exist). Let's face it, qualitative research is complicated. Those qualitative scholars and writers who provide you with an easy five or 10 steps to a successful study are sacrificing and watering down much of the beauty of this inquiry, mainly that it exists as a way of interrogating life in all its complexities. Even more, quick guides ignore the idiosyncrasies of one's lived experience. And life is complex. Yet, knowing how to design a study and write research questions that will get at all of this complexity, including life oddities, is only one piece of the puzzle. Much of our time spent as qualitative researchers in the field has been devoted to dealing with the ethical and moral dilemmas that are inherent in research. And by *ethics,* we mean the kind of stuff that keeps you up at night pondering whether or not you made the right decision or whether you hurt the people you were researching.

One of the reasons these ethical dilemmas keep us up at night is because institutional research is a colonial practice. Whether we are doing positivist or naturalistic research, our research modalities are embedded in a practice that has historically and currently centered settler colonial ideologies (Smith, 2012). We borrow Linda Tuhiwai Smith's wise words:

> The ways in which scientific research is implicated in the worst excesses of colonialism remains a powerful remembered history for many of the world's colonized peoples. It is a history that still deeply offends the deepest sense of our humanity. (p. 1)

As Black and Brown researchers who have made academic careers from educational research, we are unsettled by this, even as we know this is true. We are perpetrators in playing this game of naming who gets to be researched, who gets to do the researching, and, most importantly, who ultimately benefits from the research that we do. We are simultaneously the Other in a space that has tried to white us out, shut us up, and pretend we are not smart enough to speak in their language. Yet, here we are as full professors who "made it" and are writing a textbook for the next generation to follow. Whatever we did to get here, the academic gatekeepers somehow let us into their private and privileged world. So, now, we pause and ask ourselves, was our admission to the academic table on the backs of our people? In what ways did *we* other Others and in what ways in our academic careers and research projects did we resist contributing to the narrative of Black, Indigenous, and people of color (BIPOC) that exists in the white imagination? How did our research protect our communities (or not)? How did our research help our communities (or not)? We have grappled with these questions throughout our careers, and we have honestly tried to do good by our people and communities first and foremost; all the while, we were figuring out—often on our own or looking to our Black and Indigenous foremothers in sociology, anthropology, and gender studies for guidance along the way—how our work might possibly matter in the academy. We know that Western research practices are inextricably linked to racism (Evans-Winters, 2019; McClaurin, 2001; Smith, 2012; Thiong'o, 1986). In this case, we mean *racism* as a systemic structure of oppression embedded in every institution in this country, as powerfully articulated by critical race and gender scholars. If racism is embedded in the judicial and educational system, it most certainly is embedded in our research practices. All research should be situated within a critique and recognition of the powerful structures of oppression that shape our lives (Anzaldúa, 1987; Collins, 2000). How, as players in this system who must navigate particular oppressions, do we make ethical research decisions in the best interests of our communities?

We reject any notion of a post-world. We are not postrace, we are not postfeminist, and we are definitely not postcolonial. At best, we exist in a borderland space (Anzaldúa, 1987) or, in different terms, the decolonial imaginary (Pérez, 1999). Many of us navigate this space daily. The colonial gaze has been infiltrated in us and we have been shaped by it. We cannot and will never return to a postcolonial world. The destruction has already been done: Our ancestors' minds, bodies, lands, and cultures have been ravaged; our minds and bodies are still under the colonial gaze and under attack. Keeping this in mind, we also recognize that there exists an "epistemological tyranny" (Kincheloe & Steinberg, 2008) or "apartheid of knowledge" (Delgado Bernal & Villalpando, 2002) in the academy. Through citational practices (Ahmed, 2017), hiring, and tenure decisions, a certain set of knowledge has been valued. This knowledge centers Western ways of knowing and being and deems all other forms as illegitimate. Knowledges that fall outside of this accepted paradigm are critiqued in harsh ways, viewed with much skepticism, or outright rejected as anecdotal or emotional. This proliferation of the status quo continues under our noses, despite our statuses as full professors. It is something we navigate as we design studies, apply for institutional review board (IRB) approval, seek external funding, or submit for publication.

Yet, as faculty who teach future methodologists and theorists, we believe in both the perils and possibilities of qualitative research. We know qualitative research has been exploitative while simultaneously being a tool to attempt to portray the humanity of the Other near and far. All ethical qualitative research requires considerations of the benefits of the study to the individual or community under investigation, but most of us would admit that community members or individual informants rarely reap the tangible rewards of academic research. Research participants are expected to enter the research process for altruistic reasons, yet researchers knowingly undertake research with an expected tangible outcome (e.g., a dissertation, job offer, grant, etc.).

When we give attention to this imbalance in the rewards of research, we can clearly admit how research can easily become exploitative or inequitable. Exploitation can take on a variety of forms, including cultural, scientific, and economic forms, with some of these systems of exploitation being deeply intertwined and intersecting. For instance, institutional research has robbed many Indigenous communities of their cultures and repackaged it and sold it back to the public in the forms of academic books (on ethnic groups), anthropological documentaries, museum artifacts, ethnic prints, cultural trips abroad, and so on.

Similarly, scientific exploitation looks similar to convincing and recruiting those who are colonized, marginalized, and poor to participate in research studies for the *sake of science* with little return to their own communities; they will be taking on all the risk of science (e.g., disclosing family secrets, discussing abuse and trauma, experimenting in educational curriculum trials, etc.). Along these same lines, economic exploitation in institutional research looks like academic scholars attaining tenure-track positions, promotion and salary increases, book deals, and speaking engagements from telling the stories or theorizing the destitution of those who gain little or nothing from sharing their stories with researchers. The scientific Other remains, for the most part, the mere object of knowledge.

We must remember that it was the so-called natural sciences that defined and declared who counted as the Other; scientific nomenclature ordered, ranked, sorted, and categorized human population groups. Of course, researchers in the social sciences—such as ethnographers—were later enthusiastically charged with describing and generalizing the categorized; and qualitative researchers continue to give the categorized Other an inscribed culture described through their eyes and interpretations. However, what happens when the Other is now the researcher? What happens when the researched Other questions the researcher and the motives of the research itself? How is research discourse shifted when the descendants of the colonized reclaim science and reject dominant narratives that depict their ancestors as savages, passive simpletons, or somehow otherworldly totems to be gawked at and posted up in museums and narrowly confined to black-and-white reels?

A new generation of qualitative researchers have the right and responsibility to ask, what has qualitative research done for me lately? The descendants of the colonized are beginning to question the motives of qualitative researchers, and the oppressed themselves are beginning to refuse the educated elite access to their communities and their sacred stories; they have come to understand that many of the benefits of academic research have not filtered down to their communities. Further, many of the descendants of colonized people also know through the oral tradition and formal academic training that Indigenous people have always had their own ways of knowing that sometimes informed traditional science and, at other times, contradicted mainstream science.

Many of us even believe that our knowledge claims were co-opted or outright stolen by Western scientists. Current generations of scholars are calling for the decolonization of qualitative inquiry and academia overall. Some of us want to know how academic research mitigates white supremacy in education, state-sanctioned violence, police brutality, and cultural hegemony. In comparing qualitative methodologies to quantitative modalities, scholars haphazardly depict qualitative research as somehow more humane or naturally benevolent. Qualitative research is not more humane because it, like all of science, has been infiltrated by scientific racism and elitism.

For some seasoned research scholars, we do believe that many institutional researchers finagle their way into people's lives. To be a part of a scientific study can be seducing for the dispossessed who have a story to tell, but it is no legitimate outlet for their joys and pains. Research from an outsider's perspective threatens to dehumanize and deprive BIPOC of multidimensionality. Any research process devoid of critical self-reflection and contextual analysis, whether facilitated by an insider or outsider of a cultural group, fails to portray the full humanity of a people. Intersectional qualitative research accepts the limitations of science and the historical and contemporary devastation that scientific investigation has caused to racially minoritized and Indigenous people.

If science that quantifies flattens the souls of Black and Brown people by depicting socially constructed realities in curves and norms, then research that qualifies people has squeezed entire groups of people's memories into rigid yet fantastical storylines. Quantitative research has been vilified as limiting because it fails to provide contextual analysis in explaining norms and trends, especially across racial, gender, and economic groups. Comparatively, qualitative research has somehow been declared our savior, since people want to hear our side of the story. But qualitative research is also limited and limiting because it continues to position the researcher as the omnipotent and omnipresent knower of other people's lives and circumstances. How do we interrupt the myth of the innocence of qualitative research while appreciating the ability of humanizing stories and memory work? Intersectional qualitative research explores ways to interrupt the inherent exploitation and voyeurism of scientific inquiry in all forms.

Qualitative research that centers intersectionality calls for more meaningful scholarship that simultaneously seeks to understand how race and gender overlap and constructs individuals and social groups' memories, stories, and perceptions about reality. As experienced research scholars, we know for sure that many graduate students, especially novice scholars of color, pursue research topics and projects that they believe are important to their professors, to their profession, or even to the general public. By pursuing what is the new and sexy topic at the time, many scholars consequently set out to simply observe and document, which requires them to separate emotionally from the topic of study and objectify the cultural experiences and insights of dynamic social actors.

Political and economic reform necessitates seeking to comprehend how people's choices and behaviors are influenced by larger social forces and how social forces are informed by people's choices and behaviors. Intersectional research thus seeks to explore the nuances and dynamics of both social forces and human actions. Qualitative researchers from racial minoritized groups and those impacted by the overlapping oppressions of race and gender limit ourselves and the possibilities of sociopolitical transformation when we disconnect from the research experience in order to pursue research simply for the sake of acquiring the degree or the status of calling ourselves "Doctor."

By centering intersectionality in qualitative research, we encourage seasoned and novice researchers to center race and gender and other marginalized identities in our research questions, methodologies, and analyses. Qualitative inquiry for some is known as a feel-good endeavor; for others, the thought of talking to and spending time with complete strangers causes much anxiety. For us, we find a sense of pleasure in telling other people's stories, and our own stories alongside those stories, as well as politicizing the stories of the marginalized and oppressed. Hence, this is why we have chosen to write this book: to remind the next generation of scholars of the moral and ethical obligations of qualitative research.

As we write this text, the world's population is experiencing a health pandemic that has shifted our way of life and the taken-for-granted ways in which we communicate, labor, and deliver curriculum. For the majority of the world, educational curriculum is being delivered remotely, business is conducted via synchronous video, and we cannot gather with friends and family in large numbers or too closely (or, at least, without wearing a mask). The pending health pandemic has had a disproportionate impact on the most vulnerable communities in society, including African Americans, Indigenous groups, and our elderly populations. It is now common knowledge that those groups already cemented to the bottom of society are the ones more likely to acquire and die from COVID-19, due to a history of structural inequality in housing, employment, and healthcare access.

The erosion of civil rights in the United States (U.S.) and the use of technology to document state-sanctioned violence, alongside a health and economic crisis, has encouraged many youth to organize and confront anti-Black racism. Here we bring up the current sociopolitical and economic context to place qualitative research within a larger conversation on race, gender, and class in the U.S. and abroad. While qualitative research may feel good or lead to positive affect, research must be considered an important scientific and political tool for documenting a social group's humanity, including their struggle against all forms of oppression.

As previously explained, once upon a time not too long ago, qualitative adventures were undertaken by privileged white men who had the economic means, physical freedom, and political clout to travel and document the ways of the life of the Other in between the pages of their travel journals. Fortunately, notable race and gender scholars such as St. Clair Drake, Zora Neal Hurston, Elijah Anderson, and Joyce Ladner systematically investigated and documented the lived experiences of their own cultural communities. Because of their methodological thoroughness and meticulous attention to forms of documentation, we have a blueprint for the most ethical and moral purposes and processes of research inside oppressed communities. The purpose of research must be not only to document humanity but also to combat the colonizers' historical and contemporary practices of utilizing science to colonize, control, surveil, and dehumanize.

Instead, what if our research projects were connected to larger liberation movements? What if our research projects presented the ways of life and memories of the oppressed and marginalized as a political tool to mitigate oppressive white supremacist patriarchal imperial capitalist regimes? What if scholars adopted qualitative research that centers intersectionality to expand the struggles and triumphs of Black and Indigenous women and others surviving under the foot of the interlocking systems of race, class, and gender oppression? In closing, this book is a call to the next generation of scholars to reimagine qualitative inquiry as a political tool in the struggle for our humanity.

References

Ahmed, S. (2017). *Living a feminist life*. Duke University Press.

Akbar, N. (1999). *Know thyself*. Mind Productions & Associates.

Anfara, J., & Mertz, N. T. (2015). *Theoretical frameworks in qualitative research* (2nd ed.). SAGE.

Anzaldúa, G. (1987). *Borderlands/La frontera: The new mestiza*. Aunt Lute Books.

Anzaldúa, G. (1990). *Making face, making soul/Haciendo Caras*. Aunt Lute Books.

Bailey, C. A. (2007). *A guide to qualitative field research* (2nd ed.). SAGE.

Barone, T., & Eisner, E. W. (1997). Arts-based educational research. In R. M. Jaeger (Ed.), *Complementary methods for research in education* (2nd ed.). AERA.

Becker, H. (1993). How I learned what a crock was. *Journal of Contemporary Ethnography, 22*(1), 28–35.

Behar, R. (1993). *Translated woman: Crossing the border with Esperanza's story*. Beacon Press.

Berger, M. T., & Guidroz, K. (2009). Introduction. In M. T. Berger & K. Guidroz (Eds.), *The intersectional approach: Transforming the academy through race, class, and gender* (pp. 1–24). The University of North Carolina Press.

Bhattacharya, K. (2007). Consenting to the consent form: What are the fixed and fluid understandings between the researcher and the researched? *Qualitative Inquiry, 13*(8), 1095–1115.

Bhattacharya, K. (2009). Othering research, researching the other: De/colonizing approaches to qualitative inquiry. In J. C. Smart (Ed.), *Higher education: Handbook of theory and research* (pp. 105–150). Springer.

Bhattacharya, K. (2017). *Fundamentals of qualitative research: A practical guide*. Routledge.

Bishop, R. (1998). Freeing ourselves from neo-colonial domination in research: A Māori approach to creating knowledge. *Qualitative Studies in Education, 11*(2), 199–219.

Blanchett, W. J., Klingner, J. K., & Harry, B. (2009). The intersection of race, culture, language, and disability: Implications for urban education. *Urban Education, 44*(4), 389–409.

Blumer, H. (1967). *The world of youthful drug use*. University of California Press.

Blumer, H. (2000). *Selected works of Herbert Blumer: A public philosophy for mass society*. University of Illinois Press.

Bochner, A. P., & Ellis, C. (Eds.). (2002). *Ethnographically speaking: Autoethnography, literature, and aesthetics*. Rowman Altamira.

Bogdan, R. C., & Biklen, S. K. (2007). *Qualitative research for education: An introduction to theories and methods* (5th ed.). Pearson.

Bogdan, R. C., & Taylor, S. J. (1975). *Introduction to research methods: A phenomenological approach to the social sciences*. Wiley.

Bolker, J. (1998). *Writing your dissertation in 15 minutes a day: A guide to starting, revising, and finishing your doctoral thesis*. Owl Books.

Boylorn, R. (2017). *Sweetwater: Black women and narratives of resilience* (revised ed.). Peter Lang.

Bruchac, M. M. (2018). *Savage kin: Indigenous informants and American anthropologists*. University of Arizona Press.

Buendia, E. (2003). Fashioning research stories: The metaphoric and narrative structure of writing research about race. In G. Lopez & L. Parker (Eds.), *Interrogating racism in qualitative research methodology* (pp. 49–69). Peter Lang.

Bulmer, M. (1984). *The Chicago school of sociology: Institutionalization, diversity, and the rise of sociological research*. University of Chicago Press.

Cannella, G. S., & Lincoln, Y. S. (2011). Ethics, research regulations, and critical social science. In N. Denzin & Y. Lincoln (Eds.), *The SAGE handbook of qualitative research* (pp. 81–90). SAGE.

Charmaz, K. (2001). Grounded theory. In R. M. Emerson (Ed.), *Contemporary field research: Perspectives and formulations* (pp. 335–352). Waveland Press.

Charmaz, K. (2006). *Constructing grounded theory: A practical guide through qualitative analysis.* SAGE.

Cho, S., Crenshaw, K. W., & McCall, L. (2013). Toward a field of intersectionality studies: Theory, applications, & praxis. *Signs, 38*(4), 785–810.

Clandinin, D. J., & Connelly, F. M. (2000). *Narrative inquiry: experience and story in qualitative research.* Jossey-Bass.

Coburn, C. E., Penuel, W. R., & Geil, K. (2013). *Research–practice partnerships at the district level: A new strategy for leveraging research for educational improvement.* William T. Grant Foundation.

Coffey, A., & Atkinson, P. (1996). *Making sense of qualitative data.* SAGE.

Collins, P. H. (1998). It's all in the family: Intersections of gender, race, and nation. *Hypatia, 13*(3), 62–82.

Collins, P. H. (2000). *Black feminist thought: Knowledge, consciousness, and the politics of empowerment.* Routledge.

Collins, P. H., & Bilge, S. (2016). *Intersectionality: Key concepts.* Polity.

Cooper, B. C. (2017). *Beyond respectability: The intellectual thought of race women.* University of Illinois Press.

Cortese, A. J. (1995). The rise, hegemony, and decline of the Chicago school of sociology, 1892–1945. *The Social Science Journal, 32*(3), 235–254.

Crenshaw, K. (1989). Demarginalizing the intersection of race and sex: A Black feminist critique of antidiscrimination doctrine, feminist theory and antiracist politics. *University of Chicago Legal Forum, 1*(8), 139.

Crenshaw, K. (1991). Mapping the margins: Intersectionality, identity politics, and violence against women of color. *Stanford Law Review, 43*, 1241–1299.

Crotty, M. (2013). *The foundations of social research.* SAGE.

Darder, A. (2012). Neoliberalism in the academic borderlands: An ongoing struggle for equality and human rights. *Educational Studies, 48*(5), 412–426.

Davis, C. A. (1999). *Reflexive ethnography: A guide to researching selves and others.* Routledge.

Davis, E. M. (2008). Risky business: Medical discourse, breast cancer and narrative. *Qualitative Health Research, 18*(1), 65–76.

Delgado Bernal, D. (1998). Using a Chicana feminist epistemology in educational research. *Harvard Educational Review, 68*(4), 555–583.

Delgado Bernal, D., & Villalpando, O. (2002). An apartheid of knowledge in academia: The struggle over the "legitimate" legitimate knowledge of faculty of color. *Equity & Excellence in Education, 35*(2), 169–180.

Denzin, N. K. (2001). The reflexive interview and a performative social science. *Qualitative Research*, 23–46.

Denzin, N. K. (2017). Critical qualitative inquiry. *Qualitative Inquiry, 23*(1), 8–16.

Denzin, N. K., & Lincoln, Y. S. (Eds.). (2000). *The SAGE handbook of qualitative research.* SAGE.

Denzin, N. K., & Lincoln, Y. S. (Eds.). (2004). *The SAGE handbook of qualitative research* (3rd ed.). SAGE.

Denzin, N. K., & Lincoln, Y. S. (2011). Disciplining the practice of qualitative research. In N. K. Denzin & Y. S. Lincoln (Eds.), *The SAGE handbook of qualitative research* (4th ed., pp. 1–20). SAGE.

Denzin, N. K., Lincoln, Y. S., & Smith, L. T. (Eds.). (2008). *Handbook of critical and Indigenous methodologies.* SAGE.

DeVault, M. (1990). Talking and listening from women's standpoint: Feminist strategies for interviewing and analysis. *Social Problems, 37*(1), 96–116.

Dill, B. T., & Kohlman, M. H. (2011). Intersectionality: A transformative paradigm in feminist theory and social justice. In S. N. Hesse-Biber (Ed.), *The handbook of feminist research: Theory and praxis* (2nd ed., pp. 154–174). SAGE.

Dillard, C. B. (2000). The substance of things hoped for, the evidence of things not seen: Examining an endarkened feminist epistemology in education research and leadership. *International Journal of Qualitative Studies in Education, 13*(6), 661–681.

Du Bois, W. E. B. (2008). *The souls of Black folk.* Oxford University Press.

Edwards, E. and Esposito, J. (2019). *Intersectional analysis as a method to analyze popular culture: Clarity in the matrix.* New York: Routledge.

Edwards, E. B. and Esposito, J. (2018). Reading the Black woman's body via Instagram fame. *Communication, Culture, and Critique, 11*(3), 341–358.

Ellingson, L. L. (2009). *Engaging crystallization in qualitative research: An introduction*. SAGE.

Ellis, C. (2002). Shattered lives: Making sense of September 11th and its aftermath. *Journal of Contemporary Ethnography, 31*(4), 375–410.

Ellis, C. (2007). Telling secrets, revealing lives: Relational ethics in research with intimate others. *Qualitative Inquiry, 13,* 3–29.

Ellis, C. (2009). *Revision: Autoethnographic reflections on life and work*. Left Coast Press.

Ellis, C. S., & Bochner, A. P. (2006). Analyzing analytic autoethnography: An autopsy. *Journal of Contemporary Ethnography, 35,* 429–449.

Emerson, R. M., Fretz, R. I., & Shaw, L. L. (2011). *Writing ethnographic fieldnotes*. University of Chicago Press.

Esposito, J. (2009). What does race have to do with Ugly Betty? An analysis of privilege and postracial(?) representations on a television sitcom. *Television and New Media, 10*(6), 521–535.

Esposito, J. (2011). Negotiating the gaze and learning the hidden curriculum: A critical race analysis of the embodiment of female students of color at a predominantly white institution. *Journal for Critical Education Policy Studies, 9*(2).

Evans-Winters, V. E. (2005). *Teaching Black girls: Resiliency in urban classrooms* (Vol. 279). Peter Lang.

Evans-Winters, V. E. (2016). Schooling at the liminal: Black girls and special education. *The Wisconsin English Journal, 58*(2), 140–153.

Evans-Winters, V. E. (2019). *Black feminism in qualitative inquiry: A mosaic for writing our daughter's body*. Routledge.

Evans-Winters, V. E., & Esposito, J. (2010). Other people's daughters: Critical race feminism and Black girls' education. *Educational Foundations (Winter–Spring)*, 11–24.

Evans-Winters, V. E., & Esposito, J. (2018). Researching the bridge called our backs: The invisibility of "us" in qualitative communities. *International Journal of Qualitative Studies in Education, 31*(9), 863–876.

Evans-Winters, V. E., & Esposito, J. (2019). Intersectionality in education research: Methodology as critical inquiry and praxis. In N. K. Denzin & M. D. Giardina (Eds.), *Qualitative inquiry at a crossroads: Political, performative, and methodological reflections*. Routledge.

Evans-Winters, V. E., & Girls for Gender Equity. (2017). Flipping the script: The dangerous bodies of girls of color. *Cultural Studies ↔ Critical Methodologies, 17*(5), 415–423.

Fairclough, N. (1989). *Language and power*. Longman.

Fine, M. (1994). Working the hyphens: Reinventing self and other in qualitative research. In N. Denzin & Y. S. Lincoln (Eds.), *Handbook of qualitative research* (pp. 70–82). SAGE.

Flores, J., & Jiménez Román, M. (2009). Triple-Consciousness? Approaches to Afro-Latino culture in the United States. *Latin American and Caribbean Ethnic Studies, 4*(3), 319–328. 10.1080/17442220903331662

Foucault, M. (1972). *The archeology of knowledge and the discourse on language.* (A. M. Sheridan Smith, Trans.). Pantheon Books.

Foucault, M. (1975). *Discipline and punish: The birth of the prison*. Vintage Books.

Galuska, L., Hahn, J., Polifroni, E. C., & Crow, G. (2018). A narrative analysis of nurses' experiences with meaning and joy in nursing practice. *Nursing Administration Quarterly, 42*(2), 154–163.

Garfinkel, H. (1967). *Studies in ethnomethodology*. Prentice Hall.

Gee, J. P. (1990). *Social linguistics and literacies: Ideology in discourses, critical perspectives on literacy and education.* Falmer Press.

Gee, J. P. (2011). *How to do discourse analysis: A toolkit*. Routledge.

Geertz, C. (1973). *The interpretation of cultures*. Basic Books.

Glaser, B. G. (1998). *Doing grounded theory: Issues and discussions*. Sociology Press.

Glesne, C. (2011). *Becoming qualitative researchers: An introduction* (4th ed.). Pearson.

Green-Powell, P. (1997). Methodological considerations in field research: Six case studies. In K. M. Vaz (Ed.), *Oral narrative research with Black women* (pp. 197–217). SAGE.

Grzanka P. R. (Ed.). (2014). *Intersectionality: A foundations and frontiers reader*. Westview Press.

Guba, E., & Lincoln, Y. (2008). Paradigmatic controversies, contradictions, and emerging confluences. In N. Denzin & Y. Lincoln (Eds.), *The landscape of qualitative research* (3rd ed., pp. 255–286). SAGE.

Gubrium, J. F., & Holstein, J. A. (1997). *The new language of qualitative method.* Oxford University Press.

Gubrium, J. F., & Holstein, J. A. (2009). *Analyzing narrative reality.* SAGE.

Guion, L. A. (2002). *Triangulation: Establishing the validity of qualitative studies.* https://sites.duke.edu/niou/files/2014/07/W13-Guion-2002-Triangulation-Establishing-the-Validity-of-Qualitative-Research.pdf

Happel-Parkins, A., & Esposito, J. (2018). "Would you wear that to church?!": The production of "ladies" in a Southern all girls' after-school club. *Urban Education.* 10.1177/0042085918802614

Haraway, D. (1988). Situated knowledges: The science question in feminism and the privilege of partial perspective. *Feminist Studies, 14*(3), 575–599.

Hart, C. (2001). *Doing a literature review: Releasing the social science research imagination.* SAGE.

hooks, b. (1990). *Yearning: Race, gender, and cultural politics.* South End Press.

Hughes, S. A., & Pennington, J. L. (2017). *Autoethnography: Process, product, and possibility for critical social research.* SAGE.

Humphreys, L. (1970). *Tearoom trade: Impersonal sex in public places.* Duckworth.

Israel, M. (2015). *Research ethics and integrity for social scientists: Beyond regulatory compliance* (2nd ed.). SAGE.

Johnson-Bailey, J. (1999). The ties that bind and the shackles that separate: Race, gender, class, and color in a research process. *International Journal of Qualitative Studies in Education, 12*(6), 659–670.

Jones, J. (1993). *Bad blood: The Tuskegee syphilis experiment.* Free Press.

Josselson, R. (1996). On writing other people's lives: Self-analytic reflections of a narrative researcher. In R. Josselson (Ed.), *The narrative study of lives, Vol. 4: Ethics and process in the narrative study of lives* (pp. 60–71). SAGE.

Juritzen, T. I., Grimen, H., & Heggen, K. (2011). Protecting vulnerable research participants: A Foucault-inspired analysis of ethics committees. *Nursing Ethics, 18*(5), 640–650.

Kendi, I. X. (2017). *Stamped from the beginning: The definitive history of racist ideas in America.* Random House.

Kincheloe, J. L., & McLaren, P. (2000). Rethinking critical theory and qualitative research. In N. K. Denzin & Y. S. Lincoln (Eds.), *Handbook of qualitative research* (2nd ed., pp. 279–313). SAGE.

Kincheloe, J. L., & Steinberg, S. L. (2008). Indigenous knowledges in education: Complexities, dangers, and profound benefits. In N. K. Denzin, Y. S. Lincoln, & L. T. Smith (Eds.), *Handbook of critical and Indigenous methodologies* (pp. 135–156). SAGE.

King, D. K. (1988). Multiple jeopardy, multiple consciousness: The context of a Black feminist ideology. *Signs: Journal of Women in Culture and Society, 14*(1), 42–72.

King, J. E. (1991). Dysconscious racism: Ideology, identity, and the miseducation of teachers. *The Journal of Negro Education, 60*(2), 133–146.

Kubota, R., & Okuda, T. (2016). Confronting language myths, linguicism and racism in English language teaching in Japan. *Why English? Confronting the Hydra,* 77–87.

Kvale, S. (1996). *Interviews: An introduction to qualitative research interviewing.* SAGE.

Lahman, M. K. E. (2018). *Ethics in social science research: Becoming culturally responsive.* SAGE.

Lamphere, L. (2006). Feminist anthropology engages social movements: Theory, ethnography, and activism. In E. Lewin & L. M. Silverstein (Eds.), *Mapping feminist anthropology in the twenty-first century* (pp. 41–64). Rutgers University Press.

Lather, P. (1992). Critical frames in educational research: Feminist and post-structural perspectives. *Theory into Practice, 31*(2), 87–99.

Leavy, P. (2013). *Fiction as research practice: Short stories, novellas, and novels.* Left Coast Press.

LeCompte, M. D., & Schensul, J. J. (1999). *Designing and conducting ethnographic research.* AltaMira Press.

Liamputtong, P. (2007). *Researching the vulnerable: A guide to sensitive research methods*. SAGE.

Lim, S. G., & Tsutakawa, M. (Eds.). (1989). *The forbidden stitch: An Asian-American women's anthology*. Calyx Books.

Limes-Taylor Henderson, K., & Esposito, J. (2019). Using others in the nicest way possible: On colonial and academic practice(s), and an ethic of humility. *Qualitative Inquiry, 25,* 876–889. 10.1177/1077800417743528

Lincoln, Y. S., & Guba, E. G. (1985). *Naturalistic inquiry*. SAGE.

Lorde, A. (2018). *The master's tools will never dismantle the master's house*. Penguin Classics.

Madison, D. S. (2005). *Critical ethnography: Method, ethics, and performance*. SAGE.

May, V. M. (2015). *Pursuing intersectionality, unsettling dominant imaginaries*. Routledge.

McClaurin, I. (Ed.). (2001). *Black feminist anthropology: Theory, politics, praxis, and poetics*. Rutgers University Press.

Mead, M. (1928). *Coming of age in Samoa*. Morrow.

Merriam, S. (1998). *Qualitative research and case study applications in education* (2nd ed.). Jossey-Bass.

Miles, M. B., & Huberman, A. M. (2013). *Qualitative data analysis* (3rd ed.). SAGE.

Mitchell, J. (1994). Recruitment and retention of women of color in clinical studies. In A. C. Mastoianni, R. Faden, & D. Federman (Eds.), *Women and health research: Ethical and legal issues of including women in clinical studies* (Vol. 2, pp. 11–17). National Academies Press.

Moe, K. (1984). Should the Nazi research data be cited? *The Hastings Center Report, 14,* 5–7.

Moraga, C., & Anzaldúa, G. (Ed.). (2015). *This bridge called my back: Writings by radical women of color*. SUNY Press. (Original work published 1983)

National Commission for the Protection of Human Subjects of Biomedical and Behavioral Research. (1978). *The Belmont report: Ethical principles and guidelines for the protection of human subjects of research*. Author.

Noblit, G. W., Flores, S., Murillo, E. G. (2004). Postcritical ethnography: An introduction. In G. W. Noblit, S. Y.

Flores, & E. G. Murillo (Eds.), *Postcritical ethnography: Reinscribing critique* (pp. 1–52). Hampton Press.

Ogloff, J. R., & Otto, R. K. (1991). Are research participants truly informed? Readability of informed consent forms used in research. *Ethics & Behavior, 1*(4), 239–252.

Padilla, E. (1958). *Up from Puerto Rico*. Columbia University Press.

Patton, M. Q. (1987). *How to use qualitative methods in evaluation*. SAGE.

Pérez, E. (1999). *The decolonial imaginary: Writing Chicanas into history*. Indiana University Press.

Pillow, W. (2003). Confession, catharsis, or cure? Rethinking the uses of reflexivity as methodological power in qualitative research. *International Journal of Qualitative Studies, 16*(2), 175–196.

Prendergast, M. (2009). Introduction: The phenomena of poetry in research. In M. Prendergast, C. Leggo, & P. Sameshima (Eds.), *Poetic inquiry: Vibrant voices in the social sciences* (pp. xix–xlii). Sense Publishers.

Prior, L. (2003). *Using documents in social research*. SAGE.

Ravitch, S. M., & Carl, N. M. (2016). *Qualitative research: Bridging the conceptual, theoretical, and methodological*. SAGE.

Ravitch, S. M., & Riggan, M. (2012). *Reason & rigor: How conceptual frameworks guide research*. SAGE.

Reay, D. (2001). "Spice girls," "nice girls," "girlies," and "tomboys": Gender discourses, girls' cultures and femininities in the primary classroom. *Gender and Education, 13*(2), 153–166.

Reinharz, S. (1992). *Feminist methods in social research*. Oxford University Press.

Richardson, L. (1994). Writing: A method of inquiry. In N. K. Denzin & Y. S. Lincoln (Eds.), *The SAGE handbook of qualitative research* (pp. 516–529). SAGE.

Richardson, L. (2000). Writing: A method of inquiry. In N. K. Denzin & Y. S. Lincoln (Eds.), *The SAGE handbook of qualitative research* (2nd ed., pp. 923–948). SAGE.

Riessman, C. K. (2008). *Narrative methods for the human sciences*. SAGE.

Roberts, D. E. (1999). *Killing the Black body: Race, reproduction, and the meaning of liberty.*

Rodriguez, M. A., & Garcia, R. (2013). First, do no harm: The U.S. sexually transmitted disease experiments in Guatemala. *American Journal of Public Health, 103*(12), 2122–2126.

Roulston, K. (2010). *Reflective interviewing: A guide to theory and practice.* SAGE.

Saldaña, J. (2016). *The coding manual* (3rd ed.). SAGE.

Saldaña, J. (2018). Researcher, analyze thyself. *The Qualitative Report, 23*(9), 2036–2046.

Sandoval, C. (2013). *Methodology of the oppressed* (Vol. 18). University of Minnesota Press.

Schatzman, L., & Strauss, A. (1973). *Field research: Strategies for a natural sociology.* Prentice Hall.

Scheurich, J. (1997). *Research method in the postmodern.* Routledge.

Scheurich, J. J., & Young, M. D. (1997). Coloring epistemologies: Are our research epistemologies racially biased? *Educational Researcher, 26*(4), 4–16.

Schram, A. (2003). *Conceptualizing qualitative inquiry: Mindwork for fieldwork in education and the social sciences.* Merrill/Prentice Hall.

Schutz, A. (1967). *The phenomenology of the social world.* (G. Walsh & F. Lenhert, Trans.). Northwestern University Press.

Schwandt, T. (1997). *Qualitative inquiry: A dictionary of terms.* SAGE.

Schwandt, T. (2015). *Dictionary of qualitative inquiry* (4th ed). SAGE.

Seidman, I. (2013). *Interviewing as qualitative research: A guide for researchers in education and the social sciences* (4th ed.). Teachers College Press.

Shavers, V. L., Lynch, C. F., & Burmeister, L. F. (2000). Knowledge of the Tuskegee study and its impact on the willingness to participate in medical studies. *Journal of the National Medical Association, 92*(12), 563.

Shea, C. (2000). Don't talk to the humans: The crackdown on social science research. *Lingua Franca, 10*(6). http://linguafranca.mirror.theinfo.org/print/0009/humans.html

Sherman, F. T., & Torbert, W. R. (Eds.). (2013). *Transforming social inquiry, transforming social action.* Kluwer Academic Publishers

Simson, D. (2013). Exclusion, punishment, racism, and our schools: A critical race theory perspective on school discipline. *UCLA Law Review, 61,* 506.

Smith, B. (Ed.). (1983). *Home girls: A Black feminist anthology.* Rutgers University Press.

Smith, D. E. (1987). *The everyday world as problematic.* Northeastern University Press.

Smith, L. T. (2012). *Decolonizing methodologies: Research and Indigenous peoples.* Zed Books.

Smith, L. T., Battiste, M., Bell, L., & Findlay, L. M. (2002). An interview with Linda Tuhiwai Te Rina Smith, March 27, 2002. *Canadian Journal of Native Education, 26*(2), 169–186.

Southern, S., Smith, R., & Oliver, M. (2005). Marriage and family counseling: Ethics in context. *The Family Journal, 13*(4), 459–466.

Souto-Manning, M., & Ray, N. (2007). Beyond survival in the ivory tower: Black and Brown women's living narratives. *Equity & Excellence in Education, 40,* 280–290.

Sparkes, A. C., Nilges, L., Swan, P., & Downing, F. (2003). Poetic representations in sport and physical education: Insider perspectives. *Sport, Education, and Society, 8*(2), 153–177.

Spitz, V. (2005). *Doctors from hell: The horrific account of Nazi experiments on humans.* Sentient Publications.

Spivak, G. C. (1988). Can the subaltern speak? In C. Nelson & L. Grossberg (Eds.), *Marxism and the interpretation of culture* (pp. 271–313). Macmillan Education.

Spradley, J. P. (1979). *The ethnographic interview.* Holt, Rinehart, and Winston.

Spradley, J. P. (1980). *Participant observation.* Wadsworth, Cengage Learning.

Stake, R. E. (1995). *The art of case study research.* SAGE.

Stanfield, J. (1994). *(Response) Empowering the culturally diversified sociological voice.* Cited in Gitlin, A. (2014). *Power and method: Political activism and educational research* (pp. 166–180). Routledge.

Stanley, L., & Wise, S. (1993). *Breaking out again: Feminist ontology and epistemology*. Taylor & Francis.

Stark, L. (2012). *Behind closed doors: IRBs and the making of ethical research*. University of Chicago Press.

Strauss, A., & Corbin, J. (1998). *Basics of qualitative research: Grounded theory procedures and techniques* (2nd ed.). SAGE.

Strauss, A. L. (1995). Notes of the nature and development of general theories. *Qualitative Inquiry, 1*(1), 7–18.

Tantaquidgeon, G. (1942). *A study of Delaware Indian medicine practices and folk beliefs*. Kessinger Publishing, LLC.

Thiong'o, N. (1986). *Decolonising the mind: The politics of language in African literature*. James Currey.

Thorne, S. (2000). Data analysis in qualitative research. *Evidence Based Nursing, 3*, 68–70.

Tillman, L. C. (2002). Culturally sensitive research approaches: An African-American perspective. *Educational Researcher, 31*(9), 3–12.

Tyson, C. (2003). Research, race, and an epistemology of emancipation. In G. R. Lopez & L. Parker (Eds.), *Interrogating racism in qualitative research methodology* (pp. 19–28). Peter Lang.

Van Manen, M. (1990). *Researching lived experience: Human science for an action sensitive pedagogy*. The University of Western Ontario.

Villenas, S. (2000). The colonizer/colonized Chicana ethnographer: Identity, marginalization, and co-optation in the field. *Acts of Inquiry in Qualitative Research*, 75–93.

Visweswaran, K. (1994). *Fictions of feminist ethnography*. University of Minnesota Press.

Washington, H. A. (2006). *Medical apartheid: The dark history of medical experimentation on Black Americans from colonial times to the present*. Doubleday Books.

Watts, I. E., & Erevelles, N. (2004). These deadly times: Reconceptualizing school violence by using critical race theory and disability studies. *American Educational Research Journal, 41*(2), 271–299.

Wax, R. (1971). *Doing fieldwork: Warnings and advice*. The University of Chicago Press.

Weindling, P. J. (2004). *Nazi medicine and the Nuremberg trials: From medical war crimes to informed consent*. Palgrave Macmillan.

Weindling, P. J., von Villez, A., Loewenau, A., & Farron, N. (2016). The victims of unethical human experiments and coerced research under national socialism. *Endeavor, 40*(1), 1–6.

White, D. G. (1999). *Ar'n't I a woman?: Female slaves in the plantation South*. WW Norton & Company.

White, R. F. (2007). Institutional review board mission creep: The common rule, social science, and the nanny state. *The Independent Review, 11*(4), 547–564.

Willig, C. (2014). Interpretation and analysis. In U. Flick (Ed.), *The SAGE handbook of qualitative data analysis* (pp. 136–149). SAGE.

Wing, A. D. (2000). *Global critical race feminism: An international reader*. NYU Press.

Wirth, L. (1928). *The ghetto*. University of Chicago Press.

Wolcott, H. F. (2008). *Writing up qualitative research*. SAGE.

Yin, R. K. (2018). *Case study research and application: Design and methods* (6th ed.). SAGE.

Index